About the Authors

ALLAN LAZAR is a graduate of Jefferson Medical College of Philadelphia and did postgraduate work at the University of Chicago, where he was also a member of the faculty. He has also served on the faculty of Columbia University College of Physicians and Surgeons as well as Fairleigh Dickinson University Dental School. In his retirement he teaches at the Institute for Learning in Retirement at Bergen Community College in Paramus, New Jersey, and in his spare time teaches dogs to play the piano and sing.

DAN KARLAN originally trained at MIT to be a biochemistry researcher, but after several years changed careers to computer programming. He combined his expertise in programming and science to establish a career as a scientific computer programmer and technical writer. His favorite authors include Joseph Conrad, Charles Dickens, Victor Hugo, Larry Niven, and Poul Anderson.

JEREMY SALTER was born in New York City, grew up in Long Branch, New Jersey, and got a bachelor of science degree in chemistry from Monmouth College. He worked in the drug industry as an analytical chemist, learning instrument repair and teaching electron microscopy, X-ray diffraction, and chromatography. He left the industry in 2002 and studied writing at the feet of Allan Lazar and his dog, Yogi.

THE 101 MOST
INFLUENTIAL PEOPLE
WHO NEVER LIVED

THE 101 MOST INFLUENTIAL PEOPLE WHO NEVER LIVED

How Characters of Fiction, Myth, Legends, Television, and Movies Have Shaped Our Society, Changed Our Behavior, and Set the Course of History

ALLAN LAZAR, DAN KARLAN, AND JEREMY SALTER

HARPER

NEW YORK • LONDON • TORONTO • SYDNEY

HARPER

HarperCollins books may be purchased for educational, business, or sales promotional use. For information please write: Special Markets Department, HarperCollins Publishers, 10 East 53rd Street, New York, NY 10022.

FIRST EDITION

Designed by Phillip Mazzone

Library of Congress Cataloging-in-Publication Data
Lazar, Allan.
    The 101 most influential people who never lived : how characters of fiction, myth, legends, television, and movies have shaped our society, changed our behavior, and set the course of history / Allan Lazar, Dan Karlan, Jeremy Salter.—1st ed.
        p. cm.
    ISBN-10: 0-06-113221-7
    ISBN-13: 978-0-06-113221-6
    1. United States—Civilization—Miscellanea.   2. National characteristics, American—Miscellanea.   3. Popular culture—United States—Miscellanea.   4. Fictitious characters—Miscellanea.   5. Mythology—Miscellanea.   6. Legends—Miscellanea.   I. Karlan, Dan.   II. Salter, Jeremy.   III. Title.   IV. Title: One hundred one most influential people who never lived.   V. Title: One hundred and one most influential people who never lived.

E169.1.L45   2006
306.4'80973—dc22   2006043486

06 07 08 09 10 WBC/RRD 10 9 8 7 6 5 4 3 2 1

Dedicated to the artists who entertain,
inform, and inspire.

And to the memory of a nineteen-year-old cairn terrier.

Contents

THE 101 MOST
INFLUENTIAL PEOPLE
WHO NEVER LIVED

Preface

We believe so strongly in the characters of television, literature, and movies that we treat them as important people in our lives. We have to see the last episode of our favorite TV series every season; we've stood in line to see the latest movie sequel or remake. Legends, myths, theater, animation—it's all the same. We identify with these characters, even if the story dates back thousands of years. We shed real tears over their setbacks and suffering. We try to emulate the greatness of the heroes and learn from the mistakes of the tragic figures. Much of fiction helps us deal with the real world. We can experience the full range of life—the exotic, the dangerous, the foolish—all in complete safety.

Fiction informs us about the world, but it also shapes it. Some individuals are so inspired by what they have read or seen, they set out to remake the world. Would Alexander the Great have tried to conquer the world without having heard the stories of the Trojan War? Would Napoleon have thought of invading Russia without the example of Alexander?

Suppose Harriet Beecher Stowe had written *Uncle Tom's Cabin* in 1885 and triggered the Civil War when Grover Cleveland was president, instead of during the time of Lincoln? The guns and artillery would have been deadlier, and a larger portion of the population would have been killed. Would enough of the United States have survived to enter World War I and help defeat Germany? Without the defeat of Germany, would Hitler have emerged, and would the Russian Revolution have taken place?

Consider the Wright brothers. Without the example of Icarus and Daedalus, the legendary Greeks who were the first to fly, would the Wright brothers have built the first airplane? Or, instead, would they have built giant bicycles to carry people cross-country? What would we have missed?

Fiction often affects us on a personal level. We adopt a character's slang or join discussion groups on the Internet. And it's often more personal than that. We can trace some of the lessons of life that we learned as children—our moral values—back to specific tales. Many of these memories are lost in the fog of our early years and bedtime stories read to us while we were half asleep. The nursery rhyme characters have an influence so subtle we are hardly aware of it. Other fictional characters have had an influence that was deliberate and obvious. Some, such as Jim Crow, have risen to an importance that was never intended.

The creation of fiction—which includes legends, folktales, and myths—is commonplace among all societies during the past three thousand years, and probably longer. The importance of these ancient stories was largely unappreciated until recently. We are, truly, a self-made species. Our lives unfold in a world defined by other human beings, often fictional ones.

This collection identifies some of the most influential among these creations and describes their impact on our lives. We did not consider the world from a Chinese perspective, or an Egyptian viewpoint. We have not looked into Celtic myths or Persian, Babylonian, Hindu, Portuguese, Russian, or Korean literature. We have considered what affects our own culture. And don't think that we authors agreed on everything. Although we put a great deal of effort into finding facts, this book rests heavily on the authors' opinions.

The influence of these characters has two facets: the number of people affected and the depth of impact. We bypassed dozens of popular characters including Darth Vader, Hedda Gabler, Charlie Brown, Sam Malone, David Copperfield, Wonder Woman, and Mr. Whipple. Many characters have been popular *favorites* of our culture, but popular doesn't always translate into *influential*. A few of our characters might have been real people, but what we know of them comes from the movies, books, and plays, not from actual histories. So we included them. And some of our characters are not people at all. We trust you'll find our selection interesting.

Beginnings: How We Got into Writing This Book

It all started on a summer's night. There was a hot philosophy meeting at the mall, and we heard it was a tough crowd. People who'd argue about truth and being and thought and morality. Dangerous people, who got personal about Plato and Socrates, and other philosophers such as Wittgenstein. Who was Wittgenstein, anyway? In any case, the meeting was held in a bookstore whose manager hoped to sell some of the philosophy books dying of old age on his shelves—those heavy books that people expect to see but just don't buy. They sit and gather dust. There isn't much dust in the mall, very little, and all of it slowly migrates to the philosophy section of the bookstore, Plato and Schopenhauer and Dale Carnegie—part of the life cycle of a book.

The bookstore was also the safest place for the gathering. Safe because books fly open when you throw them, and flop to the floor like wounded pigeons. So when you toss a hefty philosophy tome at the person who insists that Jean-Paul Sartre was actually three people, no one gets hurt. But Macy's was next door, and a dozen philosophy people rushed over to the kitchen department and purchased carbon steel chef's knives, those ultrasharp metal masterpieces that can filet a philosopher quicker than you can say "existentialism."

After the meeting, during which we decided that truth depends on the kind of carpet you're standing on, the injured were taken away. On our way out, Dan picked up a copy of *The 100: A Ranking of the Most Influential Persons in History* by Michael Hart. Dan didn't actually buy the book. (That's something most people who go to philosophy meetings don't do. They resent having to pay for knowledge; they would rather figure it out for themselves. They're lousy tippers, too. That's just how they are.) Dan leafed through the book and pointed out a chapter about a Chinese man who invented paper. Allan said, "I'll bet we could write a book like that. What about fictional characters?" Dan bought into it right away, and Jeremy followed along, muttering the way he sometimes does.

We started the following week during one of our regular outings, this one to the Montclair Art Museum. Professional interest, you understand. Dan is a sculptor, and Jeremy paints— mostly in acrylics because they dry quickly and don't smear on the car seat during the drive home. And Allan's a colorful character who earned his way through college as an artist, taking commissions for paintings that would go well with the buyer's couch. (Remember now, a lot of beige.) Jeremy will often point out that Rembrandt started the same way: a painter and upholsterer. You bought the painting and the couch together, as a matched set. But then the kids jumped on the couches, and the springs went soft, and the fabric got beer and dog pee on it. After a few years, only the paintings survived.

Normally on our outings we discuss the merits of Dutch and English bread making, but we started talking about fictional characters and decided to compile a list. Allan picked Satan, whom he doesn't believe in, except for the times they go at it hammer and tong at philosophy meetings. Jeremy selected Nora Helmer, the heroine of an Ibsen play. Dan chose Big

Brother, George Orwell's nightmare dictator. And so it went, until we had about thirty names. We each worked on our own list, and we met again and added more names: Brünnhilde and Santa Claus and Miss Piggy and Sam Spade and Loki and Thor. And also real people, such as Marilyn Monroe and Buffalo Bill and Elvis Presley, who had become their own legends.

We kept going. We asked our friends Victor, Victoria, Vinny, Veede, and Vecee, among others, for suggestions. They contributed several who had escaped our attention. During a trip to the Griswold Museum in Old Lyme, Connecticut, we divided the list into categories.

The Griswold is truly a remarkable place, with the beautiful Lieutenant River behind it. We went to visit the paintings from the Hartford Steam Boiler collection. (That's what they are called even though they are not actually painted on steam boilers.)

At dinner that evening—a good burger, clams, and fries at a place a few miles up the road in Niantic—a large seagull came over to beg for French fries. In exchange for a few tidbits, he suggested that we include some Russian characters: The Brothers Karamazov, Ivan Ilyich, Uncle Vanya, and, of course, the Firebird. We didn't use any of them.

Later, we dropped all of the essays we had written about religious characters, on the advice of a deity we aren't allowed to name, and we cut out all the real people except for Siegfried, Saint Nick, and King Arthur, who were very different from the stories told about them. They came from the Dark Ages, that rowdy era when hordes of pre-Nietzschean philosophers stormed across Europe in search of debate, pillage, and bookstores.

Then we started writing, and correcting one another's work, and we got used to it. It gets to be a habit, writing.

One day we were in a bookstore, one of the large ones with a café and a jazz combo, a little Brubeck, the smell of strong coffee and cinnamon. A classy blonde in a tight blue satin dress engaged us in conversation and eventually asked, "What do you do?" We were not quite ready to admit that we're writers, so we told her we're philosophers, the rowdy kind.

The 101 in Rank Order

The following is our list of most influential characters, arranged in order of influence, most influential to least. Note that this measure is completely subjective.

1. The Marlboro Man
2. Big Brother
3. King Arthur
4. Santa Claus (Saint Nick)
5. Hamlet
6. Dr. Frankenstein's Monster
7. Siegfried
8. Sherlock Holmes
9. Romeo and Juliet
10. Dr. Jekyll and Mr. Hyde
11. Uncle Tom
12. Robin Hood
13. Jim Crow
14. Oedipus
15. Lady Chatterly
16. Ebenezer Scrooge

17. Don Quixote
18. Mickey Mouse
19. The American Cowboy
20. Prince Charming
21. Smokey Bear
22. Robinson Crusoe
23. Apollo and Dionysus
24. Odysseus
25. Nora Helmer
26. Cinderella
27. Shylock
28. Rosie the Riveter
29. Midas
30. Hester Prynne
31. The Little Engine That Could
32. Archie Bunker
33. Dracula
34. Alice in Wonderland
35. Citizen Kane
36. Faust
37. Figaro
38. Godzilla
39. Mary Richards
40. Don Juan
41. Bambi
42. William Tell
43. Barbie
44. Buffy the Vampire Slayer
45. Venus and Cupid
46. Prometheus

47. Pandora
48. G.I. Joe
49. Tarzan
50. Captain Kirk and Mr. Spock
51. James Bond
52. Hansel and Gretel
53. Captain Ahab
54. Richard Blaine
55. The Ugly Duckling
56. Loch Ness Monster (Nessie)
57. Atticus Finch
58. Saint Valentine
59. Helen of Troy
60. Batman
61. Uncle Sam
62. Nancy Drew
63. J. R. Ewing
64. Superman
65. Tom Sawyer and Huckleberry Finn
66. HAL 9000
67. Kermit the Frog
68. Sam Spade
69. The Pied Piper
70. Peter Pan
71. Hiawatha
72. Othello
73. The Little Tramp
74. King Kong
75. Norman Bates
76. Hercules (Herakles)

77. Dick Tracy
78. Joe Camel
79. The Cat in the Hat
80. Icarus
81. Mammy
82. Sindbad
83. Amos 'n' Andy
84. Buck Rogers
85. Luke Skywalker
86. Perry Mason
87. Dr. Strangelove
88. Pygmalion
89. Madame Butterfly
90. Hans Beckert
91. Dorothy Gale
92. The Wandering Jew
93. The Great Gatsby
94. Buck (Jack London, *The Call of the Wild*)
95. Willy Loman
96. Betty Boop
97. Ivanhoe
98. Elmer Gantry
99. Lilith
100. John Doe
101. Paul Bunyan

1. Greek and Roman Myths

The gods we know best are the ones passed down to us in Greek and Roman stories. But what has made these deities so interesting for so long? The Greek god Dionysus invented wine, quite an impressive accomplishment to some people. But others were more impressed by the sobering, palpable presence of the gods in their everyday lives. They were not just the gods behind the forces of nature; they were the very forces themselves.

These gods lived full lives of intellect, temperament, and emotion. They exhibited vanity and jealousy; they engaged in love and war. While other cultures' gods were snakes or bulls, the Greek and Roman gods looked human and, much of the time, acted like humans. They married, had children, and battled among themselves. They had favorites among us mortals: people whom they met, spoke to, helped, or cursed. And many human women bore children by them. These offspring were demigods who often became heroes in their own right.

Are these gods and heroes fictional? That's the wrong question. Myth is a seductive, poetic enterprise by which we express our deepest wishes, as well as our most profound anxieties.

In this chapter, we visit these gods and examine their influence on how we resolve moral issues today. The beauty of these stories can only be realized when the characters remain where they belong, neither in the world of truth nor the realm of fiction, but beyond the world of reason.

Prometheus—#46

Prometheus is the god who created man, a claim he shares with dozens of other deities. But he also brought man the essential gift of fire, which is more than we can say for Yahweh, Allah, or any other Western divinity.

Prometheus, whose name means "to think before acting," was a god to both the ancient Greeks and Romans, and his history has grown under the pens of such writers as Hesiod, Apollodorus, and Ovid.

Prometheus was the son of the Titan Iapetus and a nymph, Clymene. Even though he was a Titan on his father's side, he sided with Zeus during the war in which the Olympic gods defeated the Titans. Following this, Zeus, the chief Olympian god, rewarded him with the task of creating humans. Prometheus did this from earth and water and then had the goddess Athena breathe life into them.

But Prometheus secretly held a grudge against Zeus and the other Olympians for destroying his race of Titans. And he always sided with humans against the gods.

When Zeus decreed that man must share with the gods each animal the humans sacrificed, Prometheus decided to trick Zeus. After a sacrifice to Mecone, Prometheus cut up the bull and hid the desirable parts under the hide and the undesirable bare bones under a layer of rich fat. Then he told Zeus to choose for all time which he wanted and which would go to the humans. Zeus, the glutton, chose the fat. When he realized that he had been tricked, he withheld fire from humans as a punishment. But Prometheus went up to Olympus and stole some burning nuggets from the sun. He brought them to earth hidden in a stalk of fennel and thus delivered fire to mankind. After man had fire, Prometheus taught them architecture, mathematics, medicine, and metallurgy. Again, Zeus became angry with Prometheus. By teaching men all of these skills, Prometheus's pets were approaching the status of the gods.

This time Zeus decided to punish Prometheus directly. He had his servants, Force and Violence, seize Prometheus, take him to the Caucasus Mountains, and chain him naked to a rock. There a giant eagle tore at his liver during the day; because Prometheus was immortal, his liver grew back during the night. This went on for many years until finally, in his infinite mercy, Zeus gave Prometheus a way out of his torment, but it required that an immortal volunteer had to die for Prometheus. Needless to say, volunteers did not come pouring in. In fact, no one took up the call for a long time. But eventually, Chiron the Centaur made the sacrifice for him and Zeus ended Prometheus's punishment.

Prometheus is the inspiration for all those who refuse to bow to authority, and we venerate him with a prominent statue in Rockefeller Plaza in New York City. We also revere him at his sacred temples, the Golden Arches, where we enjoy the desirable cuts of sacrificed animals that Prometheus secured for us.

This May Fire You Up

As a god of craftsmanship, Prometheus had a shrine in the potter's quarter of Athens, near Plato's Academy.

Apollo and Dionysus—#23

These two gods of ancient Greece embody the opposite personality types of the Rational and the Free Spirit. We all are combinations of calm restraint and emotional abandon, which is what separates us from the stereotypes of myth, legends, and fairy tales. "Who you are" is reflected in which of these two influential gods dominates your personality.

The Apollonian side of life is order, reason, truth, and virtue—important aspects of life, but not the things that give you a rush. By contrast, Dionysus is the god of wine, revelry, risks, disorder, and freedom.

Apollo was one of the few Greek gods not renamed when brought into the Roman pantheon. He was known as the god of light, medicine, music, and poetry. As protector of the nine Muses, he was the guardian of all culture. As the god of theater, he inspired the playwrights Sophocles, Euripides, and Aeschylus, whose works are still performed. Writers such as these produced new plays and poems for the annual festival of Dionysus. The theater that was dedicated to him in Athens still survives, though ticket sales are not what they used to be. Various groves were sacred to Dionysus, and presumably all the nightclubs and all the gin-joints as well. Dionysus, as god of the grape, has inspired the vintner's art from Dom Perignon to Thunderbird.

The classical Greeks believed that balancing your internal powers of Apollo and Dionysus brought you great personal strength. In the late 1800s, the influential German philosopher, Frederic Nietzsche, wrote about the ancient Greek concept of the man who lives beyond good and evil, the man who lives in the worlds of both the Apollonian and Dionysian. Nietzsche urged us to emphasize the Dionysian side.

The twentieth-century Greek writer Nikos Kazantzakis gave us a superb window into the realm of Apollo and Diony- sus in his novel *Zorba the Greek,* which was made into a movie in 1964. In the film, the Apollonian narrator is Basil, a writer. On his way to Crete, he befriends the middle-aged Zorba, a Dionysian free spirit who accepts the world as it is. He lives life with passion. For him, the realities are freedom, love, delight, and pleasure. He is impetuous, unreflective, and irresponsible. Basil reopens an abandoned lignite mine and Zorba, as his right-hand man, leads the venture into disaster.

In the aftermath of the calamity, they realize that they will go their separate ways, but first Zorba tells his friend that to be free, a fellow needs a little lunacy. And, as a final gesture in the film, Basil asks the Greek to teach him how to dance. Starting off side-by-side, in the sensuous Greek style, they are soon laughing and dancing wildly—the first pure delight we see Basil enjoy.

Zorba and his friend are not the only examples of the Apol- lonian/Dionysian. There are Mr. Spock and Captain Kirk; Fe- lix Unger and Oscar Madison (the Odd Couple); Leo Bloom and Max Bialystock (the Producers); among many others.

As for us, we identify ourselves with the enlightenment of Apollo; however, those who know us best probably see us as Dionysian, and we'll drink to that.

To learn more about Apollo and Dionysus, we suggest
  Mythology by Edith Hamilton.
  The Greek Myths by Robert Graves.

Venus and Cupid—#45

These two Roman gods, mother and son, who were called
Aphrodite and Eros by the Greeks, have wrought havoc on the
world since its inception. For simplicity, we will refer to them
as Venus and Cupid even though many of the stories about
them originated in the Greek culture before being adopted
into Roman mythology. In both cultures, Cupid's arrows
could strike any creature and arouse in him or her the reaction
we call love. With just one shot, Pluto the king of the underworld fell in love. Cupid even caused Apollo, the god of reason, to fall in love.

Venus, the goddess of sexual pleasure, has been resoundingly rejected as inherently sinful, especially since the writings
of Augustine in the early 300s. But let's consider Venus and
Cupid as the personifications of the positive aspects of normal
people.

Love is not something we can define. How can I resolve
the meaning of the word if I claim to love my wife, my children, my dog, and my car? The only things they have in common are that they all cost me money and have to be washed,
but that is not an acceptable analogy for love.

We really cannot separate romantic love from Venus and
her incarnation of sexual desire. But to preserve the ignorance

of children, we depict love as the cute little cherub, Cupid, and celebrate him on Valentine's Day, when we are careful not to mention his mother.

Picturing Cupid as a chubby, playful, childlike god alludes to his Roman essence. By contrast, to the Greeks he was a lusty man and an awe-inspiring primordial force—the most beautiful of all the gods. Just the sight of him could make humans go limp, and he could control the heart of anyone he chose. Eros (Cupid) was a primitive, uncontrollable force who often caused people to fall in love with an unrealistic mate—an example of love's power over rationality. This theme has recurred throughout history and is brought to its comic best in Shakespeare's *A Midsummer Night's Dream*. A modern treatment of this scenario is found in Isaac Asimov's story "The Up-to-Date Sorcerer." In it people under the influence of a love potion fall madly in love only to be cured by the reality of marriage.

Cupid too fell in love. In that myth, Venus felt threatened by the beauty of a mortal, Psyche, and dispatched Cupid to make the maiden fall in love with a monster. But when Cupid saw Psyche, he became enraptured and married her. In retaliation, Venus struck Psyche dead, but Cupid resurrected his bride and she became a goddess, as did their child. Yet another story of death, resurrection, and elevation to the status of a deity. Love can do that.

The power of Cupid is a source of anxiety for those who yearn for an orderly, harmonious life. One might be living a carefree existence before romance blossoms, when suddenly he or she becomes a slave to love.

As long as Cupid's arrows fly, any of us can be struck without warning, perhaps repeatedly. The random nature of such events makes life unpredictable. However, the passage of time can diminish our lust and bring Cupid under control. As a philosopher once so wisely observed, old age can clip our wings, cool our passions, and allow our intellect to finally function unimpeded. But just when we thought we were safe, along came Viagra.

Pandora—#47

Pandora is the original scapegoat, the target of a primitive need to point the finger, to find someone to blame. While we no longer recognize a specific individual as responsible for all or even most of the ills of mankind, we haven't completely shed the need to blame someone else when anything goes wrong or even merely not according to expectations.

In Greek mythology, Pandora was the first human (mortal) woman, the Greek analog of Eve. To make her especially attractive to men, the Olympian gods each contributed something to her construction: Aphrodite made her beautiful, Apollo made her musical, Hermes made her seductive, and the other gods enhanced her as well; hence her name, from *pan* and *doron*, meaning "all-gifted."

When Prometheus stole fire and gave it to humans, Zeus was determined to have his revenge on both parties. For humanity, he created a trap. While Pandora was still on Mount Olympus, he gave her a sealed jar (in later versions, a box) with the instruction not to open it. He then sent her to live on earth with Epimetheus, Prometheus's brother. But she was unable to resist the temptation. She eventually opened the jar, allowing all the diseases, plagues, and other afflictions to escape and bedevil mankind. (Other animals and even plants also get sick. What *they* did to offend Zeus isn't recorded.)

If Pandora were alive today, she would find herself served with countless lawsuits. No matter that she doesn't have deep pockets—or, for that matter, any pockets. Our penchant for accusing, blaming, and then suing someone for a problem for which we don't want to accept responsibility has become the stuff of future legends.

On the other hand, Pandora, when given the jar, was instructed not to open it. How much sense does that make? Get real! It has become a staple of many stories that revolve around someone doing something he was told *not* to do while given every incentive *to* do it. What kind of a god orders a human—notorious for our curiosity and orneriness, not to mention reluctance to follow directions—to resist a temptation placed in his path by that very same deity? Can you say "entrapment"?

Ulysses was familiar with this legend, which might have awakened in him the possibility of smuggling something sinister inside an attractive package. This might have been the source of his inspiration to construct a large wooden horse to achieve victory in the Trojan War, hence the derogatory proverb, "Beware of Greeks bearing gifts." People have assumed that this referred to Ulysses and his Trojan Horse trick—but perhaps it really alluded to Pandora.

As a sign that not all is lost, however, Pandora discovers Hope in the bottom of the vessel: Hope that, somehow, mankind will overcome the sickness and sorrow she has unleashed. In Genesis, Eve similarly falls victim to temptation, but in her case there is no hope. Are women more curious than men, or less able to resist temptation? It doesn't matter. The damage has been done. The blame game, once started, is difficult to conclude—much to the delight of the 300,000 lawyers in the United States.

Pandora's Box has become a metaphor for any potential to unleash additional troubles into a world already chock-full. The expression "Open Pandora's box" has been used to refer to the European settlement of the New World, the Industrial Revolution, and the introduction of atomic power. It covers industrial, agricultural, and medical technology. Pandora was the first person with "the gift that keeps on giving," and her influence has been felt from antiquity to the present day.

Helen—#59

Helen of Troy (also known as Helen of Sparta) was the most beautiful woman of her time—the most beautiful woman of all time. Men fought over her. Armies fought over her. Entire kingdoms were lost over her. And while we were writing this essay, we fell in love with her. But she being the daughter of a god, we're not surprised that she didn't answer our amorous e-mails.

Homer wrote *The Iliad,* one of the most heroic tales in all literature, about the war triggered by her abduction. Other great epics grew from the story as well: Homer's *The Odyssey,* Virgil's *The Aeneid,* and Euripides's *The Trojan Women* as well as his *Iphigenia at Aulis*. There are hundreds of other titles inspired by Helen and the Trojan War.

In the story, Helen was flesh and blood, even though her father was the god Zeus. From the beginning, she was different. Zeus had disguised himself as a swan when he had sex with the beautiful Queen of Sparta, Leda, and she produced an egg. Yes, we really mean she laid an egg. After all, she was impregnated by a swan, so she laid an egg, and from it sprang Helen.

From birth she was proclaimed for her beauty and those features stayed with her for life, and even afterward. When Helen reached puberty, the aging Theseus, king of Athens, kidnapped her. He took her to Aphidna, a small city north of Athens, and there he took her virginity. Helen's brothers gathered an army, destroyed Aphidna, and then took their sister home to Sparta. There, legions of affluent suitors soon arrived.

Among the suitors was Odysseus, who suggested that each suitor swear an oath. They would stand behind whomever Tyndareus, Helen's earthly father, selected, and they would defend the marriage. After everyone agreed to these terms, Tyndareus chose Menelaus not because he was handsome or glamorous, but because he had wealth and power through his brother, Agamemnon.

Several years later, Paris, a prince of Troy, fell in love with her, and she with him. The meeting between Helen and Paris did not come about by chance. It was the gift to Paris from the goddess Aphrodite.

As Aphrodite decreed, the lovers ran off to Troy where they married.

Agamemnon was furious about what he considered the abduction of his sister-in-law. He reminded her former suitors of the oath they had sworn, recruited an army, and built a thousand ships. Before long, the Greek forces reached Troy and after a siege of ten years, the city fell to the Greeks. Helen, with no expression of remorse, returned to her husband Menelaus with whom she lived out a happy life. And her beauty persisted. Even after she died and descended into the underworld, the spirits of many men courted her there.

Beauty in a woman is a major asset, and in this regard, Helen was truly wealthy. And she used her gifts to great advantage. The expression "The face that launched a thousand ships" refers to her (see sidebar), and it has become a synonym for feminine allure that we still use today.

Amaze Your Friends with This

"The face that launched a thousand ships" was first used by Christopher Marlowe in his play *Doctor Faustus*, written before 1604.

Odysseus—#24

Odysseus (known by the Romans as Ulysses) is the exemplar of cunning and duplicity. He was the first Greek warrior to live by his wits, not bravery or strength. When his countrymen drafted him to fight in the Trojan War, he tried to avoid service by pretending to be insane; that plan having failed, he tried to join the Air National Guard in Texas. When that didn't work, he reluctantly joined the Greek troops, who spent ten years unsuccessfully trying to breach the walls of Troy. They were trying to rescue Helen, the most beautiful woman in the world, and return her to her husband, King Menelaus.

Odysseus was one of the leaders of the Greek forces, and ultimately he was the decisive factor in the conflict because he designed the Trojan Horse. This clever trick involved hiding a squad of soldiers inside the enormous construction. The Trojans took it into their city and the hidden Greek soldiers snuck out that night to open the gates. The massed Greek army rushed in and destroyed the city, thus ending the conflict. The ruse was so influential that we still use the expression "Trojan horse" to indicate a clever deception.

In Homer's epic tale *The Odyssey*, which dates from about 800 B.C.E., we follow Odysseus on his many harrowing and often inglorious adventures on his trip home after the war.

When he and his men reached the land of the Cyclops, the huge one-eyed monster ate some of Odysseus's men. The rest escaped after cunningly blinding the monster. However, the Cyclops called on his father, Poseidon, the god of the sea, to punish Odysseus. The deity did so with storms that resulted in a ten-year journey of a few hundred miles home.

Along the way, Odysseus's ship sank and his entire crew was lost. Alone, Odysseus was cast up on the island of Ogygia, where the nymph Calypso made him her lover and refused to let him leave for seven years. When Zeus finally intervened, Odysseus sailed away on a small boat, only to be shipwrecked by another storm. The Phoenicians saved him and, finally, with the help of the goddess Athena, he reached his home island of Ithaca.

His wife, Penelope, had remained true to him during the twenty years of his absence. But after so many years, she was presumed to be a widow and several nobles tried to persuade her to remarry.

Pressured by her suitors, she declared that she would marry the man who could bend an extremely stiff bow that belonged to Odysseus. In the meantime, Odysseus, who never tackled a problem head-on, had snuck into his home disguised as a beggar. After all of the suitors failed to bend the bow, he succeeded, and then killed all of them. After that, naturally, Odysseus and Penelope lived happily ever after. However, we suspect that Odysseus, using some scam, occasionally snuck off to Ogygia to visit Calypso.

After all, he was the master of deception.

In the real world, Odysseus's trick has been used again and again to hide a bomb in a car, cyanide in yogurt, Queen Cleopatra in a rug, and computer viruses in free software. Any long or meandering journey is called an odyssey. Even a long book—*Ulysses* by James Joyce—carries his name. The stories of Odysseus, Helen, and Achilles commemorate the end of the Bronze Age and the emergence of a warrior government. Like the Germanic raiders who sacked Rome, Odysseus (and his new Greek culture) is the descendant of Northern warriors, and his target is one of the great cities. But—as noted in the Book of Joshua—great cities fell easily unless they had chariots of iron, the key material of the coming age. For a time, an early armored battle-tank was enough to resist the hordes of spear-throwing warriors and their lighter-weight laminated armor. Throughout *The Iliad* and *The Odyssey*, Homer glorifies the golden polished bronze armor and weapons of the Greeks, and he speaks distrustfully of cold gray iron, the new weapon that neither the Greeks nor Trojans have in abundance. On his way home, Odysseus encounters witches and Sirens, island holdouts from the late Neolithic, women too powerful or too remote to have been swept into the Bronze Age culture now vanishing as Odysseus and the glory-hungering warriors sack the major trade cities. Odysseus's wife, patient Penelope, is another Neolithic throwback, not property to be carried off like Helen, but a queen in her own right, declining to accept a new husband, ruling for a time on her own, but ultimately faithful to her wandering husband.

Taken alone, Odysseus's journey is the story of a remarkable adventurer, the triumph of wits. Taken in context, it's a more remarkable survey of the history, weaponry, and culture of the Bronze Age, an era still beginning to yield its secrets to archaeology.

Midas—#29

"Be careful what you wish for" is the moral of the story of King Midas. His blinding greed warns us of the trouble that can follow when we act on impulse, on any blind motivation. When we ignore the possible consequences of our actions, tragedy will follow.

As with many myths, the central character is someone who really did exist. He was one of several kings of that name in Phrygia, in Anatolia (modern Turkey) in the eighth century B.C.E. We know little about him; however, the myth that has surrounded his name is rich in narrative and detail.

In the myth, Midas did a favor for the Greek god Dionysus and the deity, as a reward, granted him one wish. In his avarice, he asked that Dionysus turn into gold everything he, the king, touched. He soon realized that this "Midas Touch" was a curse. He discovered that he was unable to eat or drink, and when his daughter tried to comfort him, tragedy struck as she too turned into gold. He finally asked that the gift be taken back. He learned how to undo the damage he had caused, and repented of his foolishness.

As a result, Midas became more generous and kind, and he was rewarded with an extension of his province, eventually taking over the realm of King Gordius (of the Gordian Knot renown). Because of the fame of these men, the kings of Phrygia were alternately named Midas and Gordius, thus leading to the mistaken belief that the famous Gordius was the son of the famous Midas.

Although Midas became more generous and kind, he did not get any smarter. He went on to make another serious mistake. He let himself be pressured into serving as a judge in the famous music contest between the god Apollo and the satyr Marysas.

This satyr had found an enchanted double flute and with it he became an accomplished musician. In time, Marysas grew to regard his musical ability as equal to Apollo's, and he challenged the god to a competition.

In the contest, Marysas and the magic flute could not meet the standards of Apollo and his lyre. But Midas, one of the judges, voiced his minority opinion in favor of Marysas.

Apollo was furious. First, he punished Marysas with a painful death. Then he chastised Midas by giving him the ears of a donkey—to reflect his tin ear as a judge in the contest. Midas hid this deformity from everyone, but his barber knew. The barber was unable to keep his secret, so he dug a hole and whispered the secret into the ground. A reed grew at the location of this whisper and passed the secret on to other reeds. Soon Midas's entire kingdom knew the truth, and Midas had the barber executed. Then, with his shame exposed, Midas committed suicide.

Midas is an object lesson in two regards: First, wishing without thinking is a dumb move. And second, challenging the vanity of the gods is even dumber.

Maybe You Hadn't Considered

The legend of King Midas is rich in the sheer quantity of specific lessons, perhaps more so than any other Greek myth:

- Beware what you wish for.
- Literal requests may be taken literally.
- Items of value, such as gold, have limited usefulness; being useful for one task does not mean an item is useful for any other task.
- The gods always win.
- A king is no judge of music: ability in one profession means little in another field.
- An honest answer is not always correct.
- Never question (doubt) a god.
- Confidants cannot be trusted, not even plants.
- Any secret will eventually leak out.

Pygmalion—#88

Pygmalion was a man who, when faced with a problem, took matters into his own hands and solved it. Many men have done this, but Pygmalion used this direct approach to solve a challenge that has plagued men from the dawn of time: how to find the ideal woman—one who would fit hand-in-glove with his disposition, love him, and be dependable forever.

We writers treat our essays as though they were our children. No matter how bad they are, we love them. In the same regard, Pygmalion, a mythical ancient sculptor, fell in love with his work, but he carried his creativity and admiration to a new level.

The story of Pygmalion was told by the Greek writers Hesiod in the eighth century B.C.E. and Pindar in the sixth century B.C.E. In addition, the Roman writer Ovid recorded the myth in his book *Metamorphoses,* written at the dawn of the Common Era.

In the story, Pygmalion, a bachelor, was put off by the many faults that he felt were natural to women. He decided to create the ideal woman and carved an ivory statue more beautiful than any woman since Helen of Troy. Then he fell in love with his creation.

The statue had all the appearance of a real woman, and he adorned her in women's clothes, rings, and long necklaces. He placed the statue on a couch and laid its head on soft pillows. He kissed it and imagined that it kissed him back.

At the festival of Aphrodite, Pygmalion made his offering of a heifer, and then asked the goddess of love to give the ivory maiden life so she could become his wife. When Pygmalion returned home, he found that Aphrodite had rewarded him. He kissed his creation and she seemed warm. He touched her breast and the ivory grew soft. She was indeed now a woman, Galatea. She felt the kisses he gave her and blushed. Soon they were married and in less than a year, Aphrodite blessed Pygmalion's bride with a daughter.

In George Bernard Shaw's play *Pygmalion,* as well as in the Broadway musical and movie *My Fair Lady*, the modern Pygmalion is Henry Higgins. He makes a lady, not out of ivory, but from a guttersnipe, a lowly flower-seller, Eliza Doolittle. And he accomplishes this by teaching her to speak proper English. From "Tha rine in Spine . . ." she advances to "The rain in Spain . . ." After this transformation, Henry passes

Eliza off as a duchess. In the end, Henry Higgins suffers the same fate as the original Pygmalion—he falls in love with his creation.

Pygmalion is a mythical character who took do-it-yourself to its ultimate limits. He is the undisputed superstar of self-help.

Icarus—#80

Icarus is important for several reasons. He is a prime example of the consequences of not following instructions. And although he was first in flight and the inspiration for the Wright brothers, he was foolish enough to exceed the manufacturer's specific limitations on altitude, and thus his wings failed. What was even worse, he had neglected to purchase flight insurance.

The story begins in Athens where Icarus lived with his father, Daedalus. The older man was so skilled as a sculptor and inventor that he was able to construct a robot that looked and functioned like a horse. However, Daedalus had a dark side. Among his apprentices was his nephew, Talos. Talos was cleverer than Daedalus, who killed him in a fit of jealousy. As a result, Daedalus was exiled to Crete, accompanied by his son Icarus.

At about this time, Poseidon, the god of the sea, sent a white bull to Crete. When King Minos refused to sacrifice the animal, Poseidon caused the queen, Pasiphaë, to fall in love with it. A queen and a bull—remember, in myth, anything goes. The queen had Daedalus construct a wooden cow in which she could conceal herself and consummate the affair.

From this union Pasiphaë bore the Minotaur, a monster with the head of a bull and the body of a man.

In an effort to hide his wife's disgrace, Minos decided to sequester the Minotaur from public view. He had Daedalus construct an intricate maze of chambers and passages, a labyrinth. The king put the beast in it and fed it humans that he forced the Athenians to send him as tribute. The Greek hero Theseus, to end the senseless sacrifices, offered himself as one of the victims. Once in the labyrinth, he slew the Minotaur and escaped from the maze by following a thread back to the entrance.

Angry because the maze could be defeated, Minos imprisoned Daedalus and Icarus behind high walls. To get away, the resourceful Daedalus made two pairs of wings from feathers and wax. Daedalus warned Icarus to keep a middle course over the sea and avoid approaching the sun. But the boy, in his excitement, flew too high. The sun melted his wings and he fell into the sea and drowned. His father, who complied with all FAA regulations, flew on to Sicily and safety.

After the tragic event, King Minos launched an investigation. First, he grilled and then fired the official who signed off on the plans. Then an independent engineer, Seymour Rappoport, testified that the wings were properly designed and should have functioned well at the altitude Icarus had reached. This led to the discovery that faulty materials were used and also uncovered other deficiencies in the military contracts that lay behind the disaster. What's worse, the investigation revealed that the contract with Mrs. Brown's Kitchen Renovation and Aviation Company had incurred enormous cost overruns.

Some things never change.

Hercules—#76

Allow me to introduce myself. In Greek legends I am known as Herakles, the god of physical power, but you probably know me by my Roman name, Hercules.

I had a difficult childhood. My mother was a mortal woman and my father was the king of the gods—Zeus. At the time, my dad was married to the goddess Hera, and she was outraged by his seemingly endless dalliances with other goddesses and human women. My mother, Alcmene, knew that as another of Zeus's bastard children, I would be in trouble with Hera. Mom tried to head off problems by naming me Herakles—the glory of Hera—but it didn't work.

While I was still an infant, Hera sent two snakes to kill me. I have been told that already I was so powerful that I crushed the vipers in my bare hands. This was a foreshadowing of my adulthood, when I became the embodiment of strength—recognized as the strongest man of all time. I wonder if my encounter with the snakes whetted my appetite for danger and killing, because those characteristics marked my adult years.

I married Megara, daughter of King Creon of Orchomenus, and we settled down. We had a few kids before the Hera-Nazi caught up with us. She caused me to have a fit and during the spell, I killed my wife and children.

As penance, the god Apollo sentenced me to hard labor. My first jobs were to kill a lion, eliminate a multiheaded monster that lived in a swamp, and capture a deer with golden horns. After I had done these tasks, I applied for parole. But even though I had been a model prisoner, I was turned down. I was sitting in my cell feeling sorry for myself when a guard came in.

"Step lively, Muscles. King Augeas needs some help down on the farm, and we're sending you."

"What kind of help?"

"Some tidying up."

Tidying up, my eyeball. The old fool wanted his stables cleaned. Now that may not sound too difficult, but the building housed more than a thousand cattle and hadn't been tended to for several decades. The piles of manure were mountainous. Worst of all, according to the contract for the job, I had to complete it in a single day. I used ingenuity. I dug a channel from a nearby river up to the door at one end of the stable and an exit ditch from the other side. Then I diverted the river into the building and drained it into a stream about a mile away. The next day I got a summons from the Environmental Protection Agency and also one from the U.S. Army Corps of Engineers—something about pollution and wetlands contamination. I couldn't understand it, so I turned it over to Shyster and Apateonos, attorneys to the gods.

When I got back to my labors, I had to kill a flock of man-eating birds, eliminate a bull that breathed fire, and destroy a bunch of man-eating horses. That done, the warden sent me out again. For some perverted reason, he wanted me to bring him the belt of Hippolyte, who was the queen of the Amazons. "Okay," I told him. "Whatever turns you on." And I was on my way.

The gal turned out to be the sister of Apollo, and she led a wild existence among a gang of chicks on the banks of the Bosphorus. I got her belt and, to score some extra points, I also brought back her battle-ax. It was to no avail; they turned me down for parole again.

My next job was to retrieve some golden apples that belonged to my nemesis, Hera. When I brought the apples back,

I told the warden I wanted to be released for good behavior, but he said I had several more years to serve. After I went on a hunger strike, we compromised. I would only have to complete one more task, but on that adventure I would have to face a real son of a bitch. The boss decided he wanted a dog. Not some cute little poodle, but Cerberus, the three-headed dog that guarded the entrance to the underworld. It turned out to be easier than I had anticipated. I hid behind a boulder, and when the beast came near I stuck out my leg. The animal took the bait and locked his jaws on my calf. It didn't let go while I walked back to Argolis.

Finally, I was released to a halfway house. Zeus took pity on me and told Hera to lighten up. Then he sent Athena on a chariot to bring me to Olympus where he made me a god. I was free at last. Free at last. Holy Zeus almighty, I was free at last.

A Man on His Way Up

In 1970, Arnold Schwarzenegger—the current governor of California—made his film debut playing Hercules in *Hercules in New York*.

2. Folktales

Imagine this: A young wife and her husband are tired of feeding her father at the table because the old man frequently drops his food and utensils. They sit him off to the side and give him a cheap wooden bowl to eat from. Later, the couple finds their young son at play, making a crude bowl. He's practicing for the day when he will treat his parents the way he has seen them treat his grandfather. This is not an Arthur Miller plot; it's one of the folktales collected by the Brothers Grimm in nineteenth-century Germany.

Folktales can originate from almost any anecdote in any location. A story about a neighbor who took a long nap might have been the source of Rip Van Winkle. And you'll find different versions of each tale because storytelling is an art—much like jazz, it's all in the performance. The stories of Mark Twain and Garrison Keillor would have ended up as folktales if they'd been written in the 1400s.

These stories are usually meant as moral lessons for children or tall tales meant for the local bar. Most of them do not deal with grand quests or national figures, but rather with animals, ordinary people, and the problems and choices of daily life. And not all of these tales deal with pleasant subjects.

For those who want a deeper understanding of this genre, we suggest Bruno Bettelheim's *The Uses of Enchantment*.

The rest of you, enter here. Santa's waiting.

Santa Claus—#4

He's number one on the *Forbes* Fictional Fifteen—the richest fictional individual in the United States—where he is listed as having infinite wealth.

Children eventually outgrow their belief in Santa Claus as the mythical, chubby, favorite uncle who brings us presents on the flimsiest of excuses—it's cold outside and we've eaten all our vegetables. But the underlying lesson endures: We're entitled to all these goodies just for living in an affluent society. It isn't necessary to justify presents on the basis of merit. Thanks to Santa Claus, we don't have to *earn* special treatment, just not having mugged anyone or started any fires this year is enough to warrant favor. In theory, only good children receive presents, but we all know just how far short of theory reality can be.

Santa Claus began as a real person, as is true of many fictional characters. Nicholas of Patara lived in the late third and early fourth centuries in what is now Turkey. His wealthy parents raised him as a devout Christian in the early days of that creed. Nicholas obeyed Jesus's instructions to "sell what you own and give the money to the poor" (Matt. 19:21, Mark 10:21). Nicholas became Bishop of Myra while still a young man, and was widely known for his generosity to the poor and his love of children.

Bishop Nicholas was initially persecuted for his faith, but the Roman emperor Constantine stopped this practice when he converted to Christianity and made it the state religion.

In 325, Nicholas was present when the Council of Nicaea decided on the details of the modern Roman Catholic religion. A few years later Nicholas died, and the anniversary of his death is remembered as St. Nicholas Day, December 6.

Over the centuries, Nicholas has been associated with stories, legends, and miracles benefiting the poor. One story tells of three poor sisters in need of dowries. Each miraculously received a bag of gold said to have been tossed through an open window, landing in a stocking left to dry in front of a fire. Thus began the custom of hanging Christmas stockings by the fire.

In his role as patron saint of sailors, Nicholas's reputation and stories made the rounds of ports far and wide, spreading the legend over the course of centuries. He became the patron saint of Sicily and Greece; of the Apulia region of Italy; and of many cities in Germany, Switzerland, Austria, Russia, Belgium, and the Netherlands. There are more than two thousand churches named for him, including three hundred in Belgium and at least four hundred in England.

Fast forward to the seventeenth century and the New World. The Dutch knew Saint Nicholas as Sinter Klaas; this was Anglicized to Santa Claus.

John Pintard, founder of The New-York Historical Society, adopted St. Nicholas as the patron saint of both New York and the Historical Society. In 1809, Washington Irving joined that society and, under the pseudonym Diedrich Knickerbocker, published his satirical *History of New York*, which made numerous references to a jolly Saint Nick–type figure; the Christmas caricature was born. In the early nineteenth century, Irving also contributed another piece of the legend when he described St. Nicholas riding over the treetops, bringing presents to children. This was when sleighs were the routine mode of travel during winter, though pulled by horses rather than reindeer.

In 1823, Clement Clarke Moore's poem "A Visit from

St. Nicholas" (also known as "The Night Before Christmas") boosted the popularity of the jolly-elf image and set the stage for illustrations that morphed into the white-bearded, pudgy, jolly old man we are familiar with—largely through the efforts of Thomas Nast, the famous nineteenth-century illustrator and cartoonist.

It is not accidental that Santa Claus is one of few characters associated with Western culture that were allowed to persist in Communist countries. Consider that both Santa Claus and Karl Marx have bushy white beards and believe in giving people what they want without regard for cost. And Santa Claus always wears a red outfit, the symbolic color of Communism.

Santa Claus has marketed everything from soft drinks to insurance. He has been the subject of many movies, books, and songs, and his image was immortalized on a U.S. postage stamp. He is the only fictional character who actually receives mail delivered by the Postal Service. Nobody would dare suggest he go on a diet—except maybe those overworked reindeer. Santa Claus is the symbol of all that is right with the celebration of the winter solstice. He favors innocent children and motivates charitable contributions. At the same time he drives the commercialization of the season. A child's belief in Santa Claus evaporates as he or she grows up, but as a parent he or she renews the tradition. And so it goes, year after year.

No, Virginia, there is NO Santa Claus. Deal with it.

The Pied Piper—#69

The Pied Piper is unique among legendary characters because it appears he was a fictional character invented to explain a real event: the disappearance of 130 citizens from the town of Hamelin on June 26, 1284. This is not the legend you're familiar with.

The common version has the Pied Piper being hired by the townspeople to rid them of a plague of rats. He does this with his magical musical ability, leading all the rats into the nearby river, where they drown. When the mayor of the town (or in some versions, the entire town) reneges on the contract, the Piper changes tunes and lures many children of the town away, into the hills. They are never heard from again. Different versions have certain children saved; in one movie, a lame child is unable to keep up; in another telling, a blind child is left behind, unable to point his elders toward the hill where his fellows disappeared. In still another movie, the mayor relents under pressure from the parents of the lost children and pays the Piper, who brings the children home, where everybody lives happily and rat-free ever after.

The name *Pied Piper* derives from the colorful garb he wore—typically bright red and yellow. And in German stories, the Pied Piper is frequently called the Ratcatcher. The town of Hamelin (also spelled Hameln) is a real place located in north-central Germany, about 40 kilometers southwest of Hannover.

The legend first appeared in print about 1440, a marginal addition to a fourteenth-century manuscript that was lost until 1936. The legend has the children entering a tunnel in the hills, through which they are conveyed to another part of Europe—Transylvania is the favored end point, but Moravia is also mentioned, even though both locations are hundreds of miles and several mountain ranges away from Hamelin. But it is at this point that the legend takes on a plausible origin.

There is some speculation, founded in historical reality and noting linguistic similarities in place names, that the Piper was a recruiting agent. He was hired by a sovereign to recruit townsfolk for new settlements in Eastern Europe—regions that had been depopulated by the Viking predations and had not recovered.

But why take only the children? That probably represents an error or confusion of translation combined with a persistent feature of political reality. Rulers have always viewed themselves as the stern parent presiding over the unruly citizenry. At one time, the citizens of a village were referred to as "children of the town" or "town children," and it is likely that it is with this sense of the term "children" that the myth reports 130 went missing. It probably refers to entire families, not just the younger generation. Some two hundred years later, this myth was blended with another story about an infestation of rats. (The disastrous Children's Crusade of 1212 might also have been on some people's minds.)

The story has been incorporated into a variety of motifs and media. In 1803, Goethe wrote a poem that Schubert set to music in 1815; in 1842, Robert Browning wrote a poem about the legend; Bertolt Brecht also cast the story in rhyme. The legend is presented in several operas, ballets, novels, songs, and both animated (Disney 1933) and live-action (1957, 1972, 1981) films, including some from Europe. Several silent movies (1911, 1926) were simply dramatizations of Browning's poem. Elvis Presley's first film was entitled *The Pied Piper of Cleveland*, about disk jockey Bill Randle; the film was never released.

In one movie version, the mayor refuses to pay the Piper his fee for cleaning the town of rats. He uses that money to build a fancy clock tower, to compete with the famous tower in a nearby town. The moral of this version is that children are worth much more than some petty rivalry. Of course, in this sanitized version the children return home.

The legend was probably composed by the remaining people of the town of Hamelin, ashamed that such a significant number of their own could be lured away from their idyllic existence in Hamelin by the promise of a better life. How could life be any better than here in Hamelin? It just doesn't make sense. They must have been tricked, by some magic, into abandoning their homes and friends.

In common language, the expression "pay the Piper" reminds us that refusing to pay someone can have very nasty consequences.

The Wandering Jew—#92

In the Gospel According to Matthew 16:28, Jesus promised that after his death, he would return to earth before some of those listening to him would die. Jesus has not returned, so the story had to be augmented to accommodate this defect. As is usually the case when a myth grows, the additional layers compound the problem that prompted the story in the first place, and this tale is no exception. The legend claims that a person from the era of Jesus is still alive, two thousand years later.

The myth first appeared in 1228 in the chronicles of Roger of Wendover. In the story, the wanderer was a pagan, a Roman soldier named Carthaphilus, who was Pontius Pilate's gatekeeper. He allegedly struck Jesus on the hand and Jesus retaliated by placing a curse on him—to walk the earth until he, the Messiah, would return, or until the end of the world, whichever came first. The story also claimed that this Roman recycles his youth. He ages normally, but every hundred years he reverts to the age of thirty. At this point, we are all sinking in the quicksand of the bizarre, and it gets worse.

In Leyden, Netherlands, in 1602 an anonymous pamphlet claimed that Paulus von Eitzen, the bishop of Schleswig, met the Wanderer in Hamburg, Germany, in 1542. The Wanderer was identified as a Jew named Ahasuerus. He had been a cobbler beside whose shop Jesus paused to rest while carrying the cross along the Via Dolorosa. The shoemaker chased Jesus away from the front of his shop and, as retribution, Jesus condemned him to wander forever.

Thereafter, the Wandering Jew became a man without a country. He became a stranger who, like Kilroy during World War II, had allegedly been in every major city in Europe. In 1868, he even turned up in Salt Lake City, where a Mormon named O'Grady encountered him. In various places, he has had different names. In France, he was called Isaac of Old; in Germany, John Buttadaeus; in Spain, John the Hope in God; in Boston, Peter Rugg.

The concept of the Wandering Jew moved into modern literature as the model for the Ancient Mariner and the Flying Dutchman. He appears in "Queen Mab," a poem by Percy Bysshe Shelley; Nathaniel Hawthorne's "A Virtuoso's Collection"; *The Holy Cross* by Eugene Field; as well as stories by Rudyard Kipling, O. Henry, and John Galsworthy. He even turned up in the 1980s movie *The Seventh Sign* opposite Demi Moore.

Søren Kierkegaard included the Wandering Jew among the three fundamental myths of European culture, the others being Don Juan and Doctor Faust. And Gustave Dore created an excellent series of woodcuts, called *The Legend of the Wandering Jew*, in 1856.

The Wandering Jew is still around. One of our less reliable sources claimed to have seen David Letterman giving him a pair of sneakers on *The Late Show*. He was also rumored to have been on with Jay Leno, who showed more imagination and gave him a Pogo Stick.

Did You See Him?

He has been seen in Hamburg, Vienna, Prague, Brussels, Leipzig, and Paris. We suggest you be more attentive when traveling abroad.

Hansel and Gretel—#52

Hansel and Gretel are fairy tale characters who bring us an important message. We must rely on our own strengths and initiatives to establish personal stability in a threatening and chaotic world. Three cheers for the children. But in the balance, the story itself is damaging considering the negative aspect of the rest of the package toward women. A Bronx cheer for the storyteller.

The story features two villainous women who independently threaten the lives of the young Hansel and Gretel. In the tale recorded and revised by the Brothers Grimm in Germany during the 1800s, Hansel and Gretel have a stepmother who reinforces the bias that stepmothers are evil. (An idea that Charles Perrault tried to sell us in the tale of Cinderella.)

The children's father, a poor woodcutter, has remarried after the death of his first wife. When the story opens in the modest hut where he and his family live, we learn that a famine has gripped the land and there is not enough food for the four people under his roof. Their ineffectual father does not know what to do, but their stepmother has a clear solution in mind. They will do away with the children by losing them in the forest, a common practice in those days. In fact, the idea may, at times, seem attractive to the parents of teenagers in the modern world, even without a famine.

On the first try, the parents take the children into the woods and desert them, but Hansel and Gretel find their way home. A few days later, the parents lead the children into the woods again, and this time the children are lost. They wander aimlessly in the forest for two days. Then a helpful bird guides them to a house made of bread and sugar, and the children think their problems are over. Not only have they found a refuge, but one they can eat. However, the house harbors the second evil woman in the story, an ugly, cannibalistic witch. So in reality their problems are not solved, they are compounded—they are in danger of being eaten by the old hag. Their luck turns around when Gretel kills the witch by shoving her into a hot oven. Following this, the children return home and, to their delight, find that their stepmother has died.

In a double standard that we still honor today, the children do not blame their father for their problems. On the contrary, now that the two evil women are out of the way, they are again secure under his roof. They have improved their condition in life by bringing home valuables taken from the witch's house. And, of course, they live happily ever after.

This fairy tale is a mixed bag of values. The scale tips to the negative side, damaging the tender minds of children. This folktale, as was true of many others altered and recorded by the Brothers Grimm in Germany or Charles Perrault in France, presents women as stereotypes based on their appearance. If they are ugly, they are evil— a notion we should not perpetuate, and the notion that stepmothers are wicked is a calumny now dead, and it's long past time for its burial. Another unacceptable lesson in the tale is never trust your parents.

What we can subscribe to is this: steer clear of strangers, resist a diet high in sugar, and by all means avoid the advice of birds, no matter how well intentioned they may seem.

Cinderella, A Rebuttal—#26

The story of Cinderella, that innocent victim of oppression, has been part of every culture, with minor variations. It may have arisen in the remote past among the Chinese, whose aristocrats prized small feet. The version that is popular in America today was written from oral tradition in the 1600s by a Frenchman, Charles Perrault, and brought to film by Walt Disney in 1950.

Cinderella's damaging influence has cast a dark shadow over us. She embodies a distortion of reality, the reality in which we are expected to earn our rewards.

One of the story's sinister features is that stepmothers are wicked. In fact, we can't even think of the word *stepmother* without mentally adding *wicked* to it. On top of that, Cinderella reinforces the passive mentality of those who accept their downtrodden lot in life while waiting for mystical forces to come to their rescue.

In the end, Cinderella becomes a princess and forgives her

oppressive stepmother and stepsisters even though they should have been brought to justice for child abuse.

Cinderella is pathetic, but we fall in love with the idea that the meek will triumph in the end. To this purpose, a fairy god-mother provides her with elegant clothes so that she can attract the eye of the prince, who happens to be looking for a girl to marry. Decked out in her finery, Cinderella gets his attention at a ball where she is nothing but a clotheshorse. She has earned nothing. She deserves nothing, except perhaps back wages at home. And yet, she gets the prince to marry her. This is not the lesson we should teach our children. There are more important values than good looks, fine clothes, and expensive trappings—intelligence, independence, self-esteem, responsibility, and self-motivation—none of which characterize Cinderella.

Let's drop the Cinderella mentality and introduce our chil-dren to the genuine values in life—namely, they have to earn their rewards. And while we're at it, let's get rid of the attitude that we are wicked if we tell our kids, "Clean your room!"

It's an Old Story

The tale can be traced to China around 860 in *The Miscel-laneous Record of Yu Tang* by Tuan Ch'eng-Shih.

3. Legends

Stories of King Arthur and his knights of the round table are the sort of tales our parents tell us with a smile. This is a magical world, the child's introduction to human possibilities. Merlin transporting the great pillars of Stonehenge . . . William Tell splitting an apple on his son's head . . . this is the stuff of, well, legend.

Some of these may be based on factual accounts, but no one will ever know for sure. The tales inform us of our values, our roots, our culture, and events too romantic or too individual to be chronicled in official histories.

How do we count the persons in this section as fictional characters? That's easy: Nothing we know about them is hard fact, while large parts of these favorite stories are definitely works of fiction. The script of Kevin Costner's movie *Robin Hood* probably wasn't taken from the meager chronicles of the 1190s.

Was Saint Valentine real? That doesn't mean the story is reliable. Did Gawain really seek the Holy Grail or was that just an excuse to leave home?

What's important and real are these characters, their wisdom, their passions, their strategies, their heroism.

Lilith—#99

This woman is quite important for her involvement in so many "firsts." The story of Lilith is an old one; so old we cannot be sure of its origin. Lilith appears on a four-thousand-year-old Sumerian tablet where she is an evil spirit, a witch, in the *Gilgamesh* epic. There she is a winged female demon. She also appears in Canaanite stories. From these various sources, she entered Jewish myth as the first wife of Adam.

Lilith does not appear in the Bible. It is in rabbinic interpretation of the Jewish scriptures dating from about the time of the Babylonian captivity that we find her. According to the men who concocted the story, God constructed her from filth and mud, not the pure dust of the earth as he had done with Adam. To establish the principle of patriarchy from the start, Adam demanded that Lilith yield to his will and assume the recumbent position during sex. But she was the first feminist and refused to do so. Adam tried to compel her by force, and we almost had the first rape. But Lilith escaped in a rage, and we had the first separation followed by the first divorce.

For thinking herself the equal of a man, rabbis called upon God to punish her. The deity who had created her the way she was in the first place was asked to punish her for being that way. Women just can't win. In his infinite mercy God decided that she would have only demons as offspring, more than a hundred of them a day. As revenge, Lilith has been responsible for the deaths of many infants, and she persists in this deadly rampage against humanity to this day.

Lilith not only kills infants but, in a Christian myth of the Middle Ages, she was a succubus, a creature who copulated with men in their sleep. To prevent such carnal nightly impositions, monks would sleep guarding their genitals with their hands and a crucifix. Superstitious Jews still protect a newborn child by writing *Lilith* on the wall of his or her room and crossing it off.

Among the various myths of creation, we find that God, untroubled by his failure with Lilith, started on a series of experiments. He built a woman using bone, muscle, and blood and covered her with skin and tufts of hair. But Adam was not pleased, so God tried again, using one of Adam's ribs.* And to enhance his creation, God decorated her with jewelry. This time the nitwit was captivated. Too bad. Had Adam stuck with Lilith, even on the terms of equality, think of how much better off we would be. We would still be in the Garden of Eden where no one would have to die, or endure the trials and tribulations now associated with life. We have to put up with all of these terrible things because Adam was the first male chauvinist pig.

Saint Valentine—#58

The history of this character is lost in obscurity. In ancient times, there were several notable men named Valentine. One was a bishop of Terni, another a priest in Africa, and a third served as pope for a few weeks back in 827. However, none of them ever made it to sainthood.

There are several differing stories about Saint Valentine and how he may be connected to the holiday we celebrate on February 14.

---

* This was a potentially disastrous point in human history. Where would we all be today if, after God had removed the rib, Adam's dog picked up the bone and buried it?

The most frequently told legend holds that in 270, during the time of Emperor Claudius II, a priest named Valentine lived in Rome. Claudius felt that married men made poor soldiers because they would not want to leave their families for battle. The empire needed soldiers, so Claudius is reported to have issued an edict forbidding new marriages.

Valentine supposedly violated the ban and secretly married couples. For this, the Romans threw him in jail. While there, Valentine allegedly fell in love with his jailor's blind daughter, and it was said he miraculously cured her. But when their illicit love affair was discovered, the Roman authorities had him beheaded. On the morning of his execution, the fourteenth of February, he purportedly sent the girl a farewell message signed, *From your Valentine*. Sometime later, the miraculous cure helped qualify him for sainthood.

Beheading seems a strange reaction to a miracle, so we looked into the matter. After extensive investigation, we found an original but anonymous and possibly unreliable seventh-century manuscript, written in modern English, in the basement archives of a high school in Brooklyn. From the document, we learned that Valentine had not restored sight to a blind girl, but had bestowed blindness to a sighted girl. (The document also claimed that the Dodgers would win the World Series in 1992. Not all legends are completely reliable.)

Valentine's Day is a Christian cooptation of the pagan feast of Lupercalia that honored Juno Februata, the goddess of high-spirited sex. It was one of several Roman holidays that were sex orgies. Annually on February 15, all single young men in Rome drew a lady's name from a jar and pinned it to their sleeves for the duration of the celebration. Hence the expression "wearing your heart on your sleeve." Men and women were thus partnered for feasting and sex-play for several days.

At the end of the holiday, all of the women expected at least a piece of jewelry, and any lady who became pregnant expected to marry her partner.

By 496, the Christian clergy had demonized all of the biologically normal pagan practices. About that time, Pope Gelasius altered the Lupercalia lottery by replacing the names of local women with the names of saints. Each person was to draw the name of a saint and try to emulate him or her during the next year. This was supposed to be an improvement on what had gone on before.

In the modern world, the importance of Valentine's Day cannot be overstated. Those of us who survive December with a few unspent dollars now have an opportunity to correct that defect while fulfilling the wishes of a lover who expects a heart-shaped box of chocolates, one of St. Hallmark's romantic cards, exotic perfume, sexy underwear, and a pricey bauble. As for the importance to our economy, this day brings substantial sales of flowers, greeting cards, jewelry, and condoms.

Let's look forward to the next logical step, the restoration of Lupercalia and orgies. And if it will keep the clergy happy, we'll even call it St. Lupercalia's Day.

King Arthur—#3

The mythical King Arthur has been so important in the minds of the English that for hundreds of years many of their kings and queens have based their legitimacy to the throne on a blood relationship to him.

Arthur has been the subject of scholarly investigation for more than a century, with several dozen people writing several hundred books and several thousand journal articles in just the past two decades. They have all been trying to unravel the layers of myth to conclusively establish whether such a person existed. Scholars are coming to the unsatisfying conclusion that there's nothing in the legends that can be firmly established as real, but the mystery and the fascination with Arthur remain.

In the legend, Arthur was crowned in the fictional city of Caerleon-on-Usk, and he became the king of the Britons. He commanded the loyalty of hundreds of powerful men, foremost among whom were the Knights of the Round Table, symbolic of Arthur's popular inclusionary mode of ruling. However, Arthur never went with his knights on their adventures; the knights went their separate ways.

After more than a decade of relative peace, Arthur gathered an army and conquered most of northern Europe, from Norway to Iceland. But when he extended his conquest into Gaul, he had to cut his mission short and return to Britain because he learned that his nephew Mordred had usurped both his crown and his queen.

Mordred's army met Arthur and his followers in Cornwall, Wales. At Camlann, on the banks of the River Cam, the armies obliterated each other, and Mordred was killed. Arthur received a mortal wound and died a few days later at the age of forty.

The legend appears as a series of fabricated stories loosely based on Welsh poems and traditions from the 600s. The story got a boost in the ninth century when *The History of the Britons*, ascribed to a Welsh monk named Nennius, appeared. Nennius ended his tale with a spiritual message: Arthur would return and come to the aid of England at some future time of great need. Apparently World War I and World War II did not qualify.

In 1135, Geoffrey of Monmouth wrote *The History of the Kings of Britain,* in which he embellished the legend. He invented the Lady of the Lake, Merlin, Morgan Le Fay, Queen Guinevere, the quest for the Holy Grail, and Sir Galahad. Then Chretien de Troyes, in the late 1100s, added damsels in distress and spiritual love. In 1470, Thomas Malory wrote *Le Morte d'Arthur,* in which he added the story of Arthur drawing the sword, Caliburn, from a large rock to establish himself as the rightful king. Malory also created a second sword, Excalibur, which Arthur received from the Lady of the Lake; Camelot; Merlin's magic spells; the code of chivalry; and Lancelot's illicit love affair with Queen Guinevere.

In 1154 when Henry II became the first member of the Plantagenet family to ascend to the throne of England, he asserted his legitimacy through the Arthurian legend. He similarly invoked his Arthurian heritage to justify his conquest of Ireland in 1171. When Elizabeth I became queen in 1558, Edmund Spenser wrote *The Faerie Queene,* reviving the legend of Arthur, which she used to support her imperialist ambitions. Edward I claimed descent from Arthur to validate his control of Wales and Scotland. Edward III established a round table to bolster his connection with Arthur. Both Edward IV and Henry VII strengthened their authority by tracing their lineage to Arthur, and Henry VIII referred to Arthur when he declared his independence from the pope in 1534. James I claimed lineage to Arthur to justify uniting Scotland with England under one king.

In fact, Arthur has proven to be the single most important anchor for the monarchy in Britain. To the British and much of the English-speaking world, Arthur is more than a king: he embodies the very idea and ideal of kingship, the standard by which British monarchs are measured.

Arthur and his legend have inspired plays, movies, musicals, television programs, journal articles, books, and comic strips. From the 1300s to the present day, he is the accepted standard for bravery, competence, and good government.

A Possible Confusion

There are two swords in the legend; confusion persists to this day. Caliburn was the name of the sword Arthur pulled from the stone. Excalibur was the name of the sword Arthur received from the Lady in the Lake. Excalibur replaced Caliburn, broken during a battle.

Robin Hood—#12

Robin Hood was a good guy who stole from the rich and gave to the poor. It's an association solidly anchored in our psyche, even though we have probably never given it a second thought. So let's take a closer look at this hero.

In spite of all of the myths, legends, fairy tales, ballads, and fanciful stories about him, Robin Hood accomplished nothing. Despite all of his taking from the rich and giving to the poor, the rich remained wealthy and the poor were still poor. The king may have lost a few deer, but he retained all of his power—everyone stayed in their social class. None of the stories finds Robin with any revolutionary ideas about reforming society, but we love him anyway. However, keep in mind that if his legend had been invented yesterday, he would be a thug who holds up convenience stores in the Bronx, keeps the cash to cover his expenses, and gives the junk food to a homeless person sleeping in a doorway. Today, "taking from the rich and giving to the poor" has become the government's job. For instance, we find it in President Lyndon Johnson's Great Society, also known as the welfare state.

The first author to mention Robin Hood was William Langland in his 1377 poem, *Piers the Plowman*. The legend of Robin Hood built up, generation by generation, to fit the fantasies of each age. The earliest Robin Hood was a common man who hunted illegally in Barnsdale Forest (not Sherwood).

If we turn to English history we find Robert Hod, a fugitive in the north of England in 1226; William Robehod, a Berkshire outlaw in 1262; and Gilbert Robynhod, a Sussex thief in 1296. But none of these was the inspiration for the myth.

All the stories of Robin Hood share two similar themes: illegal hunting in royal forests, and evil sheriffs. Robin was the most skilled archer in England, but he did not become a Saxon hero fighting the Norman oppressors until Sir Walter Scott gave him a walk-on in his 1819 novel *Ivanhoe*.

In the 1400s, we find Robin celebrated in songs and ballads. His friends were knights, squires, and common men, while his enemies were sheriffs, bishops, and archbishops. Hollywood brought him to the big screen in several movies, the best of which, *The Adventures of Robin Hood* (1938), starred Errol Flynn.

The familiar story includes several heroic episodes: Robin wins an archery contest with stunning accuracy, he assists King Richard in recovering the throne, and he rescues Maid Marion from evil Prince John. The story is so well known that it lends itself to parody. Mel Brooks wounded the myth, almost fatally, with his movie *Robin Hood: Men in Tights* (1993). The hero took an additional knock from *Monty Python's Flying Circus*: Dennis Moore is a Robin Hood wannabe. One of his followers tells him that if you take from the rich and give to the poor, the rich will become poor and the poor will become rich. Moore is stunned. This scheme is trickier than he thought. And to that we can all say, amen.

William Tell—#42

The inspirational account of William Tell is set in the late 1200s. He was a man of independence and honor, who would not pay homage to the foreign tyrant who ruled his homeland. His resistance spurred the overthrow of their Austrian rulers, and a new nation, Switzerland, was born. That's an impressive accomplishment for anyone, but for an imaginary person, it's particularly noteworthy.

The clash allegedly began when Emperor Albert of Hapsburg appointed Hermann Gessler as the local governor in the Canton of Uri. Gessler set a hat on a pole in the town square of Altdorf as a symbol of imperial power and ordered everyone who passed to salute it as a sign of subservience to the Austrian authority. William Tell crossed the square without acknowledging the hat and, at Gessler's command, guards seized him. As punishment, Gessler ordered Tell, known to be an expert archer, to shoot an apple off his son's head.

Tell, shaken by the prospect, aimed his crossbow; his bolt sped and cut the apple in two. The governor noticed that, before shooting, Tell had stuck another bolt under his belt, ready for action. The governor asked why. Tell, still emotionally overwrought, blurted out, "It was for you. Had I shot my child, know that you would have been next."

A few days later, in an act of revenge for his ordeal, Tell killed Gessler. Following this, the oppressed citizens revolted against the Austrians, and Switzerland became an independent country in 1315.

Of all the characters in this book, William Tell is the one most people believe was real, and for good reason. In Altdorf, at the site of the lime tree to which Tell's child was allegedly bound, a large plaque commemorates the event. And a life-size statue of the unerring archer stands at the spot where Tell is reported to have stood. At the arsenal in Zurich, one can see the crossbow he was supposed to have used in his amazing feat. The crossbow was regarded as emblematic of Switzerland, and it appeared on many official documents, including postage stamps.

However, no one named Tell is mentioned in any of the many chronicles written at the time he was supposed to have lived. In fact, the first mention of him was in a ballad from about 1470. This was more than 160 years after the battle of Morgarten and Swiss independence.

John of Winterthur, a Swiss monk and an exceptional chronicler of the Middle Ages, was alive at the time of the rebellion and describes all of the incidents in great detail, but nowhere does he say a word about William Tell. In 1598, François Guillimann expressed the first doubts about the legend in his work on Swiss antiquities, calling the story a pure fable—but he proclaimed his belief in it, citing its popularity! In 1835 the Swiss historian Joseph Kopp conducted an exhaustive search of Swiss archives and concluded that William Tell never lived, nor did anyone named Gessler ever rule there.

Many earlier mythical heroes form the basis for the story. Saxo Grammaticus, a Dane, wrote a similar tale of Palnatoki in 950. In a Persian poem, Farid–Uddin Attar (born 1119) wrote of a prince who was forced to shoot an apple from the head of his favorite page. In the Icelandic *Saga of Thidrik*, the Tell–like hero is Egil. In Norwegian literature there are two stories with the same outline. In English literature, the *Ballad of William of Cloudeslee* has the same plot. And there are similar tales from India, Germany, Finland, Turkey, and Mongolia. John Fiske, in 1870, suggested a common origin in Central Asia for all these stories. The story has been rendered into drama by Schiller (1804) and opera by Rossini (1829). William Tell's spirit of resistance and rebellion might have played a role in the European revolutions of 1848.

In all of these stories, an unerring archer, at the capricious command of a tyrant, shoots from the head of someone dear to him a small object, such as an apple, a nut, or a coin. The archer always readies a second arrow, with which to kill the tyrant, and the tyrant always asks the archer why he prepared it—always receiving the same rebellious reply.

We warn you not to take the myth of William Tell lightly. In 1760, Simeon Uriel Freudenberger, from Berne, was condemned by the Swiss canton of Uri to be burned alive for publishing his belief that the story of William Tell had its origin in an old Danish myth, and copies of the French version of his work were burned in Altdorf.

Things have changed in Switzerland since then (see sidebar). The Swiss writer Max Frisch certainly made his contribution to this change in perception with his novel *Wilhelm Tell für die Schule* (*William Tell for Schools*) (1791). Here, the famous incidents are told as a series of coincidences and failures and are due to the narrowness and the opportunism of a not very open and rather uncultivated peasantry. Since then, the cross-bow has been retired as a symbol of Switzerland.

The story of William Tell is a powerful example of a simple myth being more believable and inspiring than real history.

Tell, The Archer

In the legend, Tell uses either a bow and arrow or a cross-bow and its short arrow, called a bolt. The crossbow, the more accurate weapon, would have had less chance of missing at close range, but its longer reloading time would have put him at risk when getting off a second shot. Crossbow bolts were sometimes made of metal, and because they were much shorter, Tell would not have been concerned that sliding the second one under his belt might have broken it, where a longer wooden arrow would have been at risk of being snapped. End of artillery lesson.

Don Juan—#40

We know Don Juan Pacheco, Marquis of Villena and Master of the Order of Santiago, as Don Juan, the seducer of Seville, a very, very naughty boy. Be careful not to confuse him with Casanova (1725–1798), an actual Italian adventurer famous for his seduction and defrauding of wealthy socialites throughout Europe.

Don Juan is a mythical figure who originated in Spanish folklore in the 1600s and has become the modern archetype of "the lover." During the time that his legend was created and embellished, aristocratic marriages were arranged for political and financial reasons. Sexual satisfaction usually had to be sought in adultery. In this regard, Don Juan's legend served an important role in Spanish society. He legitimized and glorified the practice of sexual romance. And in modern society, he still represents the wish fulfillment of almost every man as well as of many women.

However, we must correct the impression that this famous and influential character was a "lover." He was not. He was a rogue who claimed more than a thousand conquests, but was never in love with anyone except himself.

In the early legend he was Portuguese and among the greatest nobles of that land. As a clever young man, he gained the confidence of the future Spanish king, Enrique IV of Castile. By skillfully managing the future monarch's important business, he attained the rank of marquis and a greater income and status than any other aristocrat. He never married, and died in great prosperity at the age of fifty-five. The central aspect of the legend is his lust. In various stories, he fathers many children out of wedlock. And it is this aspect of his legend that we preserve.

Among the many variations of his story, we have Tirso de Molina's play *El Burlador de Sevilla* (*The Trickster of Seville*); *The Stone Feast,* a play by Molière; *Don Juan,* an epic poem by Byron; *Don Giovanni,* an opera by Mozart; and *Don Juan,* a lyrical tone poem by Richard Strauss.

In the play by Tirso, Don Juan is a powerful, dangerous psychopath with a dark side that both attracts and repels us. He is quick to resort to the sword to attain his goals, and makes no apologies for his behavior. He is like the conquistadors of the New World: he takes what he wants as if by divine right and has no moral conscience regarding the consequences.

In Byron's poem and Molière's play, Don Juan is impulsive, irresponsible, and insincere. He has no sense of right and wrong, no feelings of guilt for his misconduct. It is worth noting that at the time he was criticizing Don Juan, Byron was engaged in a sexual relationship with his own half-sister.

In Mozart's opera *Don Giovanni,* the scoundrel is about to seduce a young noble lady when her elderly father, the *Commandatore,* discovers him. They duel; Don Juan kills him and escapes. A few weeks later, while he is returning home from one of his successful seductions, he passes by a statue of the dead Commander and lightheartedly invites him to dinner. Unexpectedly, the statue arrives at the appointed time, takes the villain by the hand, and drags him down to Hell.

In the end, we'll all probably end up in Hell. But Don Juan made the most of it.

Don Juan Gets His Start

The legend may be based on the seventeenth-century Spanish nobleman Don Juan Tenorio. The first recorded account of Don Juan is *El Burlador de Sevilla* by Tirso de Molina, written sometime between 1620 and 1635.

Interlude: How We Did It—
The Ranking Method

When we started this project, we quickly thought of a few dozen characters who were important to our culture and to the words and phrases we use. When we had built up a large list, with a few contributions from friends, we started to rank them. For each character, each of the three of us gave a rank of 0 to 5, for a best combined score of 15.

We then sorted the list by total score in a spreadsheet. And we divided the list into categories, so we were comparing gods to gods, legends to legends, and so on. We had about five hundred. We cut the list to about the top three hundred, and did a second ranking. This time we gave each character a rank of 0 (forgettable) to 10 (important). A few characters were added late—Jim Crow (The Katonah Museum's exhibit), Uncle Sam, Rosie the Riveter (Burt), The Cat in the Hat, The Little Tin Soldier, Rochester. That's the first two rounds.

Here are our rationales:

Jeremy: I set aside about twenty 10s, and I made my way through the list asking myself "Was this character really important to our culture or our history?" I went through again until I had given out all the 10s. I repeated this with the 9s, 8s, 7s, and so on. A character I had proposed and then rated 0 was Max Goolis, the street-sweeping man, who somehow managed to inspire very few careers in sanitation.

Dan: I went through the list trying to place each character in historical, social, and cultural context. When I had clarified my own thoughts on what was going on at the historical time, I then estimated how influential the particular character had been.

Clearly, the older characters have been through many generations of storytelling, and if they've survived that, they probably have had some influence. It's harder to gauge the more recent ones because they don't have the benefit of a shakedown period. I also applied my own bias that influence is most lasting when it hits young: children, when influenced, don't realize they've been influenced.

Allan: We weren't able to get an answer from Allan, who is suffering from the side effects of genetic disharmony. Last we saw him, he was about to have some sort of foot operation that was supposed to be either a cure or a diagnostic method, depending on which hospital is going to do the procedure. So we talked to his dog, Yogi. We've suspected for some time that Yogi does all the writing. Here's his reply:

"I had Allan print out all the direct references on the Internet for each character, weighed the resulting stacks of paper, and then had the neighborhood kids haul it down to the dump at 20 cents a pound. A 10-rating cost Allan $9.62. If it smelled like meat, it got 2 points extra."

We assembled the list in the spreadsheet and took a simple sum of the votes: A, D, J. That was okay, but the total score for each of us ranged from about 1,000 to 1,500. So our individual degree of enthusiasm could make one's vote more influential than another's. The next step was to normalize the ratings: calculate rank divided by total score, or relative enthusiasm. For each of us (The letter stands for each person's score):

A (rank) ÷ sum of all A rankings

The pure average, even corrected, wasn't quite satisfying, so Jeremy made a test set of about nine character ratings to play with the possibilities without printing out two pounds of paper each time through. The sum of the inverses, the way electrical conductivity is calculated, seemed to be the best approach, but it wasn't. He also tried sum of the average of the logarithms, the sum of the differences—squared—as in variance statistics, and so on, but none of these proved satisfying. To highlight the difference between characters, he took a least squares sum for each character, the way total electrical power is calculated (RMS power). That worked—it kept the intuitively correct rank.

Add: A-squared + D-squared + J-squared = X, then take the square root of the sum.

The least squares sum was still a bit off, so Jeremy added a fourth term: I-squared, I being the sum of our total first-round vote. Lastly, for the final rank, he added two bias factors: 1 point for every woman in our circle who had mentioned the character as important. And, if we'd completed an essay, that was worth 3 points. It would be a superbly scientific method if Allan had voted on more than half the characters, if we had fifty more people from a variety of cultural backgrounds voting, and if half of them were women.

Then our agent, Claudia, relayed Amos 'n' Andy and Mammy, suggestions from her partner, Manie. Of course we included them. Then we dropped all the religious characters after the Great Squash, a gigantic godly vegetable, appeared before Allan's writing group. The Squash insisted on being first rank among the deities, so we dropped any god who couldn't be degraded to Mythology without being offended. Even so, the god of potholes nearly took Jeremy's foot off at 27th and Broadway.

And finally we dropped all the real people except for Siegfried, Saint Nicholas, and King Arthur, who were from the Dark Ages and could have been fictional.

You could also say that we picked the five hundred most recognizable fictional characters an American would think twice about, and then ranked them according to how quickly we could finish an article about them. That's not too far from the truth.

But Allan just kept on writing, and when we'd finally stopped at about 130 articles, we had to cut the pack by eliminating the least relevant ones. Then we voted a third time on the top 112 on a 1–10 scale. This time Dan simply added the scores. We shifted two characters into comic intermissions, cut the list to the top 101, and revoted the top 121 characters on a scale of 80–200, no number reused. Then we separated individual rankings (four 98s on the 80–200 scale, for example) by throwing mustard packets at one another. But we're all scientists, and that's how science is done — don't let anyone tell you otherwise.

4. Monsters

onsters populate virtually every folk tradition from Scandinavia to Australia. Most of us don't encounter any.

We use *monster* to designate anything ugly, evil, or large, and any creature with all of these qualities is a bona fide member of the club. *The Beast from 20,000 Fathoms* was a shoo-in. Our instincts tell us that anything large is out to get us. We really fear such things, and we suspect that they're out there in the dark, waiting for an opportunity to pounce on us.

We love movies about twenty-foot sharks, and any dusty museum with a safely fossilized *Tyrannosaurus rex* draws large crowds. We speculate endlessly about dinosaurs—as if some *Lost World* really exists, or in some future *Jurassic Park* they may be re-created. Some people even go so far as to falsify "evidence" of nonexistent monsters, such as the Loch Ness monster. Half of them come back. Nessie eats the others.

Be watchful when you walk by Shadow Lake, and always have your camera ready. We need all the evidence we can get.

Dr. Frankenstein's Monster—#6

He was born in response to a dare, a challenge among story-tellers, and he became the poster creature for science run amok. The 1818 tale of the monster and his origin was both the first horror story and the first science fiction story—decades before Edgar Allan Poe and Jules Verne. Dr. Frankenstein's Monster is a scientific project gone monstrously wrong. That is the horror: ascend to the power of the gods and there will be consequences that cannot be anticipated.

Long before there was a Chernobyl or *Jurassic Park*, Mary Shelley created the image of the mad scientist, an enduring cultural icon. If we have a lingering distrust of engineers and scientists who work at improving the world we live in, Dr. Frankenstein shows us why. Watchdog religious and technology organizations often use him as the image of science gone mad. And this theme resonates with practical horrors, from the railroad and bridge disasters of the mid-1800s to the loss of the space shuttles *Challenger* and *Columbia* in 1986 and 2003.

Mary Wollstonecraft Shelley was a genuine revolutionary and one of the earliest feminists. Her lover and soon-to-be-husband was the famous poet and rascal Percy Bysshe Shelley. His initial journey to France with her, in today's climate, could have earned him a charge of statutory rape as well as adultery: She was only sixteen years old.

An exceptional woman, she probably knew of Luigi Galvani's demonstration that electricity causes frogs' legs to twitch. She elevated this reaction into the spirit or animus that separates the living from the dead.

One rainy evening, Mary Shelley sat among a group of artists and writers in Geneva. They decided to amuse themselves by creating ghost stories. Mary was the only one who took up the challenge with serious consideration. The result, *Frankenstein*, soon became the standard for horror stories and tales of unintended consequences.

Today, almost two hundred years after her shocking story, the opponents of genetically modified crops can point to a host of problems as evidence that all scientific disciplines are still in need of serious oversight, which the fictional Dr. Frankenstein did not have. They even call the new inventions "Frankenfoods."

The full title of Mary Shelley's book was *Frankenstein, or, the Modern Prometheus*. The original Greek mythical figure earned the wrath of the gods for stealing fire and giving it to mortals. The Frankenstein referred to in the title was not the monster but his creator, and the *creation* is the act of defiance. The creation of life is not permissible for men, according to most of those of a religious inclination.

Yet it's not Victor Frankenstein's surgical techniques that cause the problem. In the book, it's the failure to be a good parent to his creature and reneging on his promise to create a bride for his Monster. In the 1931 movie (and the 1974 Mel Brooks parody *Young Frankenstein*), the disaster resulted from the use of defective parts. But in both the book and the movies, it's the consequence of work for ego's sake, and the danger of working in isolation. A linchpin of science, as practiced for the past three hundred years, is the submission of one's work to oversight and review; when these are omitted, all bets are off. The Monster causes a great deal of damage and the community rises to stop him. The Monster, in various movie versions, flees or suicides.

On the positive side, the vast popularity of the Frankenstein story has inspired such medical advances as organ transplants, cardiac defibrillation, and reattachment of severed limbs. Truly, a significant impact on our lives.

Loch Ness Monster—#56

Of all the fabulous animals in the world, the Loch Ness Monster—Nessie—is the most famous, the inspirational father of hundreds of similar beasts throughout the world. As the most popular tourist attraction in Scotland, Nessie's influence on the cash flow of that country has been significant.

The monster was first recorded in a biography of no less a person than St. Columba in the year 565 when he was bringing Christianity to the Scots. While he was preaching in the Loch Ness area, he came upon some Picts burying a man who had been killed by the beast. Miraculously, he restored the man to life. Soon thereafter, another of the Picts was swimming across the lake as the fiend arose from the depths. It was about to devour him when St. Columba raised his hand and gave the sign of the cross. He invoked the name of the Lord, and then said, "Thou shalt go no further nor touch the man—return with all speed." The monster obeyed the priest and disappeared beneath the water. When in 2005 an interviewer for *People* magazine asked the beast if this may have had some religious significance in his life, he said, "My ancestors have been pagan monsters for two hundred million years, and I'm not about to become a Christian monster at this late date."

In 1933, during the Great Depression, Mr. and Mrs. Mackay, owners of the failing Drumnadrochit Hotel on the lake, told a reporter for *The Inverness Courier* that they had seen an enormous creature rolling and plunging in the water. The story was picked up by several other Scottish papers and soon became a worldwide sensation. On December 21, 1933, *The Daily Mail* carried the headline. MONSTER OF LOCH NESS IS NOT A LEGEND BUT A FACT. Marmaduke Wetherell, a fellow of the London Zoological Society, based the accompanying story on his first-hand investigation. He described the beast as about twenty feet long and photographed its hippopotamus-like footprints. However, the entire incident was later exposed as a fraud when others discovered that Wetherell himself had made the footprints with a stuffed hippo foot that he borrowed from a museum.

In one of the first reported sightings of the creature out of the water, Arthur Grant said that he was riding his motorbike one night in 1934 and nearly ran into the creature as it was crossing the road. He reported seeing a long-necked animal with a small head, thick body, and a long tapering tail. This too was later confessed to be a fabrication.

The most famous picture of the monster, a black and white photograph taken in 1934, shows a head and long neck emerging from the lake. It also turned out to be a hoax. Christian Spurling, a skilled model maker, had trumped up the scene. He built a one-foot-high, eighteen-inch-long monster and placed it in the lake. Then Robert Kenneth Wilson, an eminent London gynecologist, snapped the photo. All of this was confessed many years later.

Nessie has also spawned hundreds of other legendary lake monsters around the globe, indirectly contributing to tourism and local economies. In Scotland, Lizzie, a three-humped cousin of Nessie, lives at Loch Lochy. In the United States we have Champ in Lake Champlain on the New York–Vermont border; Memphré in Lake Memphrémagog, on the U.S.–Canadian border; the Flathead Lake Monster in Montana; and recently, Eerie, in Lake Erie.

Dr. McRae, a retired physician, made an amateur movie of Nessie in 1935. He claimed that just after dawn one morning he saw Nessie floating on the surface of the lake. He said he shot a five-minute movie and asserted that it clearly showed the monster with a long neck, three humps, a pointed head, narrow slanting eyes, and small horns. McRae is deceased and the original film is allegedly in a London bank vault and cannot be released until such time as the public takes the matter seriously.

An attempt to find the animal took place in October 1987. It involved twenty-four boats spread across the lake. They methodically swept the loch with sonar equipment, but found no evidence of the monster.*

Just when Nessie had been firmly relegated to myth, he appeared on a stamp issued by the Maldive Islands. This raised the possibility that the beast may be real. We doubt that any country would put an imaginary animal on a postage stamp.

Gary Campbell, president of the Official Loch Ness Monster Fan Club, has his life insured for $400,000 against being eaten alive by the monster. He operates a gift shop at Loch Ness and says his bestsellers are plaster casts of the monster's footprints. He explains, "Although they're actually casts of the impressions made by pushing my casserole dish into the ground, they're very popular, although occasionally someone will ask why the monster has the word *Pyrex* engraved on its foot."

---

* The search was ill conceived from the start. Everyone in the vicinity of the loch knows that Nessie goes on vacation in October.

King Kong—#74

The giant ape climbing the Empire State Building is one of the enduring images of the movies. And the idea of a big gorilla abducting a woman is just as persistent. King Kong brings together elements of sexuality, racism, myth, and reality in a way that few films have before or since. *King Kong* has been rereleased several times, remade twice, and sired at least ten related films. The director of the 2005 version, Peter Jackson, has said that he was inspired to become a moviemaker by the 1933 film.

The plot isn't complicated. A film director and his team of adventurers go to Skull Island in the Indian Ocean and find huge beasts—in particular, a giant gorilla, King Kong, whom the natives fear and worship. The American film crew captures him and brings him to the United States for exhibit. Kong breaks free, abducts a beautiful girl who was part of the expedition, and carries her off to the top of the newly finished Empire State Building, then the tallest building in the world. The military attack him there with the latest aircraft. Wounded, he puts the girl aside before falling to the pavement, dead.

When David O. Selznick released the original film on March 2, 1933, at both Radio City Music Hall and the RKO Roxy Theater, it played to an audience of fifty thousand on the first day and earned a record $100,000 in its first week. The film saved both RKO and the Roxy Theater from bankruptcy.

King Kong is a story that white audiences saw as a scary-beast movie with overtones of the *Beauty and the Beast* fable. But some black people saw a story frighteningly similar to that of their own ancestors: kidnapped from the tropics, brought to America in chains, exploited, emancipated, and killed for trying to rise in society.

In slang, a gorilla can be any forceful man, especially one with long or hairy arms. In the movie, a young woman asks what the fuss is all about. When she is told it is about a gorilla, she complains that there are enough of them in New York.

The film ends by saying it was beauty that killed the beast, but others might think it was bigotry.

Even the British Love Him!

King Kong, the giant ape who ran amok through Manhattan, has been voted by the BBC NEWS audience as the most terrifying movie monster of all time.

Godzilla—#38

Godzilla—the Japanese film monster—stomped, belched, and overacted his way through thirty films between 1954 and 1995. In the process, he helped lift the Japanese out of their post–World War II depression by restoring a portion of their national pride and revitalizing the Japanese movie industry. He is the best-known movie monster of all time, and he was the first mass media character to warn us of the true horrors unleashed by atomic weapons.

The original Godzilla movie was first produced in 1954 and reworked by Hollywood in 1956. Japan emerged from the destruction of World War II with these niche films: low-budget movies in which rampant destruction and overacting combined with excessive and silly dialogue. The movie was so obviously bad that it became an instant cult classic.

With each new monster presented to the movie-going public, an "arms race" ensued in which the newest ogre had to be more powerful and fearsome than the last.

Godzilla was one of the first monsters born in the Atomic Age. Because in various films he ranges from destructive to beneficial, he carries the schizophrenic attitude of our civilization toward atomic power. Nuclear bombs are destructive, but atomic power can also produce electricity; radiation from the bombs killed more people than the actual blasts, but radiation therapy can save lives by killing cancer cells.

The United States, which had unleashed the scourge of the atomic bomb on the world, was Godzilla's antagonist. In the story, one of the U.S. bombs awakens the destructive potential in a creature that had been no threat to humanity. (How do you wake a sleeping monster? If you have any sense, you don't.) Just as the atomic bombs devastated Hiroshima and Nagasaki, so does Godzilla destroy Tokyo and other cities in Japan. Humanity is helpless against him.

But a curious thing happened with this arms race. Just as the Soviet Union emerged to challenge and threaten the United States, so did other monsters arise to challenge Godzilla. Then Godzilla morphed into a more beneficent creature and saved mankind from those other villains, just as Japan relied on the United States relative to the Soviets.

In fact, there are two distinct types of Godzilla movies. In the first, a succession of monsters from a wide variety of sources face off against Godzilla. This series ran from 1962 through 1989. There is no coherent political statement made in this series, which is regarded as the "true" classics. They are pure "Godzilla vs. Monster X" formula movies. These monsters include Gigan, The Thing, Mothra, and Megalon. Megalon, for example, was unleashed onto humanity by a society of humanoids living deep beneath the surface of the earth. They sent the monster as retaliation for the threat to their subterranean home posed by underground nuclear testing. Incongruously, these subterranean people sent their monster to attack Japan, even though the underground nuclear testing that threatened them was being conducted by the United States. However, the logic of the story was much less important than the battle between Godzilla and Megalon.

In the second series, lasting from 1991 to 1995, rescuers from the future try to avert the cascade of monsters by interrupting the original nuclear bomb that would awaken Godzilla. However, in this series, an even worse nuclear explosion—an accident—awakens an even more fearsome Godzilla, who thumbs his reptilian nose at the time travelers and wreaks havoc on humanity until he melts down from his own radiation. Though this series attempts to make a political statement—returning to the "Nuclear-Energy-Is-Evil" theme of the first movie—the statement is much weaker than it was in the original.

Several Godzilla movies made in the United States in the 1990s persuaded the company that produced the original 1954 movie to re-enter the arena. In 2004, the twenty-eighth Godzilla movie presented itself as the true sequel to the first film. What the future holds for this adaptable monster is anybody's guess.

The original movie is a classic, presenting a thinly veiled political statement about the horrific dangers of atomic weapons. But, as with most enterprises, the creature took on a life of its own—several lives, in fact—as moviegoers thrilled to the action and carnage in an attempt to escape from the realities of the political world around them.

5. Stereotypes

The characters in this chapter are unique and important. Yes, there are dozens of stereotypes, and you'll find several in other chapters of this book, but the following have insinuated themselves into our culture.

We invent personality types to rationalize our lack of understanding of the people around us. You know what to expect of an Aries or a Lothario, and also someone designated by an ethnic slur. There are no surprises.

A great many women at some point in their lives look for their Prince Charming, but do such unrealistic expectations keep them from finding true happiness? Has Prince Charming set the standard too high? Perhaps his intrusion in our lives has contributed to the high divorce rate.

We perpetuate a great disservice by continuing to circulate these myths. For instance, insisting that we will not settle for anything less than Mr. or Ms. Right.

You may have noticed that the authors of this work are good at defining the problem, although if you want solutions you've picked up the wrong book.

But while you're here, keep reading.

Prince Charming—#20

The most eligible bachelor on the planet is not a handsome actor or a business tycoon, but a seventeenth-century aristocrat. Prince Charming is the ideal man, the one women seek, the standard men are measured by.

Look in any magazine or newspaper advice column and you'll see the same titles: WHEN YOUR PRINCE CHARMING FINALLY ARRIVES; PRINCE CHARMING CARRIAGES FOR YOUR FANTASY WEDDING; WHAT WOMEN WANT IN THEIR PRINCE CHARMING, and so on.

Yet, there is hardly a more enigmatic, less deserving character. He has no personality, no accomplishments, no skills, no character . . . only a castle and a dream.

The prince is a blank slate on which any girl can write her fondest dreams. He has the basics: he's rich; he doesn't have to work, so he's got time for her; he has no hobbies, nothing to distract him from her; and he's polite. Charming. In some ways he's still a little boy, and that's part of his attraction. This is not Machiavelli's Prince, a murderous practical politician; not a muscular warrior on a horse or a motorcycle; not an old man obsessed with soy futures and bumbling around in rumpled pajamas filling the castle with Lithuanian stamp collections and video porn. No, this is a healthy young man with a responsible future, the respect of a kingdom, and a facility for dancing. He has a large house with a dance floor, transportation (horses—how quaint), and a servant staff to do the housework.

There are only three cautions: One, he lives with his parents.

While this does show long-term family loyalty, it raises a question about your in-laws and how much influence they will have. Two, he can't make a decision on his own—he will need a wife's opinion to guide him. Although, now he's got the prime minister, the head of staff, and his father—and with all that advice he couldn't get a dating service? Three, he's not going to be a good father. As writer T. Velazquez pointed out, he can't recognize the love of his life, so what happens if one of the kids gets lost—is he going to go to the mall with a box of their shoes making all the neighborhood children try them on?

Prince Charming is not found in the Grimm's fairy tales, the collection of earthy and wishful folk stories from Germany. He's found in the French stories, first in 1697 as King Charming in "The Blue Bird" by Countess D'Aulnoy; then in Charles Perrault's children's stories (1696–1697). More than a century later he hits the London stage as Prince or King Charming in productions by James Robinson Planché.

In our own time, he's found in or associated with *Cinderella*, *Sleeping Beauty*, and *Snow White and the Seven Dwarfs*—mainly in the Disney animated films. In Disney's *Snow White*—the ground-breaking 1937 version that was the first feature length animated film (or the first to hit American audiences)—Prince Charming appears at the end to rescue Snow White from a poison-induced coma, lifting the lid of her glass coffin and awakening her with a kiss.

In Perrault's version of *Sleeping Beauty*, or, more literally, *The Beauty in the Sleeping Woods*, the prince awakens the sleeping maiden, no kiss, and is charmed *by her*.

In *Cinderella*, both the Disney film and the Rodgers and

Hammerstein musical, he's got the girl's glass slipper to help him find his love. Is he cheating on Snow White? No. In these three popular tales, he's expendable, interchangeable, a stock character. (Disney, taking no chances, specifies Prince Philip in *Sleeping Beauty,* but we still think of him as charming.)

That's where his importance lies. He's a standard character in our vocabulary. The unrebellious young adult who becomes the perfect husband. What could be more influential than that?

"Dear, I'll get the kids at soccer practice, then pick up the sitter, and be back to change for the opera.

"Champagne at the Hyatt later? Good."

Titles You Won't Find

- *Prince Charming and the Temple of Doom*
- *Foot Topology for Dummies*
- *Sleeping Women and Sexual Harassment: Case Studies in Medieval Europe 1300-1550*
- *Kingly Charm: How to Win Friends and Seduce Dusty Women*
- *50 Ways to Leave Your Frog*

Note: T. Velazquez is an artist and freelance writer living in Oregon's Mid-Willamette Valley. From *Prince Charming and Other Fairy Tales,* unpub. Used with permission.

To learn more about Prince Charming, read
   The Oxford Companion to Fairy Tales, edited by Jack
Zipes.
   The History of Animation: Enchanted Drawings by Charles
Solomon.

Jim Crow—#13

There was a time when bus stations had separate waiting rooms
for whites and "coloreds," when a Caucasian could not legally
marry a Negro, when even a traveling circus had to maintain
separate ticket windows for the black and white races. The
racial segregation system established in the Southern states after the Civil War was called Jim Crow, the code word for any
African American, a name now remembered as the symbol of
the two-hundred-year subjugation of blacks in America. But
we'll bet you didn't know that Jim Crow was famous as a
white actor's song and dance act.

At first, Jim Crow was a mythical scalawag and trickster in the
folk tales of rural blacks. In 1827, Thomas Dartmouth Rice
(1808–1860), a traveling actor and comedian, heard a Negro
song called "Jim Crow" and built it into a comic routine. He
combined the song with a "jump," a whirling dance that he
probably copied from a black farmer in Ohio. As early as
1830, Rice jumped Jim Crow, dressed in worn clothes and

"corked up"—with blackened face. In the first stanza, with half a dozen misspellings, Rice's character declared himself Jim Crow, born in Tuckahoe, and told how he would wheel around and turned around, and gave the dance the name Jump Jim Crow.

The 1832 version, perhaps the earliest recovered, has forty-four stanzas, each ending with the chorus of the last two wheeling lines. Soon there were hundreds of lyrics. Some lampooned the local mayor, others told of Jim's romances and misadventures, many were made up on the spot. A decade before the first blackface minstrel show, T. D. Rice was performing "Jim Crow" as a solo act and had toured St. Louis, Pittsburgh, New Orleans, and Baltimore.

The act was a national sensation, popular with both blacks and whites, a hero to the lower classes in an era when a free black was only a minor oddity of American life. Jim was a character who could get into and out of any sort of trouble, and he did so repeatedly and with great pleasure. By 1836, Jim Crow was the central character in a new play, and more than a dozen Jim Crow plays were produced. The act was an international hit. T. D. Rice performed in Paris and staged at least three plays in London.

But back in the mid-1800s, two events changed Jim Crow's success into a different kind of notoriety. In 1837, Queen Victoria assumed the throne of Great Britain, and in the rigid morality of her reign Jim Crow's exploits were dangerously amoral. Then, from 1861 to 1865, the American Civil War, the abolition of slavery, and the political chaos called Reconstruction took place. To the surprise of the victorious North, the freed blacks did not immediately become noble industrious Republicans. They needed protection from murderous white militias, and they needed help adjusting to the new responsibilities of freedom. Jim Crow, the irresponsible drifter, was not anyone's idea of a good role model. Worse, cultural reforms were blocked by the southern Democrats, many of whom were former Confederate officers pardoned by presidents Lincoln and Johnson. In a twist of fate, the count of blacks as whole persons gave the South more political power than it had before the war, and the new South slid past the North's reforms and turned out antiblack laws by the dozen.

Blacks and whites could not associate in any way. Blacks could not inhabit a building where a white lived, play baseball within two blocks of a white team, lease property outside a town, or practice a trade without a license (which limited them to farm labor). The races could not ride in the same coach, read the same books at a library, eat at the same counter, be educated in the same school, be imprisoned in the same jail, be buried in the same cemetery. Separate and inferior was the practical effect of the "Separate but Equal" decision (*Plessy* v. *Ferguson*, 1896), and it stayed that way until 1954. Practical integration took more years of legal and street battles. Congress passed a stronger civil rights act in 1964, but even today racial inequality and prejudice are not extinguished, after fifty years of effort. Driving while black will still elicit harassment from police.

Jim Crow would be quite surprised. After all, he was for the Union, for freedom, and for brotherhood.

Did You Know

- In Mississippi and Missouri, the antimarriage law applied to persons of mixed ancestry, even to one-eighth part (one black great-grandparent).
- Lincoln wanted Negro slaves established in colonies of their own, and he supported a settlement off Haiti. It failed.
- The contested election of 1876 was settled with the presidency going to Rutherford Hayes in exchange for the withdrawal of Northern troops from the South.

To learn more about Jim Crow, read
Jump Jim Crow: Lost Plays, Lyrics, and Street Prose of the First Atlantic Culture by W. T. Lhamon, Jr.
The Banjo: America's Mythic Instrument by Robert Shaw.
Reconstruction: The Ending of the Civil War by Anthony Craven.

Mammy—#81

This overweight, smiling, submissive character was perhaps the first black completely trusted by whites, and she may have been a key force in the Civil Rights movement. While black men were being lynched, beaten, and attacked by dogs in the South, it was a woman—little Rosa Parks, fined for riding in the white section of a bus—who triggered the Montgomery Bus Boycott, one of the first victories of the Civil Rights Movement.

A black man wouldn't have taken such a risk for fear of being killed. But a black woman, that was different. People all over the country knew the black woman as Mammy, the reliable servant. The Mammy we first thought of was the steadfast housekeeper in *Gone with the Wind* (1939), played by Hattie McDaniel. When McDaniel won an Oscar that year—best supporting actress—she was the first black to receive an Academy Award. Her winning role was not a single character, but a stereotype that continues into the present day.

There is very little worth saying that hasn't already been said or summarized by Dr. David Pilgrim, curator of the Jim Crow Museum of Racist Memorabilia at Ferris State University in Big Rapids, Michigan. And, with his permission, we present much the same material. In addition to the articles on the museum's website (*www.ferris.edu/jimcrow*) you'll find images of Mammy on all types of products, from Soap-O-Lene cleanser to Aunt Jemima pancake flour.

The tradition of using conquered peoples as servants dates back to biblical times. But in an era when blacks were distrusted and abused, again and again Mammy presented a comforting image of the black woman as a trustworthy, asexual servant. You can find traces of Mammy in *Uncle Tom's Cabin* (1852), D. W. Griffith's *The Birth of a Nation* (1915), the savvy Delilah in Woody Allen's 1984 *The Purple Rose of Cairo,* and Nellie Ruth "Nell" Harper, played by Nell Carter, in the

1981–1987 TV series *Gimme a Break*. And it's not at all odd that Al Jolson's 1927 monster hit song was "My Mammy," sung in blackface.

Hattie McDaniel played at least thirty and possibly a hundred Mammy or maid roles in her film career, including Mammy Lou in *The Golden West* (1932), Malena Burns in *Alice Adams* (1935), and the title character Mammy of the radio series *Beulah*. Her sister Etta McDaniel played at least twenty Mammy roles in her parallel film career. Louise Beavers took the Beulah role for the TV series from 1950 to 1953. In film, Beavers played Mammy characters in *She Done Him Wrong* (1933), *Mr. Blandings Builds His Dream House* (1948), and at least thirty other films. Characters named Mammy can be found in several dozen more films, played by stars including Ruby Dandridge, Pauline Dempsey, Lucretia Harris, May Hicks, Francis Miller, and Jennie Lee, the white actress made up in blackface for *The Birth of a Nation*. In that movie and in *Gone with the Wind*, the maid defends her owner's home against Union troops. That's how reliable Mammy was: You could leave your children with her. You could leave your husband with her. You could leave your cooking and household chores with her, too.

In commercial life, Mammy's reliability in all things domestic made her the ideal spokeswoman for coffee, flour, ovens, cleaners, medicines, and, yes, pancake mix. The RT Davis Mill Company bought the product and advertising idea from Charles Rutt, a newspaper editor who had come up with the recipe in 1889. They found a model—Nancy Green, a former Kentucky slave who was born in 1834—and as Aunt Jemima, she served pancakes at the Chicago World's Exposition of 1893. The product was a hit, and she continued with the company until her death in 1923, when she was replaced by Anna

Robinson. The third Aunt Jemima was Edith Wilson, who worked the role from 1948 to 1966. As the stereotype finally begins to dissolve, Mammy retains her well-earned reputation. The modern incarnation is a prim woman whose tightly curled hair has a mature touch of gray. She looks a bit like Mrs. Doubtfire. Another step toward equality.

Did You Know?

- "My Mammy," written by Sam Lewis and Joe Young (lyrics), and Walter Donaldson (music), 1921, was used in *The Jazz Singer*—the first talking picture noticed by American audiences. However, the song's actual title was "The Sun Shines East, The Sun Shines West."

- Aunt Jemima pancake flour, a self-rising flour, is still sold in addition to the original, buttermilk, and whole wheat pancake mixes.

To learn more about Mammy, read
The Plantation Mistress: Woman's World in the Old South by Catherine Clinton.
Ceramic Uncles & Celluloid Mammies: Black Images and Their Influence on Culture by Patricia A. Turner.
Toms, Coons, Mulattoes, Mammies, & Bucks: An Interpretive History of Blacks in American Films by Donald Bogle.
Visit the Jim Crow Museum at *www.ferris.edu/jimcrow*, and at Ferris State University, Big Rapids, Michigan.

6. Adventure

We all want excitement. Few of us ever actually climb Mount Everest or sail the Atlantic solo. Most of us are too busy or never seem to get rid of the mundane daily pressures and priorities, such as work and family. And real adventure is inconvenient, not to mention dangerous. And expensive.

Fortunately, we have writers and tale-spinners to entertain us with fictional tales of derring-do, romance, glory, riches, and exploration. Those stories were the grist for this chapter. Characters in other chapters might easily have found their way here, but this chapter is reserved for those special personalities whose adventure was their primary accomplishment.

Go . . . run a marathon or bike cross-country. When you return home and need to relax, read one of the stories of these characters. Please, don't try to battle pirates on the Indian Ocean or swing through the trees of the state forest. We want you around to read the next chapter.

Sindbad the Sailor—#82

Sindbad the Sailor (Sinbad) is one of the star characters in a group of legendary stories compiled as *The Thousand and One Nights,* also known as *The Arabian Nights*. Sindbad, depicted as a heroic character in recent Hollywood films, is a villain, a scoundrel, a murderer, and a cheat in the original stories. As such, he may be more of a representation of Europe's negative image of Arabs than the representation of the rising influence of foreign trade for the Arab nations.

The basic idea for the book came from a Persian book, *A Thousand Tales,* which was translated into Arabic in the ninth century. Antoine Galland introduced *The Arabian Nights* to France in 1704, and the earliest English version appeared two years later.

There are many different stories in various collections called *The Thousand and One Nights*. Before the printing press, a person would hire a scribe to make a copy of the tales from an existing manuscript, simultaneously making any changes the new owner wished. Hence, material was continuously dropped (if it reflected badly on the new owner) and added (to flatter him). The Arabic texts from as recently as the 1600s do not contain the stories of *Ali Baba and the Forty Thieves* or *Aladdin and the Wonderful Lamp*. They were added later, perhaps by Europeans.

Many of the tales originated in India, Persia, and Egypt and predate the year 1000. The name *Sindbad* means "traveler" in Sind, a dialect of India.

Sindbad's seven trips each begin with him, a merchant, embarking on a journey and becoming shipwrecked. And the stories all end with him acquiring great wealth and safely

returning to Baghdad. The adventures are what happen in between.

Two of the stories recapitulate Middle Eastern creation
myths, in which the earth was born when the backs of giant
animals emerged from the oceans. In one, he lands on an Eden-
like island that is really the back of a huge whale. In the other,
he visits a continent that is the back of an enormous cow.

Another tale repeats the Cyclops episode from *The Odyssey*.
Sinbad lands on an island inhabited by a one-eyed giant who
eats some of his fellow passengers. The survivors blind the giant with a burning timber and try to escape on a boat they
have built. But other giants hurl large rocks at them and kill
many of the men as they are leaving.

On a different trip, he marries the daughter of a king. She
dies and is regaled with all her jewels for burial. However, by
local custom, her husband must be interred with her in a com-
munal grave in a large, closed cave. Sindbad is placed in the
chasm along with the body of his wife and enough bread and
water for him to survive for a few days. A week later, a woman
is placed in the cave with her dead husband, who is decked out
in all his jewels. Sindbad kills her and steals her food and water
as well as the gems. After that, he kills others placed in the cave
and gathers great wealth in jewelry and enough food and water to search the cave until he finds an outlet and escapes. He
makes no effort to help these unfortunate spouses; he simply
murders them.

On his last trip, he marries yet another daughter of a king.
Her father dies and Sindbad inherits enormous wealth. He then
returns to Baghdad where he and his wife live happily ever after.

Sindbad brings us the message that murder and mayhem are
a normal part of the business world. In the name of Allah, let's
reject that idea.

Robinson Crusoe—#22

The 1719 novel *Robinson Crusoe,* by Daniel Defoe, helped set the French and American revolutions in motion by changing European attitudes toward government and society. Robinson is shipwrecked on an island, but this story is not only about survival, it also concerns "character."

Crusoe, an adventurer, establishes himself as a minor plantation owner in Brazil and ventures on a clandestine voyage to Africa to buy slaves. The trip ends in disaster when his ship is driven off course by a storm and is wrecked on a sand bar. He is twenty-seven years old when he finds himself washed up on an uninhabited island. He is the only survivor.

He salvages guns, powder, seed, tools, food, cloth, and other useful items from the wreck before another storm destroys it. And although the island is uninhabited, it has fresh water and is rich in wood, lemons, grapes, tobacco, and sugar cane as well as wild goats, which he domesticates for their milk, meat, and skins.

The thrill of adventure embraces us as we identify with Crusoe's independence, determination, and resourcefulness. We applaud his success as he builds a home and provides for his needs, and we look on in frustration as he plans his escape.

After fifteen years on the island, Crusoe sees a human footprint, which arouses his terror of cannibals. But it is not until eight years later that he finds human bones and a fire pit to confirm that cannibals had been there.

In his twenty-fifth year of isolation, he sees savages with their prisoners, and as he watches from a distance, one of the prisoners runs off. Crusoe comes to the man's aid, and the two of them kill his pursuers. Robinson names the rescued man

Friday for the day when he saved him. From this comes the expression "my man Friday," meaning an assistant.

He teaches Friday about God and Jesus, but Friday refuses to believe in Satan. He wants to know why God, being so much stronger, does not kill the Devil. Crusoe can't provide an adequate answer, but says that God will punish Satan—later. For a writer in the early 1700s, that was a unique proposition. Even more radical is Defoe's depicting Friday as a good, moral, reputable man well before his conversion, and it seems that his people are of the same character. He acknowledges that they eat prisoners of war, but Friday believes this will soon end.

Finally, an English ship appears, and on it, a mutiny is in progress. The rebellious crew maroons the ship's captain on the island, thinking it is uninhabited. After the seditious crew falls asleep, Robinson, Friday, and the captain retake the ship, and they sail back to England.

Robinson Crusoe is hailed as one of the great English novels and the beginning of the alone-on-an-island genre. He spawned *The Swiss Family Robinson* (1812) about a stranded family; *Lord of the Flies,* William Golding's 1954 tale of schoolboy violence; the science fiction movie *Robinson Crusoe on Mars* (1964); the sultry *Blue Lagoon* about shipwrecked, sexy teenagers (1980); and Tom Hanks's *Cast Away* (2000).

The excitement of survival against the bare forces of nature has given birth to the reality genre of television, with programs such as *Survivor* and *Lost*—and don't forget *Gilligan's Island.*

For Jean-Jacques Rousseau (1712–1778), Defoe's work showed that men could behave well without a government to oversee them and that some non-Christian savages are just as moral as Christians. Rousseau proposed the inherent goodness of man in *Discourse on the Origin of Inequality* and *The Social Contract.* And Crusoe's underlying message of the value and equality of all men helped fuel the literary hotbeds that resulted in the French Revolution in 1789. From the theme of Liberty, Equality, Fraternity, it was only a short step to Communism and the 1917 Russian Revolution. All of this emanating from Robinson Crusoe. No wonder we consider him so influential.

Buck—#94

After we read Jack London's story of Buck, a tame, city dog who must revert to the feral state in order to survive, we knew we had experienced something special. A window into the beauty and glory of nature that transcended anything we could adequately express. With this in mind, we decided to let someone closer to the story write this essay. We turned to a terrier, Yogi, who helped us write this book.

"Yogi, have you read *The Call of the Wild*?"

"Sure. It's a five-woof story, a real tail-wagger. All of us dogs read it. It's the first book we're assigned to read in obedience school. It is one of the few serious books written from the point of view of an animal. By the way, I'll bet you didn't know that the book was the first novel to gross a million dollars in sales, and that Jack London was the most widely read author of his time."

"That's very interesting. Now do us a favor and tell us about Buck from your point of view."

"*The Call of the Wild* is the most remarkable and touching animal story ever written and it should be required reading for everyone, man and dog alike. It would certainly help you humans treat us animals better, and it might even help you treat one another with more kindness and understanding. I've noticed that the way you treat us animals is a good gauge of how you will behave toward each other."

"Yogi, what about the story?"

"Buck was a Scottish Shepherd-Saint Bernard mix who lived on an estate in southern California back in the 1890s. He was a big, strong fellow who knew his way around, but some unscrupulous men shanghaied him. They shipped him to Alaska where he would bring top dollar as a sled dog during those days of the Gold Rush.

"Well, sad to say, along the way Buck is mistreated by almost everyone he meets and he quickly learns he can't depend on humans. In the bitter cold of that northern realm, he had to rely on himself, which meant digging up instincts long buried under millennia of domestication. And he inspired us all when he did it.

"All of us were thrilled when he developed leadership qualities and became the alpha dog in his sled team. But there were a lot of inexperienced people in Alaska at the time, and Buck had to survive a lot of human ignorance and cruelty. He was constantly hungry and worked to exhaustion; his coat was ragged, his ribs showed through, and he had marks where men had beaten him. That part upset me, but I was rooting for Buck to prevail, and he did.

"At long last Buck met up with some men who understood him and treated him well. They let him wander away from camp and exercise his survival skills. He even slept away from camp at times. But then tragedy struck. Savage Indians attacked. When Buck returned to camp, he saw that all of his friends were dead or dying. He went on the attack and killed many of the barbarians.

"By then the last vestige of his domestication was gone, and

Buck was a wild animal. He joined a pack of wolves and became their leader. After that, the Indians spoke of a ghostlike wolf/dog that led his pack and would kill any Native American who crossed his path.

"The story should help you understand how all of us dogs yearn to live out our bond with nature. Deep down, we all want to return to our roots in the wild. Buck did it and he's our ideal. He overcame all of the obstacles thrown in his way by greedy humans and triumphed on his own. He inspired us all to hope for a taste of the same freedom before we die, because when it comes right down to it, we all have a bit of Buck inside of us."

"Thanks, Yogi. That's swell. It's comforting to know that there's a dog who can write better than we can. What can we do to thank you?"

"Just treat me with kindness and understanding. And if the time ever comes when you intend to ship me out, make it to Disneyland."

Tarzan—#49

Tarzan is the emblem of our species' conviction of our supremacy over the rest of the animal kingdom. Even when snatched from an outpost of civilization and brought up by uncivilized beasts, he dominates and tames the wild jungle. Nature trumps nurture.

During the twentieth century, developmental psychologists investigated whether nature or nurture plays the greater role in a person's makeup.

In Nazi Germany and Communist Russia, the decisions

made on the basis of the debate affected the lives of millions of people. If nurture (culture) had the dominant effect, social engineering could be justified from the earliest years of a person's life. If nature (genetics) had the major role, brutal selection could be justified in an attempt to improve the race. That both factors might diminish in significance as a person matures, with inner-directed free will taking over in importance, was not considered in the debate.

Edgar Rice Burroughs entered the controversy with his 1912 novel about a child of privileged parents who grows up in the wilds of deepest Africa. The story is an important tale that serves to focus attention on the questions of just what it is that makes a person civilized and how he gets that way.

The setting for this parable is simple, and almost plausible. In the closing years of the nineteenth century, an adventurous English lord and lady set up a small camp on the shore of western Africa, near the equator, on a beach just outside the jungle. A fight and mutiny among their support crew leaves them abandoned. They struggle to survive, but the woman—Tarzan's mother—goes insane and dies with the infant in her arms. By this time, encroachments from a tribe of fierce gorillas in the nearby jungle threaten the father and his boy. The father is killed, and a female ape—still carrying the body of her own recently dead infant, unable to sever the maternal bond—swaps her dead child for the living English boy. The tribe raises Tarzan as a gorilla, and in the process he learns their language and their lifestyle. He grows up to become a leader of the tribe, thanks to the combination of his strength and cunning.

Burroughs writes that Reason is the spark that separates man and brute. He believes that this faculty is innate, a part of the inherent biological uniqueness of the human species. Hence, Tarzan possesses rationality in spite of having no contact with other humans since he was less than one year old. Tarzan's curiosity leads him back to the shack from which he was kidnapped and, using the books he finds there, he is able to teach himself the language of his parents.

Later on, he encounters a band of American adventurers, rescues them, and learns of his true heritage. He falls in love with an American girl (Jane) in this company, after saving her life. But after he has lived in the United States for a while, he realizes that he doesn't—or doesn't want to—fit into civilized society. He gives up his love to return to the only home he knows.

There is much in this that is quite improbable, and more that turns out to be impossible, and some that Burroughs explicitly refuses to try to explain (quoting Burroughs, "With Tantor, the elephant, [Tarzan] made friends. How? Ask not."). But at the time the book appeared, this scenario was almost believable. It made for great drama, and it also opened the door to the ultimate Hollywood money-maker: unlimited sequels. With a savior in their midst, the animals in the jungle benefit from human justice, reinforcing the superiority people feel over the rest of the animal kingdom.

There was also a racist component: the white man invades and takes over the black man's jungle world.

Darwin's proposal that humans are related to the apes was a much-visited topic in the years prior to Burroughs's book, probably stimulating his story about a boy actually raised among our distant primate cousins. Tarzan swung into the center of that controversy, and in the process spawned an entire industry of more than two dozen additional novels, no fewer than forty movies, comics, radio and TV shows, and spin-off merchandise such as underwear, toys, and lunchboxes. Several actors established their audience through the character of Tarzan. It was the vehicle for converting Johnny Weissmuller's Olympic swimming gold into commercial gold.

With the movement toward independence for many African colonies following World War II, Tarzan faded from popularity. But in 1962, a Los Angeles librarian tried to have the Tarzan books banned because the cohabitation of Tarzan and Jane promoted living in sin. This silly plan backfired, and the entire Tarzan culture was revived. It turned out that only the 1932 movie created that impression of immorality. The outcry from faithful readers caused a resurgence in popularity of the Tarzan stories, starting in the mid-1960s. In subsequent decades, there were five Tarzan TV shows—three live-action and two animated. Through magazines, newspapers, books, comics, and radio, Tarzan was certainly one of the most popular fictional characters of the twentieth century.

There is a myth that Tarzana is the only town in America named for a fictional character. In fact, the town already existed when Burroughs bought a tract of land there and moved to California before writing his Tarzan stories. Just think: If he had purchased land in a different place, we might be discussing the merits of *Pasadeen of the Jungle*.

Luke Skywalker—#85

The hero of *Star Wars,* a cosmic action-adventure film, Luke is a simple farm boy who happens to intercept a distress call from a beautiful princess. Soon, Luke is off to rescue the girl on a journey that spans three of the most popular films ever made. *Star Wars* (1977) had the most amazing visual effects of its day, and it made director George Lucas a giant of Hollywood. The

Star Wars trilogy has fed the imaginations of two generations. In the entertainment world, Star Wars consists of the three movies of the trilogy and the three full-length prequels, plus dozens of derivative novels and thousands of toys, posters, parodies, and lunchboxes. It so dominated the cultural landscape that its language and imagery spilled into international politics.

It's both a hero's adventure and a coming-of-age story, as we follow young Luke (played by Mark Hamill) on a quest for his father's approval. The essence of the plot is that Luke gets the help of a wise old man to rescue a princess and save the galaxy from an evil Empire and its chief henchman—Luke's father, the menacing Darth Vader. Luke has to fight his father or come to terms. The psychological theme of the story is the essential conflict between father and son that Freud described. "Every boy must make this confrontation with a father figure of some sort if he is to reach real maturity."*

But this is no mere psychodrama. Inspired by the work of renowned mythologist Joseph Campbell, the story treads a classic path common to folktales from all over the world. Luke is not just a replaceable figure, he's *every* hero.

The formula is universal: First, there is a call to adventure—a reason to leave the familiar world. Next, the aid of a supernatural helper. Then, various trials and new friends along the way. Finally, a one-on-one confrontation with the enemy . . . and victory. The hero returns home triumphant, with something more than a trophy—food, treasure, or magic, a marriage gift, or a princess.

---

* Jane Adelman, LCSW.

The films have a second theme, the spiritual journey, that of Skywalker the magician. In religious terms, the hero's journey is that of leaving the world of day-to-day life, entering the realm of the gods, and returning with a magic power. Luke is taught the use of the "Force," an energy created by living beings, and a powerful friend it is. Revealed to him by Obi-Wan Kenobi, a master of the mystic arts, it will lead Luke safely through dangers, let him speak with the dead, and guide his hand in combat.

In the climactic scene of the first movie, *Star Wars,* Luke's targeting computer misses the most crucial target. Luke has to override the computer and use his intuition—the Force—to fire the shot that brings victory.

But the enemy is resilient, and in the second movie, *The Empire Strikes Back,* Luke trains with an even older Master, Yoda, to become fully proficient with the Force and its other uses: levitating objects, flying, and telepathy.

In the last movie of the trilogy, *Return of the Jedi,* Luke confronts his father's boss, the evil emperor. Lord Vader has to sacrifice himself to save his son, and Luke emerges as a complete adult in harmony with the spirit world and secure in his own destiny.

In the real world of the 1980s, President Ronald Reagan referred to the Soviet Union as the "Evil Empire" and spent billions on a "Star Wars" missile defense system, which can be credited at least in part with the end of the Cold War. *Star Wars,* through the military programs it inspired, defeated the Soviet Union, not by battle, but by pushing them into bankruptcy.

Intuition, in the Star Wars sense, may be the most important and most ignored part of our machine-oriented world. When do you look beyond the rational, the routine, to see what is really around you? Trust your feelings, your "instincts." In science, you need to know when your equipment isn't working properly. We're obsessed with high technology, yet a few bad sensors can cause the meltdown of a megawatt nuclear generator, and a small chunk of foam insulation can destroy a billion-dollar space shuttle and its crew.

Skywalker, strong in the Force, knew when to use his computer and when to ignore it. Do we?

Maybe You Didn't Know

In a survey of three New Jersey bookstores in 2005, one of the authors found that Star Wars books had more shelf space than established science fiction writers, in each case exceeding Asimov, Bradbury, and Heinlein combined.

To learn more, read
  The Hero with a Thousand Faces by Joseph Campbell.
  Practical Intuition by Laura Day.
  The Masks of God: Primitive Mythology by Joseph Campbell.
  Star Wars: The Magic of Myth by Mary Henderson.
  The Foundation Trilogy by Isaac Asimov.

Interlude: Categories

B y now you've noticed that very few of the characters of fiction belong in only one category.

Where do you put a well-dressed vampire? Folktales? legends? movies? monsters? theater?

King Arthur's been everywhere, from English legend to the *Prince Valiant* newspaper strip to the Broadway musical *Spamalot*. These days, just about everything's been made into a musical, movie, opera, or ballet. (*Godzilla* the ballet? No. Not everything.)

Do we list Superman as a hero of the comics, movies, television, adventure, crime, or Americana?

Do you know Hercules from the TV series? the myth? the cartoon? the movies? Is it general adventure or literature?

Do we list Uncle Tom under adult literature, theater, Americana, movies, or propaganda?

We've tried to put each character where his or her influence is strongest. Of course, you have your own favorites, from Christopher Reeve's Superman movies to *Snow White and the Three Stooges*. No, we didn't use these examples. Everyone's got to be someplace. Press on . . .

7. Crime

Even the most law-abiding among us is fascinated by crime and detective work. We revel in the fantasy of doing things that are forbidden, and we love the thrill of watching the mystery being solved. We allow ourselves the feeling of superiority, as if we too could solve the latest mystery, or would know how to avoid being the victim of crime. It's a reassuring illusion.

When reality doesn't satisfy our desire for justice, we retreat into a world where the criminals are always caught and punished. Stories of villains who meet a violent death satisfy our desires for judgment and vengeance. When the imaginary offender is caught, somehow, all is right with the world. This chapter includes both crime-fighters and felons, and our heroes are both those of realistic fiction, as well as those of pure fantasy.

There are many similar characters in this genre, for the business is routine, no matter which side you're on. But a few characters stand out, and we have included the most interesting and relevant, the strongest and most original. Those on the correct side of the law have set standards for intelligence, insight, bravery, persistence, technology, and technique. Those on the wrong side reveal how a criminal excuses his deeds, as well as how he operates.

Sherlock Holmes—#8

The ultimate intellectual detective, he is a man of impeccable logic who solves mysteries for the police by his powers of careful observation of details, keeping a logical approach to the crime, and following every lead no matter how far afield it may seem at first. He practically invented the forensic crime laboratory and showed us how the scientific and logical approach to solving crime was the wave of the future, our era.

Filling out four full-length novels and five collections of short stories, the adventures and intrigues of this most famous detective have spawned numerous movies, full take-off novels written as if Arthur Conan Doyle (1859–1930) might have written them, and many spin-off characters.

How much of Holmes's words, attitudes, and actions did Doyle dream up and how much were reality-based? Doyle himself made it clear that much of the character, born in 1887 (see sidebar), was rooted in a teacher, Dr. Joseph Bell, from Doyle's days as a medical student at the University of Edinburgh, Scotland. It was the time when medicine was being transformed from a black art into a solid science.

Bell and Doyle became friends when Bell invited Doyle, in his second year as a medical student, to be an assistant in Bell's hospital ward. This gave Doyle an opportunity to observe close-up Bell's habits of logical thinking, his fervent attention to detail, and his imaginative ability to rule out some explanations and rule in others.

Bell had gone further than academia with his capacity for logic. On more than one occasion, Bell had assisted local law enforcement officers at solving difficult cases—exactly as Holmes would later do. Bell always insisted on remaining anonymous and behind the scenes, deriving his satisfaction from the successful completion of a job well done, and this was the same approach Doyle used with Holmes.

The image of Holmes as a private detective quickly became an audience favorite, spawning such spin-offs as Sam Spade and Nero Wolfe. All of these characters learned their craft from the original master: pay attention to seemingly insignificant features; carefully observe personal habits, mannerisms, and inflections; and remain open to outlandish or hidden possibilities. Do not invoke supernatural explanations: seek out the evidence that will establish an ordinary motive and method for the circumstances being investigated.

Sherlock Holmes moved on to a second career as a movie hero just as Hollywood introduced talking films. In this new medium, Basil Rathbone established the living persona of Holmes and set a standard for future movie detectives.

The public's attachment to Holmes became evident when Doyle tried to close out his detective. The public outcry over Holmes's death at Reichenbach Falls (1893, *The Final Problem*) compelled Doyle to revive him in 1902. Doyle continued the series with another two novels (including the most famous, *The Hound of the Baskervilles*) and three collections of short stories before Holmes retired.

The public delighted in the stories' surprise twists, rooted in solid logic and stern reality. It played out as a game: author against audience, who could outwit the other. And in this game of one-upmanship, either the author successfully surprised his audience or the reader was able to guess the crucial element before Holmes himself does. Even today's readers enjoy this challenge.

Sherlock Holmes set the standard for noticing important yet seemingly trivial particulars in incidental features. And he established a standard of logic that is valid for all of us, in living our lives. Every detective, fictional or real, is measured by the benchmark of Holmes. The popularity of such television shows as *Quincy, ME*; the CSI franchise; and *Crossing Jordan* rest in the whole story and behind-the-scenes forensic work. They are all the descendants of Sir Arthur and the ever-logical Sherlock Holmes.

Elementary

The character was introduced in the novel *A Study in Scarlet* in 1887, which was followed by the novel *The Sign of Four* in 1890. The popularity of the character really took off with the first six short stories, published in the *Strand Magazine* in 1891.

Batman—#60

A double murder. A boy watches as both parents are gunned down. He vows revenge on *all* criminals, and this obsession shapes his destiny.

Inheriting a large fortune, he dedicates his life to a battle against crime. It won't be easy. He molds himself into a warrior who is strong, cunning, and terrifying. He will become the ultimate vigilante and in that role will influence the shape of our society. He's Batman.

This is a story of wish-fulfillment, of a rich man protecting the innocent. It's a story of secret power—a caped crusader who stalks through the city, pouncing on criminals before they act, instilling in them a fear of something beyond the law. It's a story of genius—strategies by the dozen, devices for stealth, mobility, and attack.

Batman was one of several masked vigilantes—his peers include the Phantom, the Green Hornet, and the Shadow. He is one of the few heroes of his era to fight with mere human strength. Dressed in black and gray, with a long black cape, he's a Homeric Achilles. No Kryptonian juggernaut, no magic green ring, no radioactive spider, just flesh and bone, nothing you or I couldn't be. Batman is a tireless warrior, and his obsession comes with a price. His long-term friendships are few: other heroes, police, and one attractive criminal (Catwoman). He adopts Dick Grayson, an orphan from an acrobatic troupe, who becomes his sidekick and partner, Robin, the Boy Wonder (the first in a series of Robins).

Batman first appeared in *Detective Comics #27* in May 1939, created by artist Bob Kane and writer Bill Finger (creator of Green Lantern). By 1941 the comic was selling 800,000 copies per issue, second only to Superman. The original comic book character was one nasty hero. In his first issue, he threw one crook off a roof and knocked another into a vat of acid.

Back then, the comics were a broad range of cheap publications. The most sensational were crime and horror comics, which showed realistic depictions of wife-beating, torture, and murder. Not the sort of thing for school children. In 1954 the U.S. Senate held hearings on the depravities. To avoid government regulation, the comic industry adopted a set of strict rules in which good triumphed over evil, gore and perversion were forbidden, and no crime was depicted in enough detail to be duplicated.

In this middle period, Batman's influence came from his emphasis on the human qualities of wariness, intelligence, and skill. The Caped Crusader turned to fighting bizarre villains: the Joker, the Penguin, Two-Face, and other deformed criminals bent on a sanitized sort of mayhem.

The comics sold. A goofy 1966 TV series featured Adam West and Burt Ward as the crime fighters. Batman was being trivialized. It had to stop.

In the 1980s the dark tone of the original resumed, and the serious side is best seen in Frank Miller's 1986 graphic novel *The Dark Knight Returns,* laced with brooding monologues that rival the Bogart film-noir classics.

The immensely popular Batman movies of the 1990s followed: a TV cartoon and juvenile print comic, more comic book titles, and the 2005 film *Batman Begins.* Most of these have a serious tone, realistic insanities, and strong motivations. The second Robin, Jason Todd, was eventually killed by the Joker (and revived in 2006), and the original Robin now continues on his own as Nightwing. Today Batman has at least two books running every month. He doesn't keep count.

In the recent works, the world is dirty and real evil lurks in the shadows. Corruption, torture, and brutality are common. Villains show both cruelty and patience. Obsession and ego mar the noblest of heroes.

In the real world, we have a long history of vigilantism, from the tar-and-feathering of the colonies to the executions of rustlers in the 1860s. The Caped Crusader's Gotham City was long understood to be New York, and Batman was admired as an example of toughness and skill. But vigilantism didn't die with the Old West. In December 1984, a New Yorker named Bernard Goetz shot four young men wielding sharpened screwdrivers. Goetz was hailed as a hero, then jailed for gun possession. That's why vigilantes wear masks. Or uniforms. The plainclothes police who gunned down an unarmed Amadou Diallo in 1999 weren't taking any chances. Hey, he had a wallet. Superheroes use much the same routine: stalking, assault, trespassing, battery. That's Batman's 1986 admission: Yes, he's a criminal. Superheroes have always been criminals. They have to be.

Batman puts an intelligent head on a vengeful soul and leaves us with a sense of power and protection. Giants still walk the earth.

To learn more about Batman, read

A Smithsonian Book of Comic-Book Comics edited by Michael Barrier and Martin Williams [containing a reprint of *Detective Comics #27,* May 1939].

The World Encyclopedia of Comics, vols I and II edited by Maurice Horn.

Comic Book Nation: The Transformation of Youth Culture in America by Bradford W. Wright.

The Dark Knight Returns by Frank Miller (writer), Klaus Janson (illustrator), Lynn Varley (colorist), and John Costanza (letterer).

The Complete Frank Miller Batman DC Comics.

A little bat told me:
- It's said no one ever dies in the comics. Or stays dead. Cast, characters, and titles change. It's complicated.
- Some recent comic titles include: *Gotham Knights*, *Gotham Adventures*, *The Batman Strikes*, *Legends of the Dark Knight*, and, of course, *Detective Comics*.

Hans Beckert—#90

Hans Beckert may not be a familiar name, but his impact on the movie industry and, through that medium, the general public, has been substantial. In Fritz Lang's 1931 German film *M* (for murderer), he is the first serial killer depicted in the cinema. His character, portrayed by Peter Lorre in his first major role, brought to the screen the characteristics that we now associate with serial killers: a creepy quiet fellow, a loner who seems quite ordinary. He lures schoolgirls into deserted places with candy and balloons and kills them. Afterward he writes letters to the police, taunting them. The film is an astonishing examination of the mind of a psychopath.

The movie is based on a real-life manhunt in Dusseldorf, Germany, for a serial child-murderer, Peter Kürten, and shows the havoc that one individual can inflict on a city. The movie is the springboard for an entire genre of stories such as *Psycho* and *The Silence of the Lambs*, and it brings into focus such real killers as Ted Bundy and Jeffrey Dahmer.

The unnamed metropolis in *M* is in a panic and everyone

is under suspicion. Without any evidence to back up their claims, citizens denounce one another to the police. One innocent man is attacked by a mob for just talking to a little girl.

The public keeps giving the police false leads and the authorities are worn down from working around the clock to catch the culprit. In their efforts to solve the case, the police crack down on all street crime. The criminals react by organizing a network to find the killer and thus reduce the police pressure on them. The various gangs work together and capture him. They take him to an abandoned warehouse and conduct a trial in a dark dungeonlike room. The criminals act as a kangaroo court—a jury of his peers—and conclude that society will be better off if he is dead.

At this point, the story takes an unexpected turn. Beckert becomes agonizingly human. He tells the men that it is impossible for him to resist the voices in his head. He says, "I have no control over my urges. . . . I want to escape from myself, but it is impossible." He gains our sympathy as he movingly confesses to the evil within him and pleads for mercy and understanding. The audience is forced to consider many difficult moral, ethical, and social questions about mental illness, which are not resolved in the movie.

Dick Tracy—#77

With the eyes and nose of a hawk and a chin like a meat cleaver, Chester Gould's Dick Tracy made his appearance in 1931, and transformed the comic strip into a form of literature. He defined the detective uniform—a trench coat and fedora hat—and his determination, incorruptible honesty, and use of violence combined to carry him quickly to the top of his profession, where he remains to this day. He represents the ideal detective: hard-boiled, dedicated to the public good, and relentless in his pursuit of criminals.

After seventy-five years on the job, Tracy is still a popular cultural icon who has not aged or slowed down. He remains the most popular detective in the comics, and he continues to entertain generations with sexy women and perilous situations wrapped in mystery and suspense.

After Sherlock Holmes, he is the most influential detective in literature. And where Holmes is all intellect, Tracy is a hands-on detective who uses his gun as often as he uses the crime lab.

Gould's use of violence in his new comic strip paralleled the bloodshed in the Chicago of the 1920s and early Depression years, where Tracy tracked down con men, pickpockets, gangsters, kidnappers, hit men, arsonists, and twisted freaks bent on revenge. Treachery was everywhere as bosses ruthlessly killed their henchmen and jilted molls betrayed mobsters. And, occasionally, innocent people were mowed down just for being in the wrong place at the wrong time.

In the strip's first story, Tracy's girlfriend, Tess Trueheart, was kidnapped and her father murdered. Tracy, as a plainclothes detective, tracked down the killers and rescued Tess. The strip soon became known for weird villains with bizarre physical distortions reflected in their names: Rodent, Little Face, the Brow, the Blank—who covered his scarred face with a sheet of flesh-colored cheesecloth. Larceny Lu, Stud, Stooge, Lips, the Tramp, Shakey, and Pear Shape are more examples of an almost endless parade of warped criminals defeated by Tracy. Then came the criminally insane Selbert

Depool, the suave, arrogant egomaniac; Shoulders; and the Nazi spy Pruneface. One of the favorite villains was Flattop, a hit man whose head was as flat as a table. During World War II, he was hired by black marketeers to murder Tracy—and almost did it—but in the end Tracy bested him in a spectacular fight scene.

A successful comic substory featured a family of inept hillbillies: B. O. Plenty and Gravel Gertie. Other additions to the strip included Liz, the policewoman; Sam Catchem, a Jewish detective; and Jr. Tracy, who captured the imagination of children.

Tracy has always led the way for law enforcement and communications technology. In 1946, an inventor in the strip, Diet Smith, gave Tracy a two-way wrist radio that he upgraded in 1964 to a two-way wrist TV; and in 1986 he traded that in for a two-way wrist computer.

Tracy added a line of comic books early on and had his own radio show from 1935 to 1948. He made his first movie in 1937, appearing in a fifteen-part suspense serial from Republic Pictures. A long series of B-grade feature films followed through the 1930s and 1940s, of which a highlight was *Dick Tracy Meets Gruesome* (1947). In it, Boris Karloff played the eponymous bad guy. Tracy had a television program in the 1950–51 season, and a major motion picture in 1990 starred Warren Beatty. The film, entitled simply *Dick Tracy*, featured Madonna as Breathless Mahoney and Dustin Hoffman as Mumbles, two of the more famous villains. Tracy's notoriety took a leap forward when the U.S. Postal Service issued a Dick Tracy commemorative stamp in 1995.

When Chester Gould, creator of the strip, retired in 1977, Max Allan Collins, a detective novelist, and Gould's assistant, Rick Fletcher, took over. When Fletcher died in 1983, the strip was passed on to Pulitzer-prize–winning editorial cartoonist Dick Locher.

Contemplating a career in crime? Don't give it a second thought. Tracy is still on the job—you can find him prowling cyberspace.

8. Americana

The characters in this chapter are part of the American experience, warts and all. They cover most of the nineteenth and twentieth centuries, a period during which this country grew at an astonishing pace and then burst on the international scene.

Some of these uniquely American personalities embody the attributes we most proudly show the world. Other characters have our flaws or represent our shameful treatment of the native tribes and our history with the slave trade.

All the characters in this chapter are 110 percent American. If anyone thinks Paul Bunyan could be relegated to folktales, he's got another think coming. Hiawatha was a true native American, and there's no way we're going to put him back in poetry or any of those other categories. He practically started the National Park System, for Pete's sake. Tom Sawyer couldn't be more American if he was born here—and he was born here, on the banks of the Mississippi River. And if anyone says G.I. Joe could have been in another chapter, well, that person's not a real American. That's just the way it is.

Uncle Sam—#61

Uncle Sam, the personification of our country, is the most readily recognized figure around the globe, the one most often burned in effigy by our enemies from Damascus to Jakarta.

Sam apparently evolved from a Revolutionary War cartoon character named Brother Jonathan, a moralistic Yankee with a penchant for lecturing people about proper behavior. Sam first appeared during the War of 1812 between the United States and Great Britain, as an unsophisticated, boondocks opponent of John Bull, the traditional symbol of British power.

There is speculation as to whether Uncle Sam was based on a real person. Some evidence points to Samuel Wilson, a meat packer from Troy, New York. During the War of 1812 he provided meat to the U.S. Army, and soldiers who saw that the crates were marked with the letters *U.S.* said that the meat was from "Uncle Sam" Wilson.

Before the 1860s, Uncle Sam was clean-shaven; however, after the Civil War he appeared with Abraham Lincoln's beard, lanky physique, and stovepipe hat. By the late 1800s, he was a familiar figure used by cartoonists to represent patriotism and national authority. He typically appeared—as today—dressed in the stars and stripes of the U.S. flag. Even when it was forbidden to use any part of the U.S. flag as clothing and Vietnam-era protesters were jailed for wearing flags as jackets, shirts, caps, and presumably more private articles of clothing, Uncle Sam was still decked out in the stars and stripes. There's no logic to tradition.

In the twentieth century, a succession of political cartoonists, from Thomas Nast to England's famed David Low, adopted him, and Uncle Sam has been busy ever since. He has exhorted young people to join the army, lamented the size of the national debt, and even appeared in National Comics with a kid named Buddy. They foiled Nazis intent on destroying us. Cartoonists have attributed to him every imaginable virtue, and in 1897, Governor Robert Taylor of Tennessee said that Uncle Sam was as brave as Caesar and as meek as Moses.

The illustrator James Montgomery Flagg was his own model for the famous poster that shows Uncle Sam pointing directly out of the army recruiting poster that said, *I want you.* The government printed more than 4 million copies between 1917 and 1918, as the United States entered World War I, and the poster was reprinted during World War II.

Uncle Sam's image has appeared on everything from lunch pails to cast-iron mailbox stands. Uncle Sam, who officially became our national symbol in 1950, has been adopted by such divergent symbols as neo-colonialism, corruption, military adventurism, and corporate greed.

Today, Uncle Sam has been replaced with slick television ads enhanced with computer graphics as a recruiter for the U.S. military. In his retirement, he runs a small umbrella store in Manhattan.

It's Official

According to the Troy, New York, official website, on September 15, 1961, the U.S. Congress recognized Uncle Sam Wilson as the original Uncle Sam.

Uncle Tom—#11

When Abraham Lincoln met author Harriet Beecher Stowe, he called her the little lady who made the big war. It was her book, *Uncle Tom's Cabin,* that inflamed the passions of the anti-slavery movement and helped trigger the U.S. Civil War, a conflict that killed some 500,000 soldiers and untold civilians. As the central character of this book, Uncle Tom, a quiet, gentle slave, may have inadvertently led to the death of 3 percent of the U.S. population.

Tom stands out as a symbol of injustice, the dangers of accepting injustice, and the gentle giant—the kind-hearted dolt. Let's start with the book, which is a fast-moving and well-constructed work. When we meet him, Tom is a dutiful slave on a Kentucky farm. He and his family live in a "cabin" that's as comfortable as any small beach house. He's gotten religion and, because he's now a dedicated Christian, he's trusted to do the farm's business in Ohio, a free state, and to carry $500 of the farm's money, an enormous sum in those days. Tom could easily escape, but having given his word, he doesn't.

Soon the master, Shelby, has gotten into debt and has to sell either Tom or the farm. To be sold "down south" is to be condemned to death by hard labor and starvation, and that's going to be Uncle Tom's fate. Tom sacrifices himself, knowing that the collapse of the farm would mean the sale of all its slaves, including his own wife and children. On the way South, he saves a white child from drowning. The girl, Little Eva, insists that her daddy buy Tom, and this interlude is the source of the second stereotype: the innocent child and the giant faithful servant. The new master then dies, and Tom is again sold, this time to Simon Legree, an evil plantation owner. He's not a Southerner or, as some mistakenly believe, a Jewish trader. He's a Vermont Christian who has rejected religion. Legree declares himself the only religion Tom will need. When Tom refuses an order to flog another slave, he is severely beaten, a pattern of the contest between authority and Tom's Christian morality. Shelby arrives in the nick of time with the money to repurchase Tom, but the slave has been whipped so severely that he dies minutes later, after giving blessings to all, and exclaiming the love of Jesus.

Uncle Tom is heavily drawn from the life of Josiah Henson, a slave who had been entrusted to move other slaves from Maryland to Kentucky. Josiah could have taken the whole group through Ohio up to Canada. He didn't. Once in Kentucky, Josiah and other farm property were taken to New Orleans to be sold. His master fell sick on the way, and Josiah nursed him and brought him home. Not one to repeat a mistake, Josiah then fled to Canada.

But *Uncle Tom's Cabin* is not his biography, it's a conglomeration of many slave stories heard by Mrs. Stowe. The narrative interweaves Tom's story with the tale of Eliza, a slave who realizes that her infant son is soon to be sold. She bolts without delay, taking her boy with her to Ohio and freedom.

Uncle Tom's Cabin was published as a serial before appearing as a book in March 1852. By the end of that year it had sold 300,000 copies, an astonishing record. In 1853 Harriet Beecher Stowe published *A Key to Uncle Tom's Cabin,* in which she supports the realism of every storyline, listing slave histories, incidents, and dozens of newspaper ads of slaves for sale.

In the real world, Abraham Lincoln was not in favor of political equality for the black race. Congress pushed constitutional amendments eliminating slavery and protecting the rights of all citizens—at least in theory. In practice, the promised emancipation was nullified by the Ku Klux Klan's lynchings and death lists. Blacks lived under a sharecropping system just a shade better than slavery, and progress was frustratingly slow.

Uncle Tom's Cabin enjoyed a revival in the silent film era, and again came into notice during the Civil Rights movement of the 1950s and 1960s. By the 1960s, Uncle Tom was again a nationally known character, but this time, *Tom* was an epithet for any black who accepted white authority, good intentions, or assurances for gradual progress. Josiah Henson admitted that he let his pride overrule his judgment, and he would probably agree that to be a Tom was to be traitorous or just plain stupid. Poor Uncle Tom, sold for trustworthiness, killed for kindness, and reviled for patience. That fictional slave bought freedom for every black in America.

To learn more about Uncle Tom, read
   Uncle Tom's Cabin, or, Life Among the Lowly by Harriet Beecher Stowe.
   Reconstruction: The Ending of the Civil War by Anthony Craven.
   The Era of Reconstruction: 1865–1867 by Kenneth M. Stamp.

Many Thousands Gone: The First Two Centuries of Slavery in North America by Ira Berlin.

A Key to Uncle Tom's Cabin; Presenting the Original Facts and Documents Upon Which the Story Is Founded, Together with Corroborative Statements Verifying the Truth of the Work by Harriet Beecher Stowe.

Hiawatha—#71

The Song of Hiawatha legitimized and reinforced the condescending and patronizing attitude toward the Indians that persists into the twenty-first century. Longfellow characterized them as noble savages, but while their nobility should have conferred respect, their savagery invited our domination and paternalism.

The lengthy poem struck a resonant chord with the American population. Before contact with Europeans, the natives didn't have any of the technology that was beginning to blacken the skies and souls of the settlers. They lacked gunpowder, iron, and wheels. They were still in the Stone Age, using technology less sophisticated than that available to Achilles 3,000 years earlier. Their weapons—the bow and arrow, knife, and hatchet—all had stone blades and tips. By the early 1800s the Indians were already headed toward extinction. By 1843, the Oregon Trail, heavy with settlers, sealed the fate of the Native Americans. All they lacked was a memorial, and that came in 1855 in the form of Longfellow's epic poem.

This is an Indian story, but it was not written by an Indian. It was written by a New Englander, steeped in centuries of

European tradition and comforted by the moral superiority of Northern abolitionism. But in the mid-1850s, the popular opposition to slavery did not overflow into reasonable treatment of the natives with whom treaties had been signed, and the era is marked by such atrocities as the Trail of Tears (1838) and the slaughter at Wounded Knee (1890).

Longfellow composed the poem to sound as if it were the product of an oral tradition of the Great Lakes Indians: the steady eight-syllable-per-line meter, without rhyme but with an almost musical alliteration and repetition, which can easily be imagined as being recited over the beat of a tom-tom to a tribe gathered around a campfire. The effect is dramatic and effective.

Longfellow opened the story with a panoramic sweep of the entire country: the myths of the natives, their habits and lifestyle. Then he turned his focus to Hiawatha, the young prince, his adventures, and his ascendance.

Longfellow described how the Indian tribes settled in the Great Lakes area, and he traced the emergence of Hiawatha's bloodline. And then a forewarning: The Peace Pipe smoke signal summoned the leaders of the tribes together. One of their own leaders complained of their constant quarrels and promised to send them a prophet to unify them and resolve their disputes. This leader also told them that if they ignored his guidance, they would fade away. Then the story focuses on Hiawatha himself.

Soon after Hiawatha was born, his father, a warrior, abandoned his mother, Wenonah, who then died of grief. Wenonah's mother, Nokomis, had to raise her grandson. As Hiawatha grew, he learned the ways of his natural world, much as Tarzan would learn the ways of the African jungle.

Longfellow expounded on the developing peace among

several native tribes that emerged with Hiawatha's marriage to Minnehaha. During this time Hiawatha invented picture writing and taught it to his tribesmen to protect their progeny from forgetting their accomplishments and history. As long as Hiawatha was content, his people prospered.

But Hiawatha's closest friend died, and with his ensuing sadness, his tribe was subjected to torments and plagues. In the resulting famine, Minnehaha died, and Hiawatha sadly saw the end of his own life.

A white man in a black robe arrived from the east and told of the Christian savior. This priest, presumably, was the prophet foretold much earlier in the poem.

With the revelation of this important new story, Hiawatha departed from his people, believing that they were safe in the white man's hands.

But these were not just any white men. These were Puritan Christians, who believed that children needed to be exposed to treatment as harsh as the New England winters they endured themselves. The problems they initiated continue to plague all of us. The Bureau of Indian Affairs still dominates the lives of most of the Indians in the United States. The damage done by condescending white people, comforted by the spirit of Longfellow's creation, persists to this day.

Maybe You Didn't Know

The public has a grossly distorted and sanitized conception of what the Bureau of Indian Affairs (BIA) does. The conquered population is paid an allowance by the conquerors while those conquerors remain the bankers, mismanaging the finances of their charges and wasting most of it.

None of the reservations ever had a consul or ambassador, so the Constitution's reference to making treaties with "the Indian nations" is a cruel and sterile fraud.

The U.S. Army Corps of Engineers and the Bureau of Reclamation, which together build dams and related improvements, are authorized to confiscate Indian reservation land for this purpose with no accountability. The injury done to many of the reservations—in violation of the sanctity of those treaties—has been enormous. And the Native Americans have seen little if any of the resultant economic benefit.

The former degree of savagery of the Indians is irrelevant if they are treated more like animals relegated to zoos than human beings with their own rights and dignity.

To learn more about the misuse of the Hiawatha story, we recommend

Inventing the American Primitive: Politics, Gender, and the Representation of Native American Literary Traditions, 1789-1936 by Helen Carr. See especially Chapter 3, "The Myth of Hiawatha."

The American Cowboy—#19

The most romantic mythical figure in all of American culture, the cowboy epitomizes the adventurous individual who is independent, strong, and courageous. He is invariably tall and handsome. We picture him in tight pants, leather chaps, and tall boots with high heels and large spurs. Characteristically, he also wears a short-waisted denim jacket and a bandanna about his neck, and he carries a poncho that protects him from rain and cold. His "Ten Gallon Hat" was derived from the Mexican sombrero galoneado, with *ten* added to denote a large size.

He lived in a paradise now lost forever—a symbolic pastoral place in our minds rather than a geographical location. The cowboy has been fixed in our minds by such luminaries of western literature as Owen Wister and his creation *The Virginian,* Zane Grey, and Louis L'Amour, to name just a few.

The mythical aspect of the American cowboy grew up after the Civil War, when population centers in the East looked to the open rangelands west of the Mississippi River to satisfy the newly burgeoning demand for beef. The first step was to build railroads into Kansas, to such legendary places as Abilene, Hays City, Wichita, Ellsworth, and Dodge City.

Adventurous adolescents and many former soldiers, especially from the South, were looking for a new and simpler way of life and found it on the ranches. Many of these men were blacks or Mexicans, but you would never learn that from the movies.

With resilience and perseverance they learned to handle cattle, throw steer, and break wild horses. But we most often picture the cowboy on the cattle drives from the Texas ranches to the railheads in Kansas. Thousands upon thousands of cattle were under his watchful eyes during the months-long trips. It was here that he developed his skills in the ways of the open range and became one with his horse. He worked hard, suffered deprivation, and risked death from thunderstorms, stampedes, rampaging rivers, and confrontations with outlaws.

After coaxing a slow moving herd along dangerous trails

for several months, the destination towns offered him the comfort of a hotel room, gambling, women, good food, and a place
to let off steam in a rowdy, impulsive, two-fisted way. However, there were limits, and the towns hired such legendary figures as Wyatt Earp, Wild Bill Hickock, and Bat Masterson to
maintain a degree of law and order.

In the early 1900s, dime novelists portrayed the cowboy as a
western hero who rode forth in an aura of honor, justice, and
righteousness. He found himself in conflict with Indians, gam-
blers, corrupt officials, evil cattlemen, rustlers, crooked bankers,
and hired gunfighters.

Movies have had a significant impact in forming our concept of the cowboy. Starting with the early silent films, the
Western moved into the era of sound and the inexpensively
made, simplistic movies of the 1940s and 50s—the so-called B
movies—in which horsemen rode at top speed for mile after
mile on tireless horses while shooting endlessly without having
to reload. John Wayne was the quintessential movie cowboy,
and he appeared in such classics as *Stagecoach, Red River,* and
The Searchers. The characters he played were honest and never
looked for trouble, but if trouble came, he was certain to prevail. One of the best western films came in 1953, when Alan
Ladd created Shane, the all-encompassing heroic cowboy. On a
lower note came the spaghetti westerns and then the western-
to-end-all-westerns, Mel Brooks's hilarious 1974 sendup, *Blaz-
ing Saddles.*

The cowboy evolved from the Spanish cow- and sheep-
herders, the vaqueros. They introduced the western stock sad-
dle and contributed to our language words such as sombrero,
lariat, lasso, pronto, savvy, vamoose, buckaroo, and macho.

The cattle drive era started in 1870 and lasted only about
thirty years, but the cowboy's image has prevailed to our day in

films, television, literature, amusement parks, popular music, and our love affair with guns.

The influence of the cowboy has spanned a century, and still affects our lives. To this day, we make fashion statements by wearing cowboy boots and Western-style clothing.

The cowboy is the way we define ourselves and project our image to the rest of the world: free, indomitable, unsophisticated, and always ready for a fight. The world recognizes "The Star-Spangled Banner," but really identifies Americans with the theme from *Bonanza*.

Tom Sawyer and Huckleberry Finn—#65

The Adventures of Tom Sawyer is one of the most innocent adventures of all time. Its sequel, *The Adventures of Huckleberry Finn*, is one of the most controversial. The same author penned them and several of the characters appear in both tales. This apparent incongruity highlights the genius of Mark Twain, the author.

The stories take place during the closing years of the 1850s, in the northeast corner of Missouri along the Mississippi River. The river figures prominently in both books, revealing the author's fascination with the waterway, but it is the way the boys play and learn along the river that serves to entertain us.

Tom Sawyer is the main character in the first story, which details the happy-go-lucky existence of boyhood. Tom shows us how to turn a chore into profit. In a famous chapter, Tom's Aunt Polly tells him to whitewash the picket fence in front of her house. Tom doesn't sulk; he pretends that it's fun and ropes all his friends into not only doing his work, but actually paying for the privilege. The lesson to all boys is clear: Use your imagination, and you can turn a tedious job into a rewarding adventure.

As the result of an erroneous assumption, the townspeople believe Tom and Huck have died, drowned in the river. Rather than reveal that they are alive, the boys hide out in the church and overhear what their neighbors say about them during the funeral service. When they finally come forward, everybody is delighted that they're not dead, and the punishment for putting the adults through the torment of the funeral is negligible.

Tom develops an attachment to the pretty Becky Thatcher, and he finally endears himself to her by taking the blame for a misdeed of hers. They're still children, so the subsequent attraction is G-rated: Tom and Becky get trapped in a cave. They end up not only rescued, but catching some thieves and getting to keep their loot as reward. Huck is part of that rescue and receives some of that reward, too. The first story ends with the children on the cusp of adolescence.

The second novel begins where the earlier story left off, but this time the focus is on Huck. Huck is forced to live with a local widow until his ne'er-do-well father returns, drawn by the loot that Huck has earned in the first story. His father gains custody of Huck and the loot too—emphasizing to readers that his parental role might not be honorable. Huck succeeds in escaping from his father with the widow's slave, Jim, and the two make a clean break from the oppressive society around them. They have several adventures on the river, and Jim almost floats into the hellhole of Southern slavery.

The pair finally break free: Jim, by the death of the widow whose will frees him, and Huck by finally deciding he can't live in that society anymore. Sometimes the only way to break free of the crushing burden of established society is to pack up and leave, and Huck intends to go west.

Huck Finn has left us with a major controversy: the enduring debate over the question of literary accuracy versus the offensiveness of *the n-word*. In the time these stories are set, accepted features of language reflected the negative social attitudes toward blacks in general, even free Negroes. Mark Twain's 1850's characters use what is now euphemistically called "the n-word" as a term for blacks.

It is now more than a century after Twain wrote the books, and society has made slow, erratic progress toward racial equality. The language of Twain's books is now emblematic of that oppressive society, and it is almost as offensive as slavery itself. Suggestions that the books be banned for perpetuating the stereotype have been seriously entertained, while the possibility of sanitizing the book's language has also been considered. But to date, no changes have been made.

Tom Sawyer taught generations of youngsters that as enjoyable and carefree as childhood might be, we all have to grow up eventually.

Huck brings us a far more serious message. By not turning in a runaway slave, Huck not only violates the law, but also violates the religious principles of the overwhelming majority of Southerners, who considered it a sin to aid a slave in his flight to freedom. Huck examines his conscience and tells us he would rather go to hell than turn Jim in. That moral lesson, from the mind of a child, is one of the most powerful expressions of moral integrity in all of literature. As Huck matured, so did American society.

Paul Bunyan—#101

Not only is Paul Bunyan the classic American legend, he captures the very essence of our country. Everything about him is big: his size, his adventures, his legend. He accomplishes everything he puts his mind to and, in the tradition of our nation, does it with ingenuity and good humor.

This truly American legend persists thanks to the diligent collection and preservation of his stories and tall tales by the Red River Lumber Company, which used them in ads from 1915 to 1949. They published a collection of these ads in a pamphlet that first appeared in 1922.

The California Gold Rush brought in $3 billion over the years 1848 to 1898, but during the same half century America had an even larger bonanza: lumber barons in Michigan alone cut $4 billion in timber. Most lumberjacks were homeless immigrants who worked twelve or more hours per day, six days a week, under harsh, hazardous conditions. Over the years these men created the legend of Paul Bunyan to bring some good cheer and esteem into their lives of drudgery.

The tales started variously in Maine, Wisconsin, Minnesota, or Michigan with Paul depicted as a rough, mean man of normal size who wore a handlebar mustache. William Laughhead, the advertising illustrator for the Red River Lumber Company of Minnesota, transformed him into a huge, powerful, brawny logger. After a time, he grew from a large human of just over six feet to sixty-three ax handles tall. Babe, his ox, similarly grew as the tall tales circulated.

As is true of so many myths, this one is alive and well, and new additions to it are welcome at any time. The tall tales, originally about a logger, later spread to oil field workers.

Here are a few samples of the stories told about Paul:

When he was born it took five giant storks to deliver him, and he grew so fast that after one week he had to wear his father's clothes. Soon Paul's clothes were so large they had to use wagon wheels for buttons. And his baby carriage was a lumber wagon drawn by a team of oxen.

On his first birthday his father gave him a pet blue ox named Babe. Babe was seven ax handles wide between the eyes. For a snack, he would eat thirty bales of hay, wire and all. Six men were kept busy picking the wire out of his teeth. It was impossible to build an ox-sling big enough to hoist Babe off the ground for shoeing, but after they logged off all of Dakota there was room for Babe to lie down for the procedure. Every time Babe needed a new set of shoes they had to open another iron mine in Minnesota. Paul and Babe were so large the tracks they made in Minnesota filled up and made the ten thousand lakes in the Land of the Sky-Blue Water.

Legend has it that Paul formed the Grand Canyon by accidentally dragging an ax behind him.

Babe's tracks were so deep that a settler and his wife and baby once fell into one of them. The son finally got out when he was fifty-seven years old to report the accident.

Paul ate so many pancakes every morning that there was no griddle big enough to make them. So he made one so large you couldn't see across it on a foggy day.

To call his men in for dinner, Paul made a horn so big that only he could sound it. When he blew it for the first time, he knocked over ten acres of pine. That would not do, so Paul shipped the horn East where it was made into the roof of Grand Central Station.

When Paul logged off North Dakota he hauled water for his crew from the Great Lakes. One day, when they were halfway across Minnesota, the tank sprung a leak. That was the beginning of the Mississippi River, and the river is still flowing.

Paul dug a well so deep that it took all day for the bucket to fall to the water and a week to haul it back up.

Paul was honored by the Postal Service when he appeared on a normal size stamp. A stamp four feet wide and six feet tall had been planned, but that too may be a tall tale.

Paul Bunyan's can-do "what's the next problem to solve" approach set the standard attitude for generations of Americans, in particular those who built the assembly line, carved Mount Rushmore, and created Hoover Dam. Paul Bunyan is also the original "super-size me" pioneer, and he almost certainly drives the largest SUV. Paul Bunyan's is an important cautionary tale: Paul ran short of material to support his lifestyle and was last seen heading for the Mojave Forest.

Everything About Him Is BIG!

Every year since 1953, the winner of the University of Michigan/Michigan State University football game holds the Paul Bunyan Trophy for the following year. The trophy is a four-foot-high wooden statue of the logger on a five-foot-high bases.

Amos 'n' Andy—#83

These characters had the longest-running radio program in broadcast history. Their fame lingers on in spite of, or perhaps because of, the controversy that erupted around them and their show when they moved from radio to television.

The series got started in 1926 as a derivative of the daily newspaper comic strip *The Gumps*. Executives at WGN, the radio station of the *Chicago Tribune*, approached Freeman Gosden and Charles Correll, two white southerners living in Chicago, about doing a radio drama along the lines of the comic strip. The Gumps had started in 1919 and was the first comic to run as a serial, rather than as isolated episodes; a radio serial was unprecedented.

Gosden and Correll first aired *Sam 'n' Henry* and made the story line revolve around a pair of black characters. When the series became so popular that they wanted to syndicate the show by sending phonograph recordings around the country, WGN management balked. So in early 1928, Gosden and Correll signed with WMAQ, the station affiliated with the *Chicago Daily News*, with the assurance of syndication. The names of the principal characters were changed to Amos and Andy, and the new series premiered in March. It was a hit for the next thirty years. Gosden and Correll voiced more than a hundred characters. Their portrayals were so evocative and expressive that when the show joined the NBC radio network, people across the country became avid fans.

Amos 'n' Andy were Amos Jones and Andrew Brown. The first episodes found them as farm hands in Atlanta, looking forward to making a new life in Chicago, just as many real-life blacks were immigrating to the industrial north. Amos was hesitant and uncertain, while Andy was a self-assured risk taker. The show followed their ambitious move north and the rocky lives of these two characters and their acquaintances in the city. The audience thrilled to the romance of Amos and

Ruby Taylor, the daughter of his employer. Then in 1931, they held their collective breath when she was near death from pneumonia. Amos and Ruby were finally married in 1935, and Amos noticeably matured and became happy and confident. The whole country got involved in suggesting a name for their fictional daughter. And everybody who has dreamed of becoming wealthy empathized with Andy's get rich quick schemes. But there was much more than just humor to this show: there was humanity.

Such characters as George "Kingfish" Stevens—the hustler who always had an angle—became staples of the show; Louisiana senator Huey Long even adopted the nickname "Kingfish."

Broadcast in many areas of the country for fifteen minutes each day for six days a week, *Amos 'n' Andy* was so popular during the Depression that movie theaters interrupted their feature show for the fifteen minutes of the radio program, and when it was over they resumed the movie.

Late in the radio series run, which ended in 1960, the format changed to a half hour once a week, with a live studio audience. That's the blueprint for the traditional half-hour sitcom today.

When CBS brought the show to television in 1950, racial issues were finally getting national attention. The stars were all black—a first and, for quite some time, the only instance of minority roles featured on television—but the potential to see the humor as racially prejudiced was too much for some people. The combination of the new racial awareness—and such unflattering black characters as Lightnin' (the slow-moving janitor), Madame Queen (Andy's love interest), and

Lawyer Calhoun (the conniving shyster)—aroused the NAACP. The move to television radically polarized the audience. White and black people responded differently, advertisers became skittish, and the show ceased production after only two years, though it was rebroadcast in syndication until 1966.

Part of the audience that the NAACP was trying to protect had welcomed the arrival of blacks on television, and the others—mostly the few in the acting business—embraced the show, noting, for example, that they could either play a janitor for $500 a week or be one for $5 a week. But the only black people associated with the television program were the actors; all the jobs behind the scenes remained pure white.

The largest group of blacks, however, reflected an emerging sentiment fostered by World War II. Black soldiers, having helped win the war against two viciously racist cultures and proven their worth, returned home to business and life—and racism—as usual. Certainly many of them asked, "I risked my life for this?" These returning soldiers cultivated an unwillingness to tolerate racism. The appearance of *Amos 'n' Andy* on television, with the derogatory stereotypes, could not have satisfied their desire for fair treatment. The *Amos 'n' Andy* television program was still playing in some markets, dying embers of the show, when Martin Luther King, Jr., led the March on Washington on August 28, 1963.

At the time the syndication finally fizzled in 1966, black actors held four important roles on television: Bill Cosby in *I Spy,* Nichelle Nichols in *Star Trek,* Greg Morris in *Mission: Impossible*, and Hari Rhodes in *Daktari*. Cosby played a competent espionage agent, Nichols played a starship communications officer, Morris played an electronics expert, and Rhodes played a modern African gamekeeper. The contrast between those characters and the caricatures in *Amos 'n' Andy* could not have been more pronounced.

On radio, Amos and Andy were the stars. On television, they were just two more characters of an ensemble, and the presentation of virtually all the other characters was perceived by some as insulting and distasteful. The least objectionable character, the diligent hard-working sensible Amos, was relegated to an incidental role in the television program, in spite of the star billing. The audience that sought equal treatment was the group that pressured the producers and network to abandon the show.

The original radio humor was derived from simple farce, some puns, and commentary on then-current events, and the deep sensitivity touched everybody irrespective of skin color. The *Amos 'n' Andy* radio show was popular among black people because for the most part the show treated black people sympathetically. During much of the period that this series was broadcast on radio, few people objected to the characters being black, and even today many think that the actors were black. The show set the stage for Americans of all races to see beyond skin color and into people's hearts and minds.

The *Amos 'n' Andy* show was inducted into the Radio Hall of Fame in 1988. There are still people alive who remember with fondness the original radio show, the actors, and the sometimes silly, sometimes touching lives they led. And there are others, younger, who remember being inspired by the television series to social and political activism.

To learn more about *Amos 'n' Andy*, we suggest
  Holy Mackerel!: The Amos 'n' Andy Story by Bart Andrews and Ahrgus Juilliard.
  The Adventures of Amos 'n' Andy: A Social History of an American Phenomenon by Melvin Patrick Ely.

G.I. Joe—#48

Millions of Americans and foreigners see G.I. Joe as a mindless war toy, the symbol of American military adventurism, but that's not how it used to be. To the men and women who served in World War II and the people they liberated, the GI was the common man become hero, the poor farm kid torn away from his home, the grunt who bore all the burdens of battle, who slept in cold foxholes, who went without the necessities of food and shelter, who stuck it out and drove back the Nazi reign of murder. This was not a volunteer soldier, not someone well paid, but an average guy, up against the best trained, best equipped, fiercest, most diabolical foes seen in centuries.

His name isn't much. *G.I.* is just a military abbreviation meaning Government Issue, and it was on all of the articles handed out to soldiers. And Joe? A common name for a guy who never made it to the top. Joe Blow, Joe Palooka, Joe Magrac . . . a working class name. The United States has never had a president or vice-president or secretary of state Joe.

G.I. Joe had a distinguished career fighting German, Japanese, and Korean troops. He appears as a character, or a collection of American personalities, in the 1945 movie *The Story of G.I. Joe*, based on the last days of war correspondent Ernie Pyle. Some of the soldiers Pyle interviewed portrayed themselves in the film. Ernie was famous for covering the human side of the war, writing about the dirt-snow-and-mud soldiers, not how many miles were gained or what towns were captured or liberated. His reports paralleled the "Willie" cartoons of famed *Stars and Stripes* artist Bill Maulden. Both men emphasized the dirt and exhaustion of war, the fragments of civilization that the men shared with each other and the civilians: coffee, tobacco, whiskey, shelter, sleep. To Egypt, France, and a dozen more countries, G.I. Joe was any American soldier, at that point the most important person in their lives.

The toy we know is a different breed. As the memories of the real soldiers faded, the toy version was introduced by Hasbro, a small company founded in 1923 by Henry and Helal Hassenfeld. They originally sold school supplies. The first G.I. Joe appeared in 1964, a lean twelve-inch articulated doll in plastic. Several figures, if not all, were modeled on real people, one of whom was Marine Lieutenant Colonel Mitchell Paige, who died in 2003. The toy came out during the brief early popularity of the Vietnam War. The twelve-inch doll went out of production in 1976, and the version that reappeared in 1982 was 3¾ inches tall, perhaps reflecting the downsizing of the American military, but more likely because the new Star Wars figures were that height. There have been several hundred Joes in the action figure line, most of them the smaller size. Typically, each figure is made for only a single year. The 2004 run had almost two hundred Joe characters, from Vietnam Door Gunner to Action Sailor #16.

There are at least two hundred characters in the G.I. Joe cartoon and comic book series. Joe has been in TV cartoons, comic books, and an occasional movie. There are dozens of parallel stories, comics, and toys, from the practical war stories of Sergeant Rock comics, to the abominable toy Forward Command Post, a battle-ravaged house inhabited by a single well-armed soldier. Any military toy eventually gets lumped in with G.I. Joe.

The G.I. Joe figures are rated for use by children as young as five. What? That's physical safety, not the emotional impact of napalming villages. Although there are plenty who argue against the desensitizing effect of violence on television, video games, and toys, violent acts committed by children are triggered by real violence within the home, not by toys, according to A. Storr, *Human Aggression,* 1968.

Children have played with toy soldiers for hundreds of years, thousands perhaps. In a classic story, "The Toys of Peace" by satirist H. H. Munro (who died in World War I), the parents of two small boys take away all their war-toys and give them model loaves of bread, wheelbarrows, and action figures of poets and astrologers and models of a library building and the Manchester Branch of the Young Women's Christian Association. The parents look in later to find that the boys have converted everything to forts and soldiers and are busily playing war.

The new Joe is no longer a symbol of the tired commoner. He's trim, athletic, and he doesn't fight traditional armies—foes who might be the next generation's allies. He fights terrorists, reptilian monster-men, and assorted politically correct evildoers. What will happen to the Colin Powell action figure when kids realize he's not General Powell or Secretary Powell, but a corporate executive? Boardroom at 10 o'clock! Move It! Move It! Move It!!!

Did You Know

Among the dozens of G.I. Joe dolls *are* an FBI *agent*, General Jimmy Dolittle, *and a* Navy Seal paradiver. An eight-inch figure has also been produced.

To learn more, read
    Human Aggression by Anthony Storr.
    The American Heritage New History of World War II revised by Stephen Ambrose, based on text by C. L. Sulzberger.
    Learning of Aggression in Children by Leonard L. Enron and Leopold O. Lefkowitz.

John Doe—#100

John Doe is an undisputed American celebrity, whose name appears on official documents, in works of fiction, and even in movie titles. But all of our research about him came to naught. We couldn't learn anything about him.

We thought we had a lead when we found the 1941 Frank Capra film *Meet John Doe* But he was a fake. We found four John Does in Manhattan, but none was the one we were looking for. We asked the Internal Revenue Service, but they weren't much help. They're also looking for him.

We've heard that he's living with Jane Doe, but so far we can't find her either.

9. Literature

Some of the most interesting characters you'll ever meet are in your local bookstore. That old fellow with the rusty armor is Don Quixote—he's a lunatic or, as he prefers to call himself, "a man of vision." If he asks you for a contribution to fight evil giants disguised as windmills, just pretend you didn't hear.

Some of these characters are best avoided. That girl browsing through the books about child abuse is Dolores Haze, but we know her as Lolita. Don't go near her unless you're prepared to spend the next twenty-five years in jail.

On the other hand, that attractive young woman with the English accent, the one looking through the books about romance, is Emma. A pleasant lady whose mission in life is to see to it that all of her friends make proper marriages.

In literature, we meet many personality types, each unique. Most of them inhabit long stories with complex plots: novels, poetry, satire, short stories, and plays. In this broad category, you'll find Dr. Jekyll, Mr. Hyde, Madame Bovary, Pudd'nhead Wilson, Nick Adams, Jane Eyre, and others. Almost half of the characters in this book started in literature.

Whether they are heroes or villains or personality disorders, these are influential people we can't ignore.

Don Quixote—#17

In the early twenty-first century a group of one hundred prominent writers selected *Don Quixote* as the greatest novel of all time.

In the story, Miguel de Cervantes Saavedra (1547–1616) shows us the negative consequences of following a way of life that is absurdly old-fashioned. He reminds us that even an intelligent person can fall victim to his own foolishness.

The central character in the story, a spare, gaunt gentleman of fifty, is addicted to books of chivalry and spends all of his time engrossed in these meandering stories of knights and squires. He becomes so absorbed he takes them literally. Eventually this leads to madness, and he convinces himself that his mission in life is to become a knight-errant.

He finds some armor that had belonged to his great-grandfather and repairs its broken helmet with pasteboard. Next, he gives his broken-down nag the name Rocinante and decides to call himself Don Quixote de la Mancha.

Nothing more is needed but a lady to be in love with and, unbeknownst to her, he chooses a buxom farm girl, Aldonza Lorenzo, to whom he gives the title Dulcinea del Toboso. She will be the inspiration for all of his exploits, even though we will never meet her in the novel.

One morning he dons his armor and sallies forth. In his first adventure as a knight, he discovers a farmer flogging a teenage boy. The man explains that he employs the boy to watch a flock of sheep, but he loses one every day. Don Quixote stops the beating and threatens to attack the man unless he pays the boy the sixty-three reals owed to him. The man promises to do so, and the knight rides away in triumph.

But, as soon as he is out of sight, the farmer resumes beating the boy worse than before.

A few miles down the road Don Quixote sees some merchants walking along and demands that they stop and swear that in the entire world, there is no maiden fairer than Dulcinea del Toboso. And they must do so immediately, without having seen her or her picture. Piqued by their delay in responding, Don Quixote charges them. However, Rocinante stumbles and falls. One of the men accosts the thrown rider, pummels him, and leaves him bruised and beaten. By chance, two of the Don's fellow villagers find him and bring him home.

Two weeks later he persuades an illiterate farm laborer, Sancho Panza, to be his squire, and they take to the road. Soon they come to several windmills, which Don Quixote imagines are monstrous giants. He declares that he will sweep these evil creatures from the face of the earth, and he calls on Dulcinea to support him in such peril. He charges at the first mill. But as he drives his lance into the sail, the wind turns the sail, the weapon is shattered, and Don Quixote is thrown to the ground. After the encounter he declares that a magician, who wanted to deprive him of the honor of the victory, had turned the giants into windmills.

Whenever he is bested, he attributes it to the spell of a magician. When he enjoys a victory, he usually does so by injuring an innocent party, such as when he attacks a funeral procession thinking they are devils carrying away a princess, and again when he misinterprets a flock of sheep as an enemy army.

Finally, Don Quixote arrives in Barcelona, where an old friend in disguise lures him into single combat and defeats him. His friend brings him home where, deprived of his illusions, he soon falls ill, renounces chivalry, and dies. He leaves behind a new word, *quixotic*, meaning hopelessly naïve and impractical, extravagantly unrealistic, doomed to failure. And thus, knight-errantry became extinct yet again.

Ivanhoe—#97

We have all heard of Ivanhoe, and that is why he is in this book. We may even recall that we met him in Sir Walter Scott's 1819 novel of the same name. But few of us seem to remember what he did in the story. That's probably because we confuse him with Robin Hood, who also appears in the novel. It might also be because for much of the novel, he was convalescent, even near death, and not particularly chatty.

The story of Ivanhoe extols the positive benefits of reconciliation, both political and religious. It is a political myth that brings together, in peace and cooperation, the Norman (French) conquerors of England and the indigenous Saxons in the 1200s. Ivanhoe personifies this reconciliation with his loyalty to both the Normans and the Saxons, to the advantage of both groups.

The novel's hero, Wilfred of Ivanhoe, is the son of Cedric, a Saxon lord who hopes to forge a cohesive alliance among the defeated Saxons by having his ward, Rowena, a descendant of Alfred the Great, marry Athelstane, a descendant of Edward the Confessor. However, Ivanhoe loves Rowena, and this threatens the plan. To move his strategy forward, Cedric disinherits his son. The young man then joins the Third Crusade and, in the company of Richard the Lionhearted, the Norman king of England, he travels to the Holy Land. The novel begins when Ivanhoe returns to England and finds that Prince John plans to depose his brother, King Richard.

The story shifts to a tournament where Prince John plans

to impress the Saxons with the prowess of his Norman knights. Ivanhoe and King Richard, both in disguises, are there and vanquish all of Prince John's men, but Ivanhoe is injured. A beautiful young Jewish woman, Rebecca, becomes his nurse. But before Ivanhoe can fully recover, a baron loyal to Prince John captures Rebecca and carries her off to his castle. There she is accused of witchcraft but escapes immediate execution by demanding trial by combat. Ivanhoe appears as her champion and saves her.

At the end of the story, King Richard reconciles Ivanhoe with his father, Cedric, who consents to the marriage of Ivanhoe and Rowena. Rebecca also loves Ivanhoe, but she knows that this love is futile. She and her father leave for Spain, where they hope to find a refuge from bigotry.

Ivanhoe was the first English novel that dealt seriously with issues of nationality and ethnicity.

The English venerated their Saxon ancestors and their ancient laws. By developing the idea of an alliance between King Richard and Ivanhoe, Scott brought the Norman king into close contact with the English people and, in the novel, he was accepted as one of them.

Ivanhoe was mythical, but real history reveals that Richard the Lionhearted was king of England between 1189 and 1199 and that John's plot to depose him actually took place, but failed. However, after Richard died in battle in 1199, John ascended to the throne as King John. In 1215, he signed the Magna Carta.

After two devastating world wars in Europe during the twentieth century, the countries have decided to try reconciliation as an alternative. Hence, we can credit Ivanhoe as the forerunner of the European Union.

Now, if by chance you should run into your high school English teacher, you can impress her with your profound knowledge of the story. Perhaps you'll even forgive her for all of the times her lessons about Ivanhoe interrupted your nap.

Ebenezer Scrooge—#16

The meanest of misers, Ebenezer Scrooge is the star of Dickens's 1843 novel *A Christmas Carol*. A cautionary character, he shows us not only mistakes to avoid, but the path to earthly salvation. Many of us talk about him as if he were a neighbor (the one who doesn't buy Girl Scout cookies) or our supervisor. In our everyday language, *Scrooge* has come to mean miserly, nasty, foul-tempered, and antisocial. We use his expressions "Bah, humbug!" and "Are there no workhouses?" to mark any unkind, callous, or selfish attitudes.

We meet Scrooge in his old age, when he's the cold-hearted entrepreneur whose only love is money. Rejected in love and hardened by his sister's death, he has turned from purposeful businessman to obsessive capitalist. The ghost of his former partner, Jacob Marley, appears to warn Scrooge of his approaching demise. Marley enlists the aid of three spirits, and during their visits Scrooge repents and emerges with a burst of happiness. All this happens on Christmas Eve, as though the spirits of charity have gotten their annual bonus. The moral lesson is that the need for community and family outweighs that of material wealth. Although it was written for adults, the story's real target is children. If Scrooge fails to repent, Tiny Tim, the youngest child of the office clerk, will die. We may read and understand the story as adults, but many of us first encountered it as children, and continue to do so year after year, from the time we watched our first television.

The role of Scrooge is a magnet for actors, and that keeps the story sharp in our minds. Such luminaries as Alistair Sim, George C. Scott, Albert Finney, and Bill Murray have played the role. Animated versions include *Mickey's Christmas Carol* (Scrooge McDuck: Bill Thompson), The Simpsons, The Flintstones, and Mr. Magoo (Jim Backus). More than forty movie versions can be found, with one dating back to 1913. There's also a version with Vanessa Williams as Ebony Scrooge, and even an *All Dogs Christmas Carol*.

The transformation of Scrooge is a difficult piece of work that takes four ghosts most of the night.

The first, Marley, tries the power of friendship. He and Scrooge were lifelong pals from their first working days, when Scrooge was still somewhat human. But Scrooge dismisses Marley's advice. Ebenezer has buried himself in business, and he only wants to get back to his routine. The Spirit of Christmas Past (the memories of his childhood) and the Spirit of Christmas Present (a look at real conditions) are not strong enough. Scrooge is moved to action only by the immediate threat of his own death, from the spirit of Christmas Yet to Come. Scrooge turns his salvation into a grand comeback, mocking his former self and enjoying life for the first time in decades.

Before his transformation, Scrooge represents the worst of capitalism: an unrepentant Kenneth Lay or Charles Keating, or Andrew Carnegie before he became a philanthropist. And Karl Marx may have had Scrooge in mind when he wrote *Das*

Kapital and *The Communist Manifesto* just a generation after Dickens's book was published. Where Marx saw revolution as the only answer to aggressive capitalism, Dickens presented a solution within traditional morality. The ghost of personal friendship and the semi-Druidic spirits of Christmas elevate Scrooge into bourgeois sainthood. But where Karl Marx saw the church as part of the problem, Dickens ignores it, neither indicting the church as ineffective nor calling on Jesus or the various saints. Human kindness is all that's needed, and the old Druid spirits help channel the joy of the holiday celebration.

Scrooge doesn't become poor by giving money away, he receives the joy that should have been his all along by embracing the lives of those around him.

A noteworthy lesson for our own redemption.

To learn more about Ebenezer Scrooge, read
  A Christmas Carol by Charles Dickens.
  The History of Animation: Enchanted Drawings by Charles Solomon.
  And see *A Christmas Carol* (1951), directed by Brian Hurst, Alistair Sim (Scrooge).

Captain Ahab—#53

Ahab is the middle-aged captain of the whaling ship *Pequod* in Herman Melville's 1851 novel, *Moby-Dick,* and he is the most influential embodiment of obsession and insanity. Ahab has come to represent any prepossessed or unreliable leader. His foe, the white whale, represents any unrealistic goal.

Ahab has been a whaler for forty years. On his previous expedition, he had done battle with the elusive, enormous old white whale that sailors called Moby Dick, and lost one of his legs. He took the encounter as a sign that violence and evil rule the world, and he swore that he would get revenge on the accursed, malicious monster.

His new command is the *Pequod,* which sails from Nantucket on Christmas Day. Once out to sea, he gathers the crew on deck, tells them of his battle and injuries, and exhorts them to vengeance. The men, energized by drink and by Ahab, swear an oath to hunt Moby Dick. They are not on an ordinary whaling trip.

At first, we cannot vilify Ahab. At sea he is a respected captain and a highly charismatic leader. On land he has a wife and a child. But he has not been on land for more than three years of the last forty, and he has been with his wife a single night, leaving her for the sea the day after their wedding. His tragic flaw is his obsession. They sail round the Cape of Good Hope and cross the Indian Ocean, where they kill several whales and boil out the valuable oil from the blubber. Then they enter the Pacific in search of Moby Dick, and slowly we begin to realize that Ahab's obsession has consumed him.

As Ahab's quest continues we see more signs of his disturbing state: his moodiness, his fitful sleep, his avoidance of other whaling ships, his nightmares. When the ship is struck by lightning, reversing the ship's compasses, Ahab declares himself the only guidance the ship will need. He sees himself as a malignant creation, a tool of fate, drawn to battle the symbol of a more malignant force. It is not mere hate for an unharvestable animal. He sees Moby Dick as the mask or agent of evil itself. He is struggling against all that he considers evil in the world, the entire unhuman, unsubmissive, uncontrollable, natural world. Unlike Jonah, who was imprisoned in a whale for refusing God's commands, Ahab is itching for a conflict. He is willing to risk everything in a contest that will pit him against all the forces of darkness. He forges his own harpoon and baptizes it in blood, in the name of the devil. In a way, Moby Dick is the evil within Ahab himself. Why his crew follows him is a tragedy of a different sort. Some cannot see where they are headed, some retreat into madness, some live from day to day. The first mate, too decent to kill Ahab in his sleep, dooms the crew by his inaction, almost as surely as if he'd murdered the whole crew himself.

After a long four years at sea, they spot the white whale. With all of his strength, Ahab rushes to battle, and we watch as the whaleboats are launched and give chase, with Ahab taking the forward position in one, harpoon in hand. Three times they set out from the ship, three days they battle. Ahab harpoons the whale. In retribution, the insolent whale turns and rams a hole in the *Pequod*. Seeing his fast-sinking ship, Ahab rages and throws a second harpoon into the whale. But the rope attached to it catches Ahab around the neck and jerks him out of the boat, pulling him under to his death. Moby Dick disappears, the symbol of invulnerable nature against which man is helpless. The closing vortex of the sinking ship drowns all except Ishmael, who survives to tell the tale.

Some men attach divine importance to the most ordinary aspects of life, to their personal needs, missions, and battles. In politics and corporate leadership, their beliefs drive wars, purges, blunders, scandals, and bankruptcies. To list them all would take eons. *Moby-Dick* is hailed as one of the great novels, so most of us read it in school. But we still follow such men, in their strange obsessions, ignoring all omens and warnings.

There's practical advice to be found here: Do not follow Ahab or any of his kind.

Maybe You Didn't Know

Melville spent time at sea, and he takes care to describe the whaler's world in detail.

Early in the book, Melville cites the case of the *Essex*, a whaleship sunk by a whale in 1820; the ship *Union*, sunk in 1807; and several other whale attacks.

The omens Ahab ignores include a sea-hawk stealing his hat, the ship struck by lightning, sperm whales encircling the ship, fish that had been following the boat switching to another boat, two reports from whaleships damaged or losing crew to Moby Dick, two boats stove in by Moby, and Ahab's artificial leg smashed by the whale.

Ahab wonders how much control we have over our own actions.

The *Pequod*'s crew is multinational, including Dutch, Danish, Chinese, Portugese, Spanish, Irish, at least two Muslims, and a cannibal.

Melville credits the success or failure of a voyage to the ship's harpooners.

Dr. Jekyll and Mr. Hyde—#10

A single character with two identities marks Robert Louis Stevenson's 1886 foray into the then-new world of psychology. He proposed that a single physical body could harbor two distinct personalities; he thereby inadvertently unleashed on society the phenomenon of split and multiple personalities, previously an obscure madness noticed by only a few professionals. When he suggested that the emergence of either of those personalities could be triggered by chemicals, he set the stage for the entire industry of psycho-active drugs. In addition, in suggesting that those different personalities could be expressed as two different patterns of behavior, he prepared our culture for the insanity defense. Stevenson anticipated Freud by presenting a conflict between good and evil within a single individual.

Stevenson introduces a lawyer, Mr. Utterson, who assists us in unraveling the story. The presentation is done in true mystery-story style. Bits and pieces of the evidence that the two "individuals" are one person are revealed to the reader in a prolonged and tantalizing manner. At no time do we actually meet Mr. Hyde, we are only given evidence that he exists and that he inhabits the same body as Dr. Jekyll. We never read anything of the actual transformation of Jekyll to Hyde or vice versa. Nor does the narrator present any direct accounts of either personality. The final resolution of the mystery is through a note written by Dr. Jekyll himself.

We see the mystery through the eyes of three of Dr. Jekyll's friends, who recount to one another various episodes in Jekyll's life. They relate their shock on realizing that a particularly grisly and unsolved murder—of a client of Utterson—must have been committed using a cane that was the treasured property of Dr. Jekyll. As they piece together the evidence, their shock turns to horror and confusion as they realize that Dr. Jekyll committed the murder. They reminisce as they try to understand how their friend could have done such a thing. While they contemplate this, the letter containing Jekyll's confession is delivered to the three.

What might be just as surprising as the radical nature of Stevenson's proposal was the strong popular reception his story enjoyed. The book sold forty thousand copies in the first six months. Within a year, stage versions of the tale had emerged. Actors delighted in exploiting the obvious challenge of changing back and forth between the radically different personalities. Movie versions appeared as early as 1908. In all of these adaptations, the transformation from Jekyll to Hyde is graphically dramatized, often using fangs and fur, taking extensive liberties with the story.

Stevenson shocked England with his dark tale of a murdering madman sharing the body of a respected doctor. It took decades for Stevenson's radical ideas to work themselves into the larger culture and affect science and sociology, and when they did, the result was astounding.

The Great Gatsby—#93

The major point of F. Scott Fitzgerald's 1925 novel, *The Great Gatsby,* is that Jay Gatsby is not great; although his is now a household name, he is the embodiment of everything that was wrong with America during the decadence of the 1920s. Gertrude Stein said that during the Prohibition Era, American idealism and spirituality were corrupted by materialism and wealth. Fitzgerald concurs. In the end, Gatsby's ill-gotten gain becomes meaningless, an unambiguous lesson for us and every future generation.

Gatsby is a recently rich bachelor in his thirties. He is a bootlegger, the quintessential self-made man of his era. He is hopelessly in love with Daisy, a beautiful woman with whom he had a fling several years previously. He wants to be her lover and manipulates a mutual acquaintance to bring them together. He is not concerned that Daisy is married to Tom Buchanan, a wealthy degenerate. And Gatsby is no better: he has no sense of decency and pursues Daisy even though she makes it clear that she will not be unfaithful to her husband.

Everything Gatsby tells us about himself is a lie. He claims to be the son of wealthy but deceased people from the Middle West; that he was educated at Oxford; that he has visited all the capitals of Europe; in World War I he rose to the rank of major and was decorated by every Allied government. In reality, he is from a poor family who still lives in San Francisco. He did not distinguish himself at school. He was not an officer, nor was he decorated during the war. Even his name is a fabrication—it is really James Gatz. He also has the irritating habit of not using people's names when he speaks to them. He calls them "Old Sport."

Fitzgerald's Jazz Age story takes place during Prohibition, when anyone could get rich if he was willing to exploit the immorality, corruption, and self-indulgence of the era.

Social class is central to the story. Daisy has married Tom for his old-money wealth and rejects Jay because a bootlegger, even a rich one, is beneath her class. In fact, Gatsby has no real friends, and he pals around with the mob that fixed the World Series in 1919. But the old moneyed have their corrupt characters too. A woman who is a friend of Daisy's is a professional golf champion—who wins by cheating.

Daisy's husband, Tom Buchanan, has a mistress, Myrtle Wilson, whose husband is an auto mechanic. Daisy, while driving Gatsby's car, accidentally strikes and kills Myrtle. Daisy does not stop at the scene and later, to protect his social standing, Tom starts a chain of rumors about the accident. As a result, Myrtle's husband—thinking Gatsby is responsible for his wife's death—shoots and kills him.

The book was made into a movie in 1974 with Robert Redford portraying Gatsby. And in 1999, The Metropolitan Opera premiered John Harbison's critically acclaimed opera based on the story.

We have a capacity for 20/20 hindsight. We romanticize past eras into "the good old days," no matter how bad they were. We remember the surface of those times, and we can recall their allure as long as we don't look behind the façade. But in his book, Fitzgerald exposes the rotten core beneath the glitter.

Because the book is required reading in many high schools and colleges, millions have been introduced to the seductive, exciting lifestyle that can come with wealth. And some have fallen into the moral trap of using lies and fraud to enter that world—a world where phony stock schemes are common and the moral bankruptcy of companies—like Enron—is all too common.

Interlude: The Writing Process

Perhaps you've wondered about our writing process. There're four of us, counting Yogi, Allan's dog. We each pick out a favorite character, do a little research on the Internet, and head down to the local library, which is usually air conditioned, even in the winter. It's a quiet place, and they have a table set up for coffee, and you can look through the romance novels while pretending you're looking for existentialist philosophy. The libraries are set up with columns of enormous shelves that run for yards until you get to the large print books. After we've each written a few pages, we gather around a card table at Dan's place, and if no one's remembered to bring the cards we get to work. The topic may be Madame Bovary, but somehow Allan will quote an eight-hundred page book that's only available in Norway. On the lower shelves of a library in Leirvik. The main branch, where they have the loganberry festival. You might wonder what the venerable Bede and Erik the Berserker had to say about Madame Bovary, but somehow Allan always finds a useful comment. Jeremy quotes out of Batman comics, Dan looks through the great issues of molecular genetics, and Yogi chews up anything that falls on the floor. Somehow, it works.

We read each essay out loud, and all four of us criticize, even contradicting our own writing. Then we go out to lunch. It's a little diner, down the street, and they have a large staff and the usual variety of sandwiches, spaghetti, creamed corn, and cheese-cakes. There's a giant zucchini out front, which takes up two handicapped parking spaces and howls about vegetable rights. We walk past it, politely putting a quarter in the collection bucket, and get a couple of blintzes, baked squash, meat loaf, and chocolate cake, and come back and rehash the days' work. Dan checks the punctuation and the grammar, putting in commas from a big bucket he keeps under the sink. Allan slips in some Nietzsche and Kierkegaard, and we go around again, back and forth like a sort of literary tennis match. Then we go to dinner.

Yogi stays in the car. He's been banned from the restaurant for peeing on a salmon filet that was overcooked. We pay the bill and leave a generous tip, depending on how many ketchup bottles we've emptied on one another.

Back at the house, our staff joins us. There's Stubb, a retired fisherman, a pudgy, middle-aged fellow with curly hair and a plaid shirt. They won't let him in the restaurant. He's imaginary, you see, and they don't serve that kind. Stubb edits words starting with *A* and any phrase including a gerund. Then there's Emma, a tall, lanky woman of about thirty-eight, with a French accent, long brown hair, and the lingering scent of vanilla. She's fictional too, but she makes good coffee, and she brings the dog in from the car. "Hi there. What's a gerund?" It's a small animal that chases cats, we tell her. Not that you'll find a gerund at the zoo, perhaps next to the pepperoni cage, but a fictional person doesn't really need to know these things.

While she starts the coffee, John enters: "Hello! Anyone at

home?" John's a real live friend of ours and walks with a limp from an auto accident. He's about fifty, short, and wide-shouldered. John comes over twice a week to check typeface. He's insistent about this because while overseas he learned that half of all books are sold by typeface. Not too fancy, though, because then people expect a punch line. Jeremy asks what he's doing in the book. "Editing. Didn't you read the last paragraph?"

Stubb: "I'd like some punch."

Dan: "You're an imaginary construct. Get your own punch."*

It's getting pretty darn crowded, even with only two fictional people. Stubb corrects us; he's imaginary, not fictional.† Some people just have to be exact. You're at a bar with a small combo and a guy on trumpet, playing a little Miles Davis, maybe. There's espresso, the strong, bitter coffee served with lemon, and white wine in small glass flutes. And some guy next to you says "No, that's a soprano valve trombone," and offers to settle the matter in the parking lot. You'd think we could write better characters to help us. Yogi wrote three characters who were great editors, but they decided they didn't need us and moved to St. Paul, where they opened a little jazz club and sandwich shop, for fictionals who can't get served in regular restaurants.

About two A.M., we start in on Moby Dick, the white whale. He was a real whale, but more of a chocolate milk color—Mocha

---

* "Imagine your own punch," Dan later decides, but the dog's lapped it all up and Stubb settles for gin, in a small glass, with one of those little paper umbrellas.

† There's no difference, but try telling him that.

Dick, from having too much espresso, probably. John asks if Moby started Greenpeace or a whale coalition. Allan quotes a passage on whaling from Kierkegaard's *Philosophy of Whitefish,* and Stubb reels off the return on investment for whaling in the 1850s, pointing out that whaling continued to be profitable into the 1980s. Not for the whales, of course. John reminds us that very few whales will be buying this book—the bookstores are too far inland and the doors are too small. And no whale access ramps. Jeremy sketches a portrait of Long John Silver for an article he doesn't intend to write, while Dan and Stubb debate the legal rights of marine creatures. After an hour of heated argument, they discover that they agree. It's about time we called it a day. Besides, it's past breakfast. Time for lunch again. And there's a giant zucchini and a whale out on the sidewalk, both threatening to sue over the lack of access ramps . . .

We plan to write them out of the next edition.

10. Children's Literature

In this category, some aspect of the story is always clearly impossible, so even though other aspects are plausible, the tale is undeniably fictional. Steam engines and rabbits can't talk, and cats aren't known to wear tall hats.

Back in ancient Greece, the slave, Aesop, composed fables, many with talking animals who taught us valuable lessons via their adventures and dealings. We hear these stories when we are children, and the tales stay with us throughout life, forming a part of our moral vocabulary.

After digesting several centuries of literature written for children (or written for adults and then set aside for children), we recognize that moral education is the real purpose of these tales, with entertainment the sugar that makes the medicine go down.

Is Lewis Carroll justified in using two hundred pages of good paper to keep little Alice Liddell amused for an afternoon? Considering the lessons learned on the other side of the Looking Glass, we can resoundingly answer, yes.

The Little Engine That Could—#31

Each of us has reserves of strength, imagination, and intelligence. If we concentrate and focus our attention, we can tap those reservoirs and meet challenges that might otherwise have seemed overwhelming. This is the simple yet powerful lesson of *The Little Engine That Could*. And it is a lesson well worth learning. It is especially worth the attention of its target audience because *The Little Engine That Could* is a morality play for children. It is also very much an American tale in which an individual accomplishes what the establishment is unable or unwilling to do.

The story originated in the early 1900s and glorified the spirit of individuality that had opened the American West. And the story contrasted that spirit with the false hopes of those who expected help from a faraway bureaucracy.

In the story, a long chain of cars is looking for an engine to pull it up a steep hill. A request to a big engine is refused as being too much to expect. A second request, to another big engine, brings the same answer. Finally, the cars approach the little roundhouse utility engine. She (yes, this little engine is female) agrees to help. She chants to herself as she pulls, repeating her belief in her own ability, perhaps the first mantra of positive thinking. And partly because she thought she could do so, the Little Engine succeeds in pulling the cars over the rise. (Note: because of trademark issues, we can't freely repeat that famous phrase. Or, we think we can't, we think we can't.)

Children are usually quite comfortable in the world as they find it. The notion of changing that world is introduced later, when they are older. That's what *adults* do. In a child's world, machines that talk are accepted as matter-of-factly as talking animals. But if you were to ask a child, "Can steam engines talk?" the immediate answer would certainly be, "No, that's silly."

Children freely move back and forth between the two worlds of reality and fantasy and that is precisely why it is so appropriate to teach important lessons—the guidance that must be absorbed early in life—through the vehicle of fantasy. This is nothing new. Aesop knew it centuries ago. The world would be a particularly dull place without fantasy.

A valuable lesson for children is that being big doesn't always make the difference. Those big engines refused to do what the tiny hero of our story accomplished. And she teaches us that we should believe in ourselves, to believe we *can* do it. With that start, we can concentrate and call upon resources of strength to accomplish a difficult task. Success starts with believing in our own potential.

Just as the little engine had to believe in herself, the child must believe in herself too. This is the lasting influence of *The Little Engine That Could:* The child who thinks she *can* grows up to become the adult who accomplishes great things.

That Can-Do Attitude

The nominal author of the story is Watty Piper, but no such person ever existed. "Watty Piper" is the generic pseudonym used by the first major publisher of the story, Platt & Munk, in 1930. Before that the story had apparently been making the rounds for decades. It was a cultural staple and appeared in several versions.

The Ugly Duckling—#55

Parents have related this story to their children for the past 150 years and will undoubtedly continue to do so unless we can find a way to successfully boycott this outrageous tale. For those of you who do not recall Hans Christian Andersen's 1844 story, here it is in brief.

On a summer's day in a farmyard, a duck hatches several ducklings, all of which are adorable except the last. He came from the largest of her eggs and was "different," ugly. Because of this, he was physically and emotionally abused.

Unable to endure this mistreatment, he ran away. During the following fall and winter, he survived many dangerous and nerve-racking adventures. He was almost killed by hunters and their dogs, but escaped and found shelter in a woman's cottage. However, she soon turned him out because he could not lay eggs.

During the winter, he became frozen to the surface of a pond. A peasant freed him and took him home, but the bird frightened his children. As a result, he was again turned out and had to spend the rest of the hard winter in misery and privation.

In the spring, he saw three lovely white swans and flew into the water next to them. Totally discouraged and depressed by his constant rejection, he told them to kill him and bent his head down awaiting death. But in the water he saw his image. He was no longer ugly, but a graceful, beautiful swan; the most handsome of them all. The older swans bowed their heads before him. In his bliss, he tells us that he could never have been this happy if he had remained an ugly duckling.

While parents may rationalize that they are merely

introducing their children, especially their young daughters, to the realities of the world, they should think of the distorted values they are promoting and stop this nonsense. In fact, it's worse than nonsense. The story is downright insulting and degrading to the overwhelming majority of us who have remained "ugly ducklings" throughout our entire lives.

The tale ignores our inherent worth, our intelligence, wealth of acquired knowledge, hard work, and creative capacities. It gives tacit approval to childhood bullying and marginalization of those who are "different," while ignoring the humanistic concept of the worth of each person.

We should encourage our children to develop mental, emotional, and physical strengths. We should teach them not to rely on physical attractiveness.

Let's stop telling our children that beauty is the central focus of their worth, that a woman's attractiveness is her "wealth" in life. The Andersen story reinforces the endless advertising messages that tell a girl that she is inferior unless she is beautiful. If you accept these values, you have stepped into a world in which her husband can be expected to reject her later in life for a younger, more attractive "trophy wife."

Please join those of us who have closed our doors to the offensive message of the ugly duckling because we treasure the intrinsic merit of all children.

Alice—#34

Lewis Carroll's Alice (*Alice's Adventures in Wonderland* and *Through the Looking Glass*) is the voice of simple unabashed reason in a world gone bonkers. That she is also a child is testament to the emerging sentiment during the closing years of the nineteenth century: The world of children is not just a simple version of the adult world, but a radically different world. Children are not just little adults, but almost an entirely different species.

Lewis Carroll wrote *Alice's Adventures in Wonderland* in 1865, and it was an instant success. The characters he introduced— Alice herself, the Mad Hatter, the Cheshire Cat, the Red Queen, and others—instantly became childhood favorites. Adults see many of Carroll's characters as metaphors for a variety of grown-up issues.

The two worlds through which Alice romps are perhaps the freest fantasy in all of literature. Where would the lunatic fancy of *Monty Python's Flying Circus* be without the imagination of Lewis Carroll to light the way? And who among us, having once read the stories, can forget the rabbit that insists it is late, the Queen of Hearts insisting on offing everybody's head, or the Mock Turtle, from which one can make Mock Turtle Soup?

Meanwhile, another aspect emerges. Some of the adventures Alice encounters reflect true oddities in the real world. For instance, in the realm of quantum physics, surprises are the rule and common sense doesn't seem to work. It might not be a coincidence that among the first generation to have enjoyed *Alice's Adventures* were virtually all the scientists who turned the world of physics topsy-turvy in the 1920s with their proposal of quantum mechanics. Lewis Carroll (Charles Lutwidge Dodgson) was a mathematician in real life, so it is appropriate that his young readers grew up to revolutionize physics with its seemingly crazy mathematics.

The transformation of children into adults is less like the growth of a tree from a sapling than it is like the metamorphosis of a tadpole into a frog. Just as most frogs probably wouldn't recognize a tadpole as any relation, most adults don't understand children. Lewis Carroll was a notable exception, as were J. M. Barrie (*Peter Pan*) and L. Frank Baum (*The Wizard of Oz*). It is particularly interesting that all these writers flourished and bequeathed to humanity their treasures during the same period, 1865 to 1910.

But with Alice, it is the adult world that is absurd while hers is sane. On the other hand, most adults regard their world as realistic and the world of children—the world of toys and make believe—as the realm of fantasy.

Children can grow up believing that the world of their adults is nutty; when *they* grow up, *they* will know how to fix things, to eliminate the lunacy and restore order. This is a good thing to encourage in children. It can be an ambition that sustains them until they actually become adults, and realize that the world of adults isn't as mad as they thought. And when they reread *Alice's Adventures in Wonderland* to their own children, they can again discover and appreciate what they enjoyed about a child's unsophisticated perspective on the world.

Alice thus serves as a bridge between the generations. This connection becomes more important as, with each generation, the chasm between youth and adult sometimes seems to widen.

For children, the lesson is more ordinary: Be prepared for the ridiculous, be prepared to be surprised. And if you learn what works in a strange world, you will be better equipped to discover what works in a more familiar world. As you go through life, you'll be prepared for the inanity of contemporary culture, and both the sane and insane people who populate it, thanks to Alice.

Peter Pan—#70

Peter Pan, the boy who never grows up, has vicariously satisfied that fantasy in adults, especially when faced with the more burdensome aspects of adult life. When life gets us down, Peter Pan can raise our spirits.

James M. Barrie first conceived the character Peter Pan in 1897 after a dinner party encounter with Mrs. Sylvia Davies. When Barrie noticed her smuggling out of the party some desserts for her children, the two conversed at length. Barrie, who never had children, befriended the Davies family and developed a special bond with George, their six year old. The theme of eternal childhood was born of his association with the Davies children.

By 1900, Barrie had the first coherent outlines of the story, developed through conversations with George, who was at the age of curiosity about other children. From these chats, Barrie wove together anecdotes about Peter—after George's younger brother—a child who could fly. Barrie suggested to George the fanciful notion that in his (George's) own not-too-distant childhood, George had been able to fly, and if he worked really hard, he could imagine a past life full of adventures among the treetops.

Barrie created a character able to relate to children, named for George Davies's brother Peter and the ancient god of forests, Pan. Thus Peter Pan emerged.

In 1901, Barrie accompanied the Davies family on a vacation to Black Lake (near Tilford, south-west of London), spending much time with the five Davies children. He took pictures of them playing, in particular their made-up swordplay adventures with pirates. From this emerged the book *The*

Boy Castaways of Black Lake Island. The location was clearly the inspiration for Neverland.

The high-tech 2003 movie *Peter Pan* sticks very close to the original Barrie story. In the story, one night, after a particularly trying confrontation between Mr. Darling and his children—Wendy, Michael, and John—Peter Pan enters the children's bedroom through the window (open even though it is winter and snow is expected). After some discussion with the children, Peter leads them to Neverland. This is a journey they are able to accomplish by flying, thanks to wishful thinking and the aid of fairy dust supplied by Tinkerbell, Peter's tiny companion. Once in Neverland, they meet the Lost Boys, other children who have left homes where they had felt unwanted. They encounter Peter's mortal enemy, Captain Hook, and his pirate crew. There are sword fights and setbacks; Peter is first captured and then rescued, and finally Hook is defeated. Wendy tells Peter she wants to return home, a desire shared by her younger brothers. Once home, they comfort their frantic parents, who have learned how much they missed the happy-go-lucky, carefree rambunctiousness of their children. The family is reunited on happy terms; the Lost Boys, also homesick, join the Darling household. Peter stays in Neverland alone with Tinkerbell, hoping to remain alive in Wendy's memory, as she grows up and tells the story to her children, and they in turn to their children.

Barrie created the kind of story he probably wanted to hear when he was a child and wanted to tell the children he never had—of life as a great adventure, to look forward to with enthusiasm and fascination. That vision is a stark contrast to the stuffy, stern, businesslike workaday attitude of Mr. Darling, somewhat shared by his wife. It is easy to imagine that the Darling children, seeing how sad their parents were, would wish they never had to grow up but remain children forever, protected from the sadness that permeates the world of adults.

Barrie developed the make-believe adventures of the Davies children into the novel *The Little White Bird*. In that story, the child Peter Pan flies out of his nursery every day, has adventures, and returns for the night. One day, however, he fails to return home and stays away for a whole year. When Peter does return home, he finds his mother caring for a new infant. This vignette grew from Barrie's own childhood. His mother became distant after the untimely death of Barrie's older brother, David, and James had to deal with his mother's subsequent pressure on James to grow up before he was prepared to.

The play *Peter Pan* emerged early in 1904 and was an immediate success. Barrie was credited with a play that cast a spell capable of bringing adults back to their own childhood. Peter represents that child in all of us who's having too much fun, who doesn't want to grow up. Yet Barrie himself insisted that he, James Barrie—not the young Peter Davies—was "the boy who wouldn't grow up." As psychologist Claudia Black has written, "It's Never Too Late to Have a Happy Childhood."

Since then, the story of Peter Pan has become a frequently produced musical and movie, in addition to the audience-interactive play first written by Barrie. Several actors and—especially—actresses have made or enhanced their fame as Peter Pan, most notably Mary Martin, from 1954 to 1961, and Sandy Duncan, in 1979. In 1953 Walt Disney made the hit animated movie. Tinkerbell has become one of the staple Disney characters, especially as the magical introduction to television's *Wonderful World of Disney*. Other writers have taken up the thread, and movie spin-offs include the Robin Williams feature *Hook* (1991), Disney's *Return to Neverland* (2002), *Neverland* (2003), and 2004's *Finding Neverland*.

In 1911, Barrie published the story as the novel *Peter and*

Wendy. In 1929, the childless Barrie donated the rights to the character to the Great Ormond Street Hospital for Children, founded in 1852. While the original copyright expired in 1987, in 1988 the British government extended in perpetuity certain limited performance rights for the story, which continue to benefit the hospital.

The popularity of Peter Pan guaranteed that the endowment would be a substantial one. In 1996, copyright terms were extended to seventy years through the European Union, retroactively recapturing the rights to Peter Pan to the Hospital until 2007 (the base year is 1937, when Barrie died). The hospital has contracted with Geraldine McCaughrean, a British author of children's stories, to compose an authorized sequel to *Peter Pan*, due to appear in 2006.

Peter Pan may grow old, but he will never grow up. Thanks to the Barrie bequest, he will continue to entertain and save the lives of children.

The Cat in the Hat—#79

At first, we left him off the list. Dr. Seuss's famous rhyming cat, the popular character of a series of children's books by Theodor Seuss Geisel, does not embody a point of view, a personality type, or a force of nature. He has caused no revolutions or social upheavals. He has no influence. The general population does not wear large or multiple hats because of him. He has not inspired more than a few lost souls to count using fish or eat green eggs with anything at all. A few days after our decision, we received this rebuttal, wrapped in brown paper and tied with a red ribbon:

April 15, 2005

Re: *The 101 Most Influential People Who Never Lived*
Dear Sirs:

I do not like to be left out.
What makes me less than Mickey Mouse?
I'd beat King Arthur in a joust.
I do not like to be left out.

I am the best from A to Z,
I teach the children how to read.
And though I sometimes make a mess
You know I'm always neatly dressed.

I am the best from Z to A.
So may I join your book today?

I brought you blue fish, red fish, too
My books are now the largest zoo:
I've got a Horton, and a Who,
Pigeons, bats, geese, and bison,
A plastic mold of Michael Jackson.

My agent has a lot of clout.
I do **not** like to be left out.

I'm wider read than Marcel Proust.
I'm more polite than Mother Goose.
I'm better known than Dorian Gray.
So may I join your book today?

Felix, Batman, Frasier Crane,
Should not be above my name.
Godzilla, Buffy, Auntie Mame,
Do not exceed my well-earned fame.
I now outrank that Hobbit, Frodo,
Uncle Sam, and Quasimodo.

Why don't you put me in your book?
I'm not an evil Captain Hook.
I'm not a vain Charles Foster Kane,
I'm not a cringing, Greedy Grinch.

I am, like Popeye, what I am.
I cook quite well, if you like Spam,
Or spinach pie, green eggs with ham.
I'll cook you lamb, I'll cook you fish
If you'll just put me on your list.

I'll bring you cherry-mulberry jam
I'll bring you shark-fin soup with clams,
Pickled beets with buttered yams,
Catfish, codfish, trout, and eels,
Onion, garlic, grilled oatmeal.
I'll cook you anything you wish,
If you'll just put me on your list

I'll rock and roll, I'll twist and shout
Just do not,
Do not,
Leave me out.

                         C.H.

We relented and put him on the list. Another five minutes of iambic begging and we'd have done anything. The publisher was less than happy that our security had been compromised, but officials at the Seuss compound deny any knowledge or involvement and assert that The Cat was vacationing at an undisclosed location.

Yeah, we've heard that before.

11. Theater

Modern theater seems to have developed from the lyric poems read before audiences about the time of Sophocles, 450 B.C.E. However, the art form went underground during the Dark Ages, and theater, as we know it today, did not fully reemerge until the 1500s.

Since then, playwrights from William Shakespeare to David Mamet have offered us a lot more than just entertainment. The melancholy Prince Hamlet forces us to wrestle with injustice and vengeance; through Romeo and Juliet we examine the follies of teenage love; Sheridan's quaint Mrs. Malaprop mangles the language in ways that would stun any politician; Molière's Imaginary Invalid leads us on a merry romp through hypochondria and the perils of medical care. In many respects, these characters help form the vocabulary of modern life.

A Broadway musical adds the impact of song to the story, and you may find yourself humming the tunes for weeks afterward. Tevye (*Fiddler on the Roof*) won't easily be forgotten, nor Grizabella (*Cats*), or Nathan Detroit (*Guys and Dolls*). Broadway's cousin, opera, was the supreme art form of Europe, from 1750 through the twentieth century; Wagner's hero, Siegfried, helped start World War II. And he wasn't the only fictional character to change history. Let's start with . . .

Oedipus—#14

In *Oedipus Tyrannous* (Oedipus the King), Sophocles, the greatest of the Greek playwrights, retold (about 425 B.C.E.) the myth of a man who tried desperately to avoid the fate that an oracle had predicted for him: He would kill his father and marry his mother. Despite all of the efforts to evade it, the prophecy came true. From this myth, Sigmund Freud constructed the Oedipus Complex, whose impact on Western culture has been immense.

In the story of Oedipus, a son was born to Laius and Jocasta, king and queen of Thebes. After they heard a prophecy of patricide from an oracle, they ordered that the child be taken to a mountain where he would die of exposure. The shepherd given the task of leaving the child decided to take him to Corinth and give him to King Polybus and Queen Merope. They named him Oedipus and raised him as their own son. When he was an adult, an oracle predicted that he would kill his father and marry his mother.

Oedipus assumed this referred to Polybus and Merope, and he left Corinth to avoid the prophecy. On his journey, he came to a crossroads and met a band of haughty men who shoved him off the road. Oedipus became angry and killed the men, one of whom, unbeknownst to him, was Laius. Thus, he fulfilled the first part of the prophecy.

Oedipus soon came to the city of Thebes, which was being terrorized by the Sphinx. Oedipus conquered the beast,

and as a reward he was made king and given the hand of Jocasta in marriage, thus unknowingly fulfilling the prophecy
of incest.

After sixteen prosperous years, during which Oedipus and
Jocasta had four children, a plague beset Thebes. The crops
died and the women became sterile. The oracle at Delphi proclaimed that Thebes was harboring the murderer of Laius, and
the plague would continue until the killer was found and van-
quished.

Oedipus, in his determination to find the murderer, con-
sulted an oracle only to discover that he—Oedipus—was the
son of Laius, whom he had killed. And in marrying Jocasta, the
prophecy had been completed. With the truth revealed, Jocasta
hanged herself and Oedipus blinded himself before going into
exile in disgrace. The play ends here, though Sophocles wrote
two other plays to complete the trilogy.

Oedipus had been marked by fate. No matter what choices
the people in this tragedy made, the fates had determined how
it would develop and end. The men and women, apparently
making free choices with the highest motives, ended in ruin.
We are left with the feeling that happiness is an illusion, that
fate predetermined by the gods is our ultimate destiny.

Freud, the father of psychoanalysis, introduced to the
world the Oedipus Complex, which describes how every boy
from about three until six years of age experiences intense
sexual feelings toward his mother and a hostile attitude toward his father. If all goes well, by the end of this stage the
child understands the nature and benefits of the parental
union and surmounts his hostile feelings. Otherwise he may
conceal stratagems, stances, and scars that cause lifelong personal problems.

Freud scares me. I want my mommy.

Romeo and Juliet—#9

Romeo and Juliet are the two impetuous, hormonally driven teenagers in Shakespeare's play of the same name. They are the original star-crossed lovers. He, sixteen years of age, she thirteen, they have no experience with the ways of the adult world as they rush into love and tragedy.

The standards for people of rank in Shakespeare's time required a courtship during which a man would earn a woman's affection. Juliet's rejection of this custom is exciting, but also dangerous in a story propelled by passion, honor, and violence.

In the play, Romeo goes to a masked ball where he sees Juliet. After a brief flirtation, they fall in love. Romeo is a Montague, and Juliet is a Capulet—two families burdened with an enmity so old its origin has been lost in time. However, the lovers' mutual attraction is not deterred by their family's quarrel.

Romeo and Juliet's passion is erotic. They have no need for a courtship, nor would their families' feud permit one. In act 2, the lovers meet on a balcony outside of Juliet's bedroom. Within minutes they decide to marry, and they are wed in secret the following afternoon.

In a duel later that day, Romeo slays Tybalt, Juliet's cousin. As a result, Romeo is banished from the city. In just two days, Romeo has fallen in love, wooed, married, killed a man, and been banished.

At the same time, Juliet's father, unaware of her secret marriage, promises her to Paris, a noble earl, and they are to be wed in a few days. To avoid the nuptials, Juliet takes a sleeping potion that will make her appear to be dead for forty-two hours.

Romeo will be told of the ruse in a letter. But the letter never arrives and a grief-stricken Romeo, hearing that Juliet is dead, hastens to her tomb where he commits suicide with poison. Juliet awakens from her trance, sees her lover is dead, takes the dagger from his belt, and plunges it into her heart.

Overcome by the double suicide, the Capulets and Montagues make peace and vow to raise gold statues of the lovers so that all will remember their tragedy.

Shakespeare's primary source for the play was Arthur Brooke's *The Tragical History of Romeus and Juliet* (1562). Another version of the tale goes back to 1476, written by Masuccio Salernitano. There are several other versions of the story that circulated in Europe for at least a century prior.

Many movies and several operas and ballets have been based on the story. On Broadway, Leonard Bernstein adapted the tale to late twentieth-century themes in the musical *West Side Story.*

Romeo and Juliet sum up the strong emotions of adolescence. For lovers, old or young, the story is the epitome of love and passion, the standard of devotion, and the language of romance.

For parents, it is a reminder to install video cameras on all of your balconies to make sure your teenager doesn't sneak out the back door at night.

The History of the Characters

These two characters first appeared as Mariotto and Gianozza in a 1476 story by Masuccio Salernitano. They became Romulus and Giulietta in a remake of the story by Luigi da Porto. Arthur Brooke adapted the tale into a narrative poem, *The Tragical History of Romeus and Juliet*, in 1562, which served as the source for Shakespeare's 1595 play.

Hamlet—#5

Hamlet, the longest and most frequently performed of Shakespeare's plays, contemplates some fundamental moral issues. Hamlet is called upon to kill his uncle as an act of revenge for the murder of Hamlet's father. Will this be a justified act of retribution, or another murder? How can Hamlet resolve his doubts?

When first we meet Hamlet, the Prince of Denmark, he has been called home from college because of the unexpected death of his father. He arrives to find that his father's brother, Claudius, has ascended to the throne. And, less than two months after his father's death, his mother, Gertrude, has married Claudius. Hamlet, outraged at the turn of events and still reeling from the death of his father, falls into melancholy.

While he is in this dejected mood, the ghost of his father appears, reveals that Claudius had murdered him, and insists Hamlet avenge the crime. Thereby the dead reach back from the grave to direct the fate of the living, and death becomes the end point of the play.

In his soliloquy "To be or not to be"—the single most recognizable passage in Western literature—we contemplate a serious issue: Is it better to endure suffering, or end one's life and take a chance in an uncertain afterlife? It's a personal question for Hamlet, but in Shakespeare's time (as in ours), there were competing versions of the afterlife. A lot of people had strong

opinions, wars were fought . . . but those who went to the afterlife, the "undiscovered country," seldom returned. Now,
having talked with the ghost, Hamlet begins to realize that
there's a lot more to earth and heaven than he had ever
dreamed of.

Now he has to sift his way through family obligations, state
politics, and heaven's requirements. He can't rely on the government for justice; Claudius *is* the government. And revenge
was a bit more significant, for *Hamlet* seems to be set in the
time of Hardecanute, the son of the Danish king who conquered England in 1016. The Danes were at that time a nation
of respected warriors, not gentle physicists and cheese makers.

Hamlet, whom some critics portray as weak and indecisive,
is exactly the opposite. He shows both courage and prudence.
He is not going to risk his life until he is sure the ghost is right.
The CSI lab hadn't been invented, so Hamlet has to trick
Claudius into revealing his guilt. Hamlet feigns madness to
throw off suspicion and buy time. Good strategy, but not good
enough. Polonius, one of the king's ministers, spies on Hamlet
and is killed as a result. A regrettable error because now Laertes,
Polonius's son, resolves to exact revenge on Hamlet for *his* father's murder.

In the final scene, all of the remaining major characters are
killed: the queen, Laertes, the king, and Hamlet. With his dying breath, Hamlet names the prince of Norway as the next
king of Denmark.

We have been challenged anew by deep-seated questions of
suicide, loyalty, revenge, justice, and responsibility. But it is
Hamlet's consuming doubts—doubts that haunt us to this
day—that give the story its universal appeal.

Hamlet is the role by which actors are judged and directors
lauded. In school we read *Hamlet* and memorize many of the

well-turned phrases that enrich our language: "Something is rotten in the State of Denmark"; "The slings and arrows of outrageous fortune"; "The play's the thing . . ."; "That one may smile, and smile, and be a villain"; "When we have shuffled off this mortal coil . . ."; "The lady does protest too much . . ."; "I must be cruel, only to be kind." Not to mention the dozens of phrases from the other characters in this play.

Hamlet, the prince of problems, stimulates us to think about the challenges of living in the real world, and perhaps there's the rub.

The History of the Character

Amleth was a legendary Danish prince, whose exploits were recorded by Saxo Grammaticus around 1200. François de Belleforest used the story in his Histoires tragiques of 1570.

Othello—#72

More forcefully than any other character, this unfortunate man illustrates the devastating results of unwarranted jealousy, and also the disaster of making major decisions based on unverified innuendo.

In Shakespeare's play, Othello is a Moor, a black man, who is a renowned mercenary general. We find him in the employ of the government of Venice and living in that city; he is frequently a guest at the home of Brabantio, a nobleman. There he entertains the assembled gentry with stories of his military adventures. Without meaning to do so, he enthralls Desdemona, Brabantio's adult daughter. She falls in love with him and they marry in a private ceremony.

She loves him unconditionally and accompanies him to Cyprus, a Venetian possession at the time. There he and his army successfully defend the island against the invading Turks. After the victory, Othello and his wife return to Venice and he promotes one of his officers, Cassio, to lieutenant. In doing so, he has passed over the more experienced Iago, who had expected to get the post. We soon see that Iago is indignant at what he considers an affront to his dignity. He is angry and determines to get revenge on Othello.

Othello is indiscriminate when trusting Iago, and this leaves him open to deception. His intense and unconditional love for his wife renders him susceptible to trickery from others. Iago uses insinuation and directs Othello into misinterpreting innocent events as he persuades the Moor that Desdemona is having an affair with Cassio.

Othello takes pride in his heritage, but Iago uses his color to raise doubt about Desdemona's love for a black man. Iago implies that many Venetians scorn his race and perhaps Desdemona is among this number. He twists Othello's mind so completely, the Moor determines to take revenge against what he believes is an unforgivable indiscretion on the part of his wife: he kills her. When he comes to the realization of her innocence, in despair, he kills himself.

His madness has consumed him. Jealousy, the green-eyed monster, has brought down a man who had never been defeated in battle.

Othello's story warns us of the dire consequences of acting on mere appearances because things are often not what they seem to be. His fatal error is a warning to us all: Be introspective. Be careful. Be very careful. Verify the information before taking action.

Shylock—#27

In the early years of the Common Era, Jews were murdered by the dozens, in the Dark Ages by the hundreds, and during the Crusades by the thousands. The Inquisitions caused Jews to be murdered by the tens of thousands and the Nazis murdered them by the millions. Shakespeare cannot be held responsible for all of these deaths, but having brought us the most famous and infamous fictional Jew in literature, the Bard has certainly played a part.

Shakespeare wrote *The Merchant of Venice,* a romantic comedy, in the 1590s. In the story, Antonio—the merchant in the title—borrows money from Shylock, a man whom he has previously abused by spitting on him, calling him a dog, and interfering with his livelihood. The abuse notwithstanding, Shylock offers the loan without interest and, "in sport," Shylock and Antonio agree that Antonio will have to forfeit a pound of his flesh to Shylock if the loan is not repaid. Antonio not only defaults on the loan but also continues to abuse Shylock, who becomes angry and seeks both justice and revenge in a court of law. He wants to collect his pound of flesh, but the court will not let him do so. In spite of the fact that Antonio is the one on trial and Shylock has not committed any crime, the judgment of the court is that Shylock has to give half of his money to Antonio and is forced to convert to Christianity, a typical outcome of a dispute between a Jew and a Christian at the time.

Shakespeare, who wrote in the late 1500s and early 1600s, knew no Jews; they had all been expelled from England in 1290 and were not readmitted until 1655. In creating Shylock, he used one of the myths and calumnies that Christians had kept alive for millennia: Jews ceremonially killed Christians and used their blood to make matzo for Passover. Hence, on the stage, Shakespeare's audience saw a Jew who was attempting to commit the ritual murder of a Christian.

During the Middle Ages, government and religion were combined into a single entity. Jews could not own land or attain membership in guilds and most professions. Lending money and charging interest—so vital to commerce—was forbidden to Christians but permitted for Jews, and that was how many earned their living. Jews were not allowed to become citizens; they had no rights and no access to legal protection.

No Christian writers of the Middle Ages depicted Jews in a positive way; one wonders what fate the writers would have suffered from their fellow citizens and clergy if they had.

Shylock perpetuates narrow-minded hatred and intolerance, even though modern society has tried to use him to promote tolerance. How successful this transformation will be remains for future generations to judge, but one thing we can all agree on is that Shylock's influence has been enormous.

Figaro—#37

As the wheels of social change grind on and new social orders emerge from the old, we tend to look back and identify key figures in the struggle forward. In the revolutionary times of the late 1700s, when the United States was born, Europe was experiencing social foment. The climax was the French Revolution of 1789, followed by challenges to many monarchies throughout the continent. Figaro was an important agent in the development of those events.

Figaro arose in the fertile imagination of Pierre Caron, a Frenchman who was a genius and a scoundrel. At nineteen years of age he invented a new clock mechanism that proved to be the high technology of his day, and he became prosperous. He married a wealthy widow and took her family name, Beaumarchais. By the age of twenty-seven he had become Count Pierre Augustin Caron de Beaumarchais, and to amuse himself took up writing in support of revolutionary causes. His play *The Marriage of Figaro* (1778) featured the clever, brazen servant, Figaro.

In the play, Figaro is a valet to a count, and Figaro's bride-to-be is the housemaid, Susanna. They thwart their master's claim to fulfill a common practice at the time—the right to sleep with the bride of his servant on her wedding night. During the play Figaro expresses a distinctly revolutionary idea when he curses the count to himself, "Because you're a great lord, you think you've got a great mind. Blood; money; rank; the choice appointments . . . what did you do to earn those many blessings? Took the trouble to be born: beyond that, you ain't much." Figaro lets us know that he considers the nobility degenerate and depraved. In the end, Figaro helps Susanna avoid dishonor by tricking his master into a liaison with an attractive young lady, arranging for the nobleman's wife to catch him. His servants have humiliated the count, so we are not surprised when no less a person than Napoleon once called the opera, "The Revolution in action."

Although Beaumarchais completed *The Marriage of Figaro* in 1778, the king's censors banned it until 1784, and Beaumarchais spent some time in jail. Those were politically volatile

times. The play aroused governmental anger because it es-
poused social equality and showed contempt for the nobility.
After the play's first performance in Paris, hundreds of people
rioted and three were killed in the brawl.

Certain changes in the social order often strike the human
community as right, and once the concepts become widespread, for better or worse, they cannot be stopped. Civilization
has witnessed the end of values that were universally held in
their time—feudalism, chivalry, and slavery, to mention a few.
In our own time, Vatican II lifted the burden of Christ's death
from the Jews, the Mormon Church ended its racist attitude toward blacks, and the concepts of sexual orientation and marriage are being rewritten.

As Victor Hugo wrote, "There is nothing more powerful
than an idea whose time has come."

Faust—#36

Faust made a deal with the devil. Mephistopheles would grant
him all of his wishes during this life, and Faust would serve the
devil—body and soul—in the next. For his part, the devil delivered. Faust had riches, knowledge, and any pleasure he
wished. He had every comfort and luxury, experienced every
excess and perversion. But in the end, Faust reneged on his
part of the bargain and God admitted him into heaven. Faust
manipulated both God and the devil and got away with it. He
pulled off the ultimate scam, and he inspires us to dream of
doing the same.

In a parallel to the tale of Job, the story starts in heaven
when God mentions that Faust is an ideal example among

men. Mephistopheles bets God that he can pervert the soul of Faust to his own ends. God is so confident of Faust that he takes up the wager.

When first we meet Faust he is a university student who has mastered metaphysics, sorcery, prophecy, theology, medicine, necromancy, and law; now he wants to understand nature, but not as words in a book. He wants to be immersed in it as God is, beyond human limits. He turns to black magic and conjures up the devil. They enter into their pact and start on the adventures that will span the following seventy years.

In his relationship with Faust, Mephistopheles relies on illusions. He takes Faust on a magic carpet ride and then entertains him in a tavern where he makes wine flow out of the tabletop. Next they go to the home of a witch, where Faust falls in love with the image of a beautiful woman in a mirror.

The following day, with the help of Mephistopheles, Faust meets Margarete and becomes enamored of her. They meet secretly that night, and the following day Margarete's brother, Valentin, learns of the tryst and confronts Faust. Faust kills him and leaves town, never to return.

Soon thereafter, Mephistopheles leads Faust to the Walpurgis-Nacht (witches' night), where he has a vision of Margarete. She has been convicted of drowning her illegitimate child, fathered by Faust. She is in jail and has slipped into insanity as she awaits execution. She prays and throws herself on the mercy of God, and as Mephistopheles shouts that she is lost, a heavenly voice announces that she is delivered.

Following this, Faust asks to have Helen of Troy as his lover. Mephistopheles creates a grand illusion in which Faust is a young man in the guise of a medieval knight. He wins Helen and they have a son, but the son dies as a young man and Helen vanishes.

During the next fifty years Mephistopheles accompanies Faust on a wide variety of adventures among gods and goddesses until, as his last exploit, Faust decides to subdue the tides and reclaim a strip of land from the sea. During the project, Faust orders the deaths of several innocent squatters. Nevertheless, the project is a success and just after its completion, Faust, who is now very old, dies.

Mephistopheles waits at the grave to take Faust's soul as soon as it leaves his body. Since Faust has committed almost every crime known to mankind, the devil is sure of his victory. However, God is not going to be embarrassed by admitting Mephistopheles won the wager. God cheats the devil by taking the spirit of the arrogant, unrepentant Faust into heaven.

Faust did not have to live a moral life to be admitted into paradise. And if this applies to him, it certainly pertains to us as well. Just be sure you catch God on a good day.

Madame Butterfly—#89

In both Europe and America, fascination with the Orient, especially Japan, flourished in the late 1800s. Several writers took advantage of this to produce anti-American literary propaganda, a popular sport in Europe at the time. Among the most successful was an Englishman, John Luther Long, who wrote the short novel *Madame Butterfly* (1897). In 1900, an American dramatist, David Belasco, turned it into a one-act play of the same name, and in 1906 the Italian composer, Giacomo Puccini, turned it into an opera that portrayed the European bias of crude and insensitive Americans. The opera is quite important because it presents the ugly American at his worst, in the person of Benjamin Franklin Pinkerton, the arch-villain of the story.

Until the mid-1800s, Japan was a closed society, an isolated nation that did not allow foreigners—either tourists or merchants—into the country. The people held to a strictly paternalistic code in which their kin formed the basic social unit and an individual, especially a woman, had little identity except as a member of their extended family. However, these values began to erode after Japan opened trade with the United States and other western nations in 1858.

In the story, Cio-Cio-San (*Cio-Cio* meaning "butterfly" and *san* being a designation of respect)—a beautiful, naïve teenage girl—marries Benjamin Franklin Pinkerton, an officer on the USS *Abraham Lincoln*.

While drinking whiskey with the American consul, Pinkerton sings of the temporary nature of his upcoming marriage to the girl and describes himself as a vagabond. In jingoistic terms he sings, "America forever . . ." to the strains of "The Star-Spangled Banner." However, after an elaborate wedding ceremony, Cio-Cio-San believes he is in love with her, as she is with him.

To marry him, she had to break all ties with her family and forgo any possible support from them in the future. She is now completely dependent on Pinkerton's good will, and he betrays that trust without a qualm or second thought. After a month of honeymoon he sets her up in a house with a female servant, leaves her some money, and returns to his ship and to America. He does not know that she is pregnant with his child.

During the next few years she does not hear from him, but remains faithful as she raises their son, to whom she has given the temporary name Trouble. She has almost run out of money and they live frugally, isolated from the rest of society.

One fine day, his ship enters the harbor and she anticipates a joyous reunion. But Pinkerton has married a "real" wife in America and, via correspondence with the American consulate, has learned about the birth of his son in Japan. His only aim now is to get the boy and bring him back to the United States.

Cio-Cio has been dishonored, and once she understands this, she has no choice. Reverence for her cultural values dictates that she kill herself. She does so with her father's ceremonial knife, leaving the boy holding an American flag while he awaits the arrival of his father.

This deeply moving story of devotion, betrayal, and degradation is quite popular with audiences worldwide in the twenty-first century. Cio-Cio-San entered marriage as do most young women—dreaming of a future in which she and her husband will face life together, in mutual consideration and support. That's not an unrealistic expectation, and if more men would accept responsibility for their half of the partnership, life would be significantly more pleasant for everyone.

Siegfried—#7

The hero of German nationalism, Siegfried, is in large part responsible for propelling Germany into both world wars. The striving of the German nation for world domination was a natural part of their warrior culture, and Siegfried, armed with sword, spear, and myth, inspired them to wars that intensified nearly to the point of exterminating their hated foes—the rest of humanity.

———

In Teutonic myth, the gods can be challenged and even insulted by powerful men. On meeting the chief Teutonic god Wotan, Siegfried broke the god's spear, clarifying that the German people were warriors on the level of deities. The name *German* is a corruption of "Schirmm-Mann," "Shield-man," or "warrior." And *Siegfried* is not merely a name, but a title meaning "Victorious Peace," or perhaps simply "Conquest."

Among the Germanic tribes, each chief usually claimed descent from Wotan. The tribesmen knew agriculture and metalwork. They preferred pillage. For centuries the Germans raided the frontiers of Rome, driven out of their homelands by the even fiercer Huns and other barbarians from the Eastern steppes. The Germans scored major victories over Rome in 9 and in the late 400s, when they overran Italy.

The story of Siegfried started in the chaotic world of the 800s and earlier, perhaps as far back as 350. The Wagnerian character derives in part from the Norse legend of Sigurd, a dragon-slayer referred to in *Beowulf* (700). Siegfried's love, Brünnhilde, was based on the real Queen Brunhild, who ruled the area around Verdun from 575 to 613—four remarkable decades of murder and war. Composer Richard Wagner took material from a poem of the 1190s, "Song of the Nibelungen," and mixed in elements from German and Scandinavian myths. The result, *The Ring of the Nibelung,* is a narrative told through four operas. In the story, a magic gold ring has acquired a curse, and Wotan has to return it to its previous owner. The god has to do this indirectly, so he sets his hopes on his human grandson, Siegfried, who succeeds in killing the dragon that is holding the ring. The hero then meets and pledges marriage to Brünnhilde, but he is killed by a treacherous host who also claims the ring.

Wotan's plan has failed, and the gods are destroyed. The *Ring* was the high point of Wagner's career, and so successful that it continues to be performed today, sustaining the myth of Siegfried.

The Germans and the warrior mentality of northern Europe contributed to the fall of Rome and launched the wars of the Reformation. Siegfried, the Aryan superman, was the greatest German hero in the nineteenth century's dominant cultural force—opera. He reminds the Germans of their divine status and the glory of battle, and his inspiration helped trigger World War I and World War II. In historical perspective, these two conflicts were not really separate events, but a single thirty-year war . . . interrupted by a twenty-year period of reloading. The hostilities were renewed by Adolf Hitler, who used themes of German superiority to justify his racist ideas. Hitler made himself the spokesman of a new order, and his riveting hate-mongering speeches turned the myth of the Aryan superman Siegfried—into pure bloodlust.

The damage is still incalculable. World War I killed more than 8 million soldiers and wounded another 20 million. The conflict cost the Allies more than $30 billion, toppled the Austrian, Ottoman, and Russian empires, scared the victors into isolationism, lost a generation of young men, and introduced the tank, the machine gun, combat aircraft, and mustard gas. Its continuation as World War II was even worse: destruction and mass murder on an unprecedented scale, killing at least 30 million people in Europe and leveling tens of thousands of square miles. All this inspired by Siegfried, bold in battle, whose crown became the funeral wreath for much of humanity.

Did You Know?

- The plot is much more complicated than presented here. In human terms, Brünnhilde is not only Siegfried's lover—as a daughter of Wotan, she's also his aunt.

- The four operas are *Das Rheingold, Die Walküre, Siegfried,* and *Götterdämmerung,* staged together as *The Ring of the Nibelung* in 1876.

- Sigebert of Metz ruled the eastern quarter of Gaul (Austrasia) and married Brunhild, a Visigoth. She acted as regent for both her son and, on his death, her grandsons.

Note: In estimating the dead of World War II due to Germany, we counted half of United States casualties and none from Italy, Japan, China, and Turkey.

If you want to learn more about Siegfried, we suggest
The Shorter Cambridge Medieval History (vol. I) by C. W. Previté-Orton.
The New Penguin Opera Guide edited by Amanda Hedden.
Dictionary of the Middle Ages, vol. 11, "Sigurd," Joseph R. Strayer, editor-in-chief.

Willy Loman—#95

Willy Loman, America's most famous failure, comes from Arthur Miller's 1949 play, *Death of a Salesman*. Willy is the quintessential American "everyman" who falls short in a society that demands success. He has relied on self-inflating, self-deluding stories, and when we meet him, that's all he has left. And, worst of all, he has brought the contagion of failure to his favorite son.

Willy has been a salesman for thirty-four years and as the play opens, he has just returned to his home in Brooklyn a few hours after having set out for New England on a business trip. He tells his wife, Linda, that he just can't seem to keep his mind on driving anymore.

We learn that his two adult sons, Biff and Happy, are upstairs in their old room having just come home for a visit. Happy is a modest success in a dull job, but Willy's thoughts are on Biff, who's an irresponsible drifter. Willy daydreams about when the boy was a senior in high school fifteen years before and starred in an important football game. Willy glorified and encouraged his son in athletics, but Biff flunked out of school, losing the football scholarship that would have taken him to college. Worse, Biff discovers his father in a hotel room with another woman.

Willy has filled his son with aggressiveness and dishonesty, which he calls "spirit." Biff let his father pump him full of hot air and, after several years away from home, he's still full of it. While Biff and his younger brother are alone together in their old room at home, they try to dream up a way to make a success in the business world. They decide that Biff will go to see a man he'd worked for many years before, and they think Biff can just drop in on him and borrow $10,000 to begin a business. When the boys tell Willy about this outlandish plan he thinks it's great.

The next day, reality crashes in on all of them. Willy loses his job as a salesman. His inflated image can't prop up an empty order book. He is so far gone, he hasn't even been making ends meet. He has been borrowing money, pretending it's his pay. Willy has outlived his era and his usefulness. His employer has used him up and discarded him, as is true of too many others in American society.

Biff doesn't bring home any good news, either. He wasn't even able to get a conversation with his old boss. That night, Biff comes to the realization that he has been living an illusion, and Willy begins to understand that his son has been a failure in life to spite his father—revenge for his father's overreaching expectations and infidelity.

Willy's more than ready for the end. He's been planning suicide, knowing that he is worth more dead than alive: The house can be paid off. And maybe Biff can use the insurance money to become successful. But it's an empty house that is paid off, and we know his son doesn't have a chance at success.

Willy created a fantasy world for himself and his family, a world in which he and his sons are great men who have what it takes—ideas with no basis in reality. Willy expects that after all the work, all the travel, the miles, the meetings, the contacts, there'll be a crowd of people at his funeral. But it's just four people around the casket. Another failure. Willy Loman arouses our pity because he cannot recognize his mistakes and because, like so many of us, his fate depends on forces outside his control.

Interlude: Who Met Whom?

It's a fact of life that fictional characters have "met" other fictional characters. A book, after all, is a whole lot of fictional characters meeting, romancing, borrowing money, and so on. But some characters go on to meet those from other stories. It can happen anywhere. It's sometimes called a guest appearance, usually limited to the character's own network or publisher. But in fiction anything goes.

This crossover effect happens most often with the gods and mythical figures. Midas not only met Dionysus, he did the god an important favor. That's what got him in trouble.

We learned in the essay on Dr. Faust that he met—and bedded—Helen of Troy. Of course this involved time travel, for Helen, anyway, but that's hardly a problem. In Scott's novel *Ivanhoe*, the title character is rescued by Robin Hood. And any regular comic-book reader knows that Superman met Batman, and the two actually fight crime together on many occasions . . . and fought each other at least once. Turns out the world *is* big enough for both of them.

In the modern era and television, it might have taken five seasons, but Buffy the Vampire Slayer actually did meet and vanquish the arch-vampire Dracula.

Among the many monsters and large animals Godzilla faced, it was not surprising that he battled King Kong and other giants of cinema, such as Mothra, Megalon, and the Smog Monster, who were inadvertently left off our list. How many people told them to pick on somebody their own size? Kong ignored that advice, and *Bambi Meets Godzilla* is one of the most thrilling—and shortest—of monster movies.

If we've missed any such encounters between characters in this book, don't hesitate to inform us of our oversight.

12. Movies

Following Edison's 1897 invention of the kinetoscope, movies quickly became the nation's favorite form of entertainment. Movies present life, fantasy, and wishful thinking as a grand spectacle to hundreds of people at the same time. It comes close to mass hallucination.

We read books individually and watch television as a family, but we attend movies in large numbers, sitting for several hours in the dark with strangers. While watching a movie, the entire audience holds its breath as one and exhales together. We laugh, mourn, and rejoice in unison. And the same movie plays elsewhere in town, as well as in Peoria, Seattle, Boston, and Memphis, bonding us into a culture of shared experiences.

Movie characters can bring out our most intense feelings. The wisdom of Ben Kenobi and the panache of Sam Spade, the cool reserve of Rick Blaine and the quiet heroism of Atticus Finch. These citizens of the silver screen captivate and motivate us. And they can change us, sometimes in ways none of us ever expected.

The Little Tramp—#73

From his birth in about 1915 through many shorts and four full-length silent films to his sentimental end in 1952, Chaplin's character the Little Tramp was one of the most recognized and beloved film personalities. He embodied the American myth of rags-to-riches and hero-winning-the-girl, and he had us all laughing at his antics. Several generations relied on the Little Tramp to brighten their days.

Chaplin created the character by accident, but he knew a success when he had one. He used his new persona in a variety of encounters, making mischief through his poverty, his earthy style, and his habit of intervening in the ordinary affairs of others. In one-reel shorts, the Tramp let us laugh at the world as it was exploding during World War I. For that escape, an entire generation counted on Charlie Chaplin.

The Little Tramp grew in stature with *The Kid* (1921). And in *The Gold Rush* (1925), *City Lights* (1931), and *Modern Times* (1936), he secured his place in cinematic history. Chaplin revived the character, in the story-within-the-story format, in his retrospective *Limelight* in 1952.

In *The Gold Rush*, the Tramp manages to reach Gold Rush—era Alaska at the end of the nineteenth century. Once there, he becomes enamored of a dance-hall girl, who seems to return the interest. The lawless Klondike is a perfect backdrop for Chaplin's anarchic approach to filmmaking and comedy, and the episode with the precarious shack on the cliff edge quickly became a cinematic icon.

While waiting for the girl to show up for a dinner he has prepared, the Little Tramp plunges two forks into a pair of dinner rolls and creates the Dance of the Rolls, with the rolls representing oversize feet and the forks spindly legs. This was so effective a vignette that at one premiere, the audience was so enthusiastic that the projectionist stopped the show, rolled the film back, and reshowed that scene. The audience responded with applause at the unprecedented encore.

In the meantime, the girl is preoccupied with her girl-friends and forgets the Tramp's dinner. The Tramp tries to bury his lovesickness in the search for gold, at which he is accidentally, but astonishingly, successful. The two not-yet-lovebirds lose track of each other, only to end up on the same ship on which the now-rich Tramp returns to the "lower forty-eight." Gushing photographers corner the Tramp and insist that he don his cheap threads for their readers. They want to capture the poor little guy who made it big. When she sees him dressed in rags, the girl realizes he is the man who tried to woo her back in the mining camp, but she had rejected him thinking he had no future. Now that he is wealthy, she worries that her rejection still stings him but he keeps the humility of his poverty and welcomes her into his new life.

In 1931, Chaplin had an additional challenge: talkies had appeared in 1927 and had taken over most of filmmaking. *City Lights* elevated comedy to a serious art form by intensifying the pathos and accentuating the contrast between the tragic and the comic. What is more poignant than a beautiful girl who is blind and cannot appreciate the beauty of the world or herself?

In the movie, a rich drunk tries to kill himself; the Tramp saves him and becomes his bosom buddy—but only when the rich man is drunk. When he is sober, he can't remember the friendship. While again drunk, he becomes the victim of an attempted robbery; when the Tramp assists him in recovering his property, he rewards the Tramp. The Tramp uses the reward money to enable the blind flower girl to regain her sight, caring only to right the tragic wrong in this corner of the world. She sees, but at first is unable to recognize her benefactor. At the end of the movie, however, she recognizes him, but we are left uncertain if the romance blossoms.

Having lived through the romantic victory of *The Gold Rush*, audiences now had to accept the romantic ambiguity of *City Lights* and its indefinite conclusion.

Modern Times is a political–social commentary on the dehumanizing effect of technology; it appeared during the Great Depression, when everything had political overtones. With millions out of work, the Tramp would not be unique, so Chaplin recast him as an outsider to the modern world. Both the Tramp and his love interest, the Gamine (Paulette Goddard), were escapees from modern society who found each other, got jostled about together, and finally walked off into the sunset together. "And they lived happily ever after" was on everybody's mind as they left the theater—just the sentiment they needed to cope with the depressed world outside.

The last Tramp film, *Limelight,* is Chaplin's reminder that even "happily ever after" comes to an end. The Tramp was less than forty, but in cinematic time that is an eternity.

For decades following his abrupt departure from the United States in 1952, Chaplin's films were not seen in this country. Entire generations grew up without the comfort of the Little Tramp surviving on the fringe of society. When his films became available again in 1972, a new audience experienced the thrill and delight in the shack teetering on the brink and chuckled at the idiocy of trying to feed an assembly-line worker while he worked.

———

The Little Tramp evolved with the film industry: he started out as a carefree kid bumming his way around, found friends and loves and—almost by accident—wealth, and finally reached sober maturity as his audience grew older. He was us.

Dracula—#33

The vampire was not originally scheduled for a place in our book until we got the following email from Eileen Watkins, author of *Dance with the Dragon*, *Ride a Dancing Horse*, *Black Flowers*, and *Paragon*, and a member of our Sunday Night Writing Group:

> Before things go any further, I have to make my case for the inclusion of Dracula among your characters. Frankly, I'm amazed that a case even needs to be made. I mean, you're including Buffy the Vampire Slayer and not Dracula? Get real! If it weren't for Bram Stoker's 1897 novel, Buffy's greatest claim to fame would be her cheerleading skills.
>
> At last count (pardon the pun), the character of Dracula has inspired 250 movies, 1,000 novels, thousands of press articles, and 4,000 clubs all over the world. Since its publication, Stoker's original novel has never gone out of print. At one point, it was supposedly the bestselling book of all time, after the Bible, and it has been translated into almost all existing languages. If that isn't "influence," I don't know what the heck is!
>
> The seventy-fifth anniversary of the book's publication—1972—spawned a flurry of nonfiction books about the character, the historical figure upon whom he was loosely based, and Stoker himself, including *In Search of Dracula* by professors

Florescu and McNally; *A Dream Of Dracula* by Leonard Wolf; and *The Dracula Myth* by *London Times* correspondent Gabriel Ronay. It also kicked off a new production of the Broadway stage play, starring Frank Langella.

Until the publication of Dracula, hardly anyone in Western Europe, Britain, or America had ever heard of the vampire myth. The only fictional piece that preceded it was *The Vampire,* a short novel by John Polidori (friend of Lord Byron and Mary Shelley), which was not successful or widely read. Stoker not only made *vampire* a household word, he virtually created the myth as we know it. An ardent Irish Catholic, he came up with the use of the crucifix, the Communion wafer, and holy water as means of repelling a vampire. These beliefs were not common even among Catholics. He took superstitions from Eastern Europe, combined them with the concept of the vampire bat from South America, added several ideas of his own, and created a modern myth that has captivated audiences for well over a hundred years.

Eastern Europeans pictured vampires as walking corpses who shambled like zombies or drifted like wraiths to prey upon their families and loved ones. Is this our image of the vampire today? No. The version that has survived is of a dark-haired, gauntly handsome, suave man with an Eastern European accent, dressed in formal clothes and a cape. And where did this come from? Stoker—but not only his novel. His Dracula, for most of the book, was gray-haired, had a mustache, and wore "severe, all-black" clothing. Our popular image is drawn from the Bela Lugosi interpretation of the 1930s, in the original play, movie, and countless spin-offs. A slightly more menacing version has evolved from the interpretation by British actor Christopher Lee in numerous Hammer Films. Try looking around you this Halloween—you can't throw a spitball without hitting a vampire based on Dracula, or a kid dressed up as the character.

Although there was an historical ruler named Dracula, Vlad Tepes, and he was a bloodthirsty tyrant, he was never rumored to be a vampire. He was a warrior prince rather than a count, and ruled a province called Wallachia in what is modern-day Romania. It was Stoker who called the character "Count" and placed him in Transylvania, a real, neighboring province. Now *Transylvania* also has become a household word.

Interestingly, the historical Dracula was a contemporary of Machiavelli's, and may have influenced the concept of the Prince.

You want influence? There's a kid's cereal called Count Chocula, for God's sake. Even Sherlock Holmes doesn't have a cereal named after him!

Here are a couple of points that contribute to Dracula's appeal. First, the idea of immortality and, to an extent, invulnerability. Who doesn't want to live forever? (At least until you really start to think about the potential drawbacks.) Second, there's something awesome and mysterious about a being who's been around for five hundred years, with all that accumulated knowledge and experience.

Yes, Dracula has been turned into a romantic figure lately, but Stoker meant him to be terrifying. There's the concept of living on other people's blood. Even if you don't kill your victims right away, what a ghastly thing to do— milk your "slaves" of their very life force! And finally, there's the mind control that comes with it—victims lose their personalities and become pale imitations of their master. He's a wonderful analogy for a lot of realistic situations. Who hasn't had the experience of being "vampirized" by someone, so that you feel drained and manipulated every time you interact with that person?

These things appeal to a lot of subconscious human impulses, and that's why the character has become, hands down, the most popular "horror" figure in our culture.

Eileen wound up her rant by listing more than twenty popular films featuring Dracula released between 1922 and 1993 alone. She noted that these are just the ones from England or America, and that many others have been produced in non–English speaking countries. We'll recommend www.rogerebert.com and www.imdb.com for filling out your own list.

Dracula has become a universal villain. He's a man of power whom women are drawn to, seduced by, and killed by. He's the dangerous side of elegance, a symbol of the horrors that lurk in the deep woods of our souls.

Want a date with that neat-looking guy in the black cape? Don't even think about it.

Maybe You Didn't Know

Bela Lugosi, whose first claim to Hollywood fame was playing Dracula in the 1931 film, was actually born in Lugos—in Transylvania. Maybe there's something in the air or water there? In recognition of that role, when Lugosi died in 1956 he was buried in full Dracula costume, including the cape.

Dorothy Gale—#91

At the beginning of the 1936 MGM movie *The Wizard of Oz*, Dorothy, who had been scolded by a nasty old woman, held her dog, Toto, and daydreamed out loud about "A place where there isn't any trouble. Do you suppose there is such a place, Toto? There must be. It's not a place you can get to by a boat or a train. It's far, far away. Behind the moon, beyond the rain."

When life gets us down, as it frequently does, we have all dreamed of escaping the rigors of this world and flying away to some enchanted, wonderful place over the rainbow, but it took Dorothy to get us there—where lovely little blue birds fly, beyond the rainbow—to the marvelous Land of Oz.

Dorothy has been a positive and welcome influence in our lives. The story exemplifies the American virtues of friendliness, sympathy for the less fortunate, common sense, and above all, perseverance.

The film starts in black and white but switches to the then newly invented Technicolor when Dorothy and Toto reach Oz. Their house had been blown there from Kansas by a tornado. The residents of Oz, a race of small people called Munchkins, greet them enthusiastically because Dorothy's house landed on a wicked witch and killed her. All seems well until they tell Dorothy that the witch's evil sister would avenge her sibling's death.

Oh my. Oz brought Dorothy new problems and, like those that had plagued her in Kansas, these too involved a sinister crone. Dorothy wanted to go home but didn't know how to get there.

The Munchkins told her to follow the Yellow Brick Road to the Emerald City, and consult the wizard there. So, she and Toto went to see the wizard, the wonderful Wizard of Oz. Along the way they met a Scarecrow, who needed a brain; a Tin Man, who wanted a heart; and a Cowardly Lion, who lacked courage. In the solid American approach to solving problems, they combined forces to reach the Emerald City.

At first, the Wizard required them to perform a difficult and dangerous task: bring him the broomstick of the evil witch whose sister Dorothy's house had crushed. They succeed, kill the witch in the process, and deliver the broomstick to the Wizard. But, alas, the Wizard turns out to be a fraud who could offer nothing beyond sentimental platitudes. Fortunately for Dorothy, all she had to do to get home was click the heels of her ruby red shoes and repeat, "There's no place like home." It works, and Dorothy awakens at home in the midst of her loving family.

> **Dorothy:** "Oh, Toto, we're home. Home! And this is my room, and I'm not gonna leave here ever, ever again, because I love you all, and—oh, Auntie Em—there's no place like home!"

Anyone who can experience that scene without a tear coming to his or her eye is a curmudgeon.

The characters were created in a series of children's books written by L. Frank Baum in the early twentieth century. The screenplay is by Noel Langley, Florence Ryerson, and Edgar Allan Woolf, and the music and lyrics are by Harold Arlen and Edgar Harburg. Here are some memorable lines:

> **Scarecrow:** "I haven't got a brain . . . only straw."
> **Dorothy:** "How can you talk if you haven't got a brain?"
> **Scarecrow:** "I don't know . . . But some people without brains do an awful lot of talking . . . don't they?"

> **Tinman:** "What have you learned, Dorothy?"
> **Dorothy:** "Well . . . if I ever go looking for my heart's desire again, I won't look any further than my own back yard. Because if it isn't there, I never really lost it to begin with!"

As an aside, we'll tell you that we have a connection, even though tenuous, to the film. One of us is responsible for a cairn terrier, Yogi, who claims that Toto was his great-grandmother. After her death he found among her effects in an old trunk, a note that read, "Auntie Em, Hate you. Hate Kansas. Taking the Dog. Dorothy."*

Sam Spade—#68

Sam Spade was the hero of the first American detective novel; he solved problems in the real world. Sherlock Holmes solved crimes as intellectual puzzles, but Sam Spade was an investigator with flesh and blood, not a mover of abstract chess pieces. In keeping with the American embrace of private enterprise, he was a *private* investigator, working for his own profit and livelihood. He was the archetype of the tough PI, dealing with the seamier side of humanity.

Because Spade constantly dealt with real people who were less than honorable, he was constantly suspicious without being paranoid. He could be generous and trusting, but only after careful scrutiny.

Dashiell Hammett's novel *The Maltese Falcon* introduced Sam Spade to the world in 1930 (see sidebar). At the time, Malta was exotic and unknown, a mysterious island; Western notions of morality didn't appear to apply. This gave Hammett ample opportunity to invent an artifact that men would fight and kill over, that women would seduce men to acquire. The novel became a bestseller, and Hollywood quickly took advantage of the opportunity to open a new genre of detectives.

---

* Carroll, Willard. *I Toto: The Autobiography of Terry, The Dog Who Was Toto*. New York: Stewart, Tabori and Chang, 2001.

The movie went through two incarnations—in 1931 and 1936—before Warner Brothers finally hit on the winning combination of director John Huston and star Humphrey Bogart in 1941. Bogart had the scarred visage of a battle-worn soldier, familiar with humanity's dark side. This lent immediate credibility to his portrayal of the detective setting out to avenge his partner's murder, uncovering treachery and deceit along the way. The setting of the story in cosmopolitan San Francisco added realism, and this was amplified in the movie.

Mary Astor, Sydney Greenstreet, and Peter Lorre, the other leading actors, added depth and interest to the movie. The film set the standard for detective/action movies.

Hammett continued the adventures of Sam Spade in several short stories: "A Man Called Spade," "Too Many Have Lived," and "They Can Only Hang You Once." In the 1940s, Spade was heard regularly on radio in *The Adventures of Sam Spade,* with Howard Duff in the title role. And a true sequel to *The Maltese Falcon,* an episode of the radio program called "The Khandi Tooth Caper," featured the same villains, now pursuing another priceless exotic relic (although two of the original villains were in prison and the third had been killed in the first story). In 1946, Sam Spade appeared in comic book form. Another comic book sequel, *The Black Bird,* spoofed the original in the early 1970s.

When the Hollywood blacklist included Hammett, the radio show simply pretended the original creator didn't exist; Sam Spade became Charlie Wild and the show was retitled *Charlie Wild, Private Eye*; all connection with Hammett disappeared. Charlie Wild eventually made it into television, not Sam Spade. But they were really the same character, played the same way, encountering the same villains. Thus was the blacklist circumvented.

Meanwhile, Hammett's success with the new genre spurred him to additional creations, including *The Thin Man*. The new heroes were husband and wife detectives Nick and Nora Charles, the basis for another sequence of six films and subsequent radio and television series. Sam Spade might have had limited exposure, but his character type is thoroughly embedded in our culture. Echoes continue in the stories of Raymond Chandler (featuring Philip Marlowe), Mickey Spillane (Mike Hammer), and Rex Stout (Nero Wolfe), and such television characters as Palladin and Thomas Magnum. Sam Spade stands at the head of a long line of intense detectives.

Maybe You Didn't Know

The Black Mask, a pulp magazine launched in 1920, printed some detective short stories, but *The Maltese Falcon* was the first full-length American novel featuring a detective.

Citizen Kane—#35

Charles Foster Kane defines the personal vulnerabilities of the people at the highest levels of American society, and his story is one of the models used to teach the art and technique of filmmaking. In our era, when movies make the deepest impressions on our view of the world, that's a colossal influence.

Charlie Kane is the star and title character of *Citizen Kane*, the movie that's on almost every top-ten list and often acknowledged as the best movie ever made. The film chronicles the life of an obsessive, lonely man who is one of the richest tycoons in the world.

Citizen Kane has held its high reputation almost since its creation in 1941—a remarkable endurance in the transient world of entertainment. The movie is one of the first gold standards of cinema, a perfect ten, a moon landing, a grand slam, a Stradivarius. Quite a feat for Orson Welles, the twenty-six-year-old actor, director, and coauthor. Hollywood's "boy genius." The characters are richly drawn, and Gregg Toland's deep-focus photography is glorious. Many of our top characters have been in motion pictures, and most of the directors of those films have learned their craft in part from Orson Welles's direction of *Citizen Kane*.

Said to be a fictionalized biography of William Randolph Hearst, the movie starts with Kane's death. The mystery of his life unfolds as reporters try to find what made the man a success in business and a failure in love and politics. They interview his few friends, and the story is told in flashbacks and recollections. Kane the tycoon, Kane the failed politician, Kane the failed husband—twice divorced, driven into isolation. And before that, poor Charlie Kane, as a child, shipped away from an abusive father to be raised by a cold guardian and the staff of private schools.

As an adult, Charlie appoints himself the savior of the common man and goes on a crusade. He picks out a small newspaper and takes it over—not just financially, but physically, moving into the editor's office. Why? Just for the "fun" of it. For personal satisfaction. Charlie has a mission: To save everyone—from people as rich as he; from trusts, conglomerates, politicians, and moneyed interests. To be a tireless spokesman for the ordinary person. Turns out that Charlie was the one ruined by riches; ruined by bankers, politicians, and moneyed interests; ruined by the fancy schools and large empty houses. And he's out to prevent anyone else from being abused, cheated, or misled.

Bit by bit, Kane shows us pieces of the puzzle, pieces of the vain, grandiose, and complex character who couldn't love, who couldn't trust, who gave his money to causes and objects and campaigns, who gave his opinions to the world but never believed in a single one of them. The scattered fragments of his life are woven into a whole as we watch him develop, celebrate, mature, and disintegrate. The speeches in *Citizen Kane* touch on memory, power, character, love, and loneliness; some of the best writing in the history of cinema is all about Kane, all surrounding Kane. And, in the end, one word, "Rosebud." His dying word, a final mystery. A woman? A horse he bought? A yacht he didn't buy? No. Something far smaller, far more personal, the only fragment of a life lost to society and obligation: a sled he had as a child. At the end, the only thing of value in his life. And, with his death, now just another piece of debris, a piece of wood burned as trash, a tiny funeral pyre for the giant whose heart it once contained, as Kane's body and memory pass from the world.

Charles Foster Kane shows us the power and pain of the highest levels of wealth, and for this we're eternally grateful. Where would we be without a window into the complex motives of the rich?

Did You Know

In the opening shots, watch the position of the window light; it doesn't change.

Citizen Kane won the Oscar for Best Original Screenplay (1941).

Recordings of Bernard Herrmann's score for *Citizen Kane* have been issued on London records and Silva. Herrmann went on to write critically acclaimed scores for several Hitchcock movies, as well as for films such as *Taxi Driver, Cape Fear,* and *The Day the Earth Stood Still.*

If you want to learn more about *Citizen Kane,* read
The Great Movies by Roger Ebert.
Citizen Welles: A Biography of Orson Welles by Charles F. Brady.
And see *Citizen Kane* (1941) directed by Orson Welles, screenplay by Orson Welles and Herman J. Mankiewicz.

Richard Blaine—#54

At a time when we desperately needed the message, Richard Blaine showed us that patriotism and courage could surpass self-interest and even take precedence over passionate love.

"Rick" Blaine entered our lives in the 1942 movie *Casablanca,* and sparked our resolve during the darkest days of World War II, at the zenith of Axis power. German forces had advanced into Russia; their U-boats threatened to cut off Britain; and Rommel's Afrika Korps was threatening the Suez Canal. On the other side of the world, following their attack on Pearl Harbor, the Japanese had conquered Singapore, Burma, and the Philippines.

Rick was an American who operated a popular nightclub in Casablanca, a city in Morocco, a colony of Free France. The French had surrendered about half of their territory to the Germans in 1940 and the remainder was called Vichy France. They were "neutral" during the rest of the war, but in reality, subjugated by the Germans.

From Casablanca, refugees could get to Portugal—also neutral—and then to safety. However, to make the passage one needed official letters of transit, and these had to be approved by the German military liaison in Morocco.

Rick has acquired two stolen letters of transit just before his former mistress, Ilsa, unexpectedly comes into his establishment accompanied by her husband, Victor Laszlo. Rick and Ilsa are still deeply in love with each other, and Ilsa wants to use the letters to get her and Rick to America. But Victor needs the letters to get him and Ilsa away so he can continue his work of organizing resistance to the Nazis.

The love aspect of the story is evoked by Herman Hupfeld's 1931 song, "As Time Goes By." When it is first played we realize the longing the lovers felt when they had been apart.

The following evening Victor and Ilsa come back to Rick's café. Victor knows nothing of his wife's plans with Rick, and the three of them drive to the airport. When they arrive, Ilsa expects Rick to walk with her to the plane, but he says, "I'm staying here."

Ilsa protests, "No, Richard, no. What has happened to you? Last night we said . . ."

Rick replies, "Last night we said a great many things. . . . Well, I've done a lot of thinking since then and it all adds up to one thing. . . . If that plane leaves the ground and you're not with him, you'll regret it. Maybe not today, maybe not tomorrow, but soon, and for the rest of your life."

Ilsa takes Victor's arm, they board the plane, and it takes off. They are on their way to safety.

The most famous line from the movie is, "Play it again, Sam." The expression has entered our language, but what Ilsa really said was, "Play it once, Sam, for old time's sake . . . Play 'As Time Goes By.' " Sam resists, because Rick has told him never to play it. Later, Rick tells Sam, "You know what I want to hear. You played it for her; you can play it for me. If she can stand it, I can. Play it."

Rick has some memorable lines in the film: "This is the beginning of a beautiful friendship." "The problems of three people don't amount to a hill of beans in this crazy world." And of course, "Here's looking at you, kid."

Rick is symbolic of the American people. He moved from a position of isolationism, as was true of America in the 1930s, to his inevitable active involvement, as America had to do when attacked at Pearl Harbor. Thereafter Rick was committed to the forces of destiny, as were we all.

Elmer Gantry—#98

Elmer Gantry, more clearly than any other character, warns us of how easy it is for a charlatan to manipulate the world of faith, a realm in which it is not always possible to separate the sincere from the unscrupulous. He personifies a promoter who takes advantage of the religious faith of his flock to gratify his excessive sensual desires. He represents everything that can go wrong with fundamentalist religion and exemplifies the sleaziness of many evangelists.

Elmer Gantry led the way for Oral Roberts to claim God was holding him hostage. Roberts claimed that if he didn't raise $8 million in ransom money in a month, God would slay him. Roberts succeeded in raising the money, but God never saw a nickel of it. Then there were Jim Bakker's adultery and theft of church funds, Tammy Faye Bakker's drug addiction, Jimmy Swaggart's prostitutes, and Billy James Hargis's life of deviant excesses. And let's not forget David Koresh, who led his faithful followers to their deaths in Waco, Texas; and Jim Jones, whose disciples blindly accompanied him into suicidal oblivion.

Some of us never learn. Because our lives reflect our wishful thinking rather than reality, we keep paying, and the evangelists keep praying—between trips to the bank.

In Sinclair Lewis's 1927 novel *Elmer Gantry,* the title character is the archetype of the hypocritical, slick-talking evangelist. He is drenched in whiskey, and spends much of his time seducing church secretaries and lining his pockets with offerings from the collection plate.

In the novel, Gantry is an ordained minister whose morals are lower than a snake's belly. Everything about him is phony. His every word is a lie, his every action a degradation of both faith and the human spirit. He has no redeeming features. His life revolves around lust, adultery, and barefaced opportunism in his ceaseless drive for sex, money, and power.

After he is ordained as a Baptist minister, he takes to the road and meets Sharon Falconer, a successful itinerant evangelist. He cons his way into becoming her manager and her lover. He steals money from her and seduces several women who work with them. But thanks to Gantry's successful, fiery sermons, Sister Sharon raises enough money to build her own church. Unfortunately, on opening night, fire destroys the new tabernacle and Sharon is killed. Without any feelings of loss—in fact, without any feeling at all—Gantry moves on.

He becomes a Methodist minister, marries well, and moves up to lead a large congregation in a Midwestern city. There he attracts a substantial following by crusading against all of his own personal vices, especially alcohol and sex. The disreputable Gantry has been rewarded with a seat at the top of his profession. The final lines of the novel sum up the entire story. Gantry tells us, "We shall yet make these United States a moral nation."

Are we there yet?

Norman Bates—#75

There's just no telling which ordinary person you meet will turn out to be a homicidal maniac. That's the lesson of Norman Bates, mild-mannered motel proprietor, occasional taxidermist, and murderer.

Norman is the mother-obsessed serial killer of the 1960 Hitchcock thriller *Psycho,* and he is number 2 on the American Film Institute's list of Top 50 Villains.

He's nuts. Not obviously dangerous, just a little withdrawn, the sort of fellow you could walk past without noticing.

Alfred Hitchcock based his film on the Robert Bloch novel of the same title, and it's the film version that everyone remembers. The famous shower scene—in particular, in which a nude Janet Leigh is attacked and killed by what appears to be an old woman in a dark veil—may be the most discussed and analyzed three-minute scene in motion pictures, for we never see the knife strike the victim, and the actor, Anthony Perkins, was actually in New York, three thousand miles away. A stand-in handled the knife, a bit of extra irony in a tale of double identities. Janet Leigh, in an interview with critic Roger Ebert, said that she was asked about the scene so often that she had to become an expert on it. It's the key event in the chronicle of Norman Bates, and it comes so unexpectedly we don't even know it has anything to do with him.

When the film opens, Janet's character, Marion Crane, steals a large amount of cash from her employer. She's leaving Phoenix to meet with her lover and start a new life. She stops on a dark and stormy night (it always is) at a motel by a foreboding Victorian mansion. That ought to have been a warning. The motel appears to be run by a demanding old woman, whose son, Norman, does the work. Marion admires his collection of stuffed vultures without realizing that "stuffing birds" is the British expression for the sexual predator's real hobby. Poor Marion Crane, feeling guilty about her embezzlement, thinks herself the worst of villains. Boy, is she wrong. She's murdered in the shower the next morning. Marion's lover and sister investigate and discover Norman's secret—that his mother's body is in the basement, and Norman is anything but normal. In a short fight, they subdue him. The film ends with a psychiatrist's explanation that Norman killed his mother and then took her place, playing both sides in the continuing battle between mother and son.

The film broke ground in a lot of ways. Murder had been

treated as a crime with rational motive. Norman has no understandable motive, not even voices in his head. In a world grown used to definable heroes and villains, the inner and outer lives of several characters are very different and almost every character has something to hide. The graphic violence was shocking. The scenes of the actress in underwear were as voyeuristic as Norman Bates. The symbolism was heavily laid, almost compulsively. Birds (Crane, Phoenix, vulture) often symbolize spirits, and Norman exerts his control by mounting them in the parlor. He is a shy fellow, raised by his abusive mother. He doesn't seem able to mount women, except as trophies of a different sort. The notion of split personality is visually foreshadowed by the repeated use of mirrors.

And, the viewer's opinion is also split. Our Norman first appears to have a gentle spirit, and when the heroine dies a third of the way through the film, we are left with no one else to sympathize with. We think he's caged by his mother's murderous jealousy. As the film slowly unpeels the layers of the mind, we see that Norman has preserved his mother's nastiest traits by splitting his personality into his and hers. But Norman started it by killing his mother years before. We never know the true relationship between mother and son that drove him to the first murder, or if that even was the first murder. There may be no end to the depths of evil.

The slasher, or psychopathic murderer, was not much of a subject in film before Norman Bates, but now it is the standard of horror movies, from *A Nightmare on Elm Street* to *Scary Movie 3*. Director Alfred Hitchcock said that we had become too numb, too secure in our civilization, that we needed to be jolted out of our senses. In his telling of the story, we are reminded that the greatest danger comes out of nowhere, or where we least suspect it.

Maybe You Didn't Know

Marion's three-minute demise took a full week to film, late in December 1959, according to star Janet Leigh in *Psycho: Behind the Scenes of the Classic Thriller*.

Janet Leigh cites between seventy-one and seventy-eight setups for the shower scene. Hitchcock used warm water, for her comfort.

Norman was played by Anthony Perkins, who also appeared in sequels.

To learn more about Norman Bates and the movie, read
   The Dark Side of Genius: The Life of Alfred Hitchcock by Donald Spoto.
   The Great Movies by Roger Ebert.
   Roger Ebert's Book of Film.
   Psycho: Behind the Scenes of the Classic Thriller by Janet Leigh and Christopher Nickens.

Dr. Strangelove—#87

Dr. Strangelove is an end-of-the-world story that rivals the Scandinavian myth of Ragnarok and the Christian story of Armageddon. But there is a major, fundamental difference: In the world of Dr. Strangelove, it is not the gods, but mankind, that knowingly bring on the holocaust that no one survives.

Dr. Strangelove's is a cautionary tale about the dangers of military technology.

The 1964 movie *Doctor Strangelove or: How I Learned to Stop Worrying and Love the Bomb* is a black comedy. An insane American Air Force general, Jack D. Ripper, suspects a Russian plot to sap our virility by fluoridating our water supply. To protect American manhood, he launches bombers under his command to strike the Soviet Union with nuclear weapons. Not even the president of the United States can recall the planes. Only Ripper has the code to do so, and he commits suicide.

The president and his military advisors phone the Russian premier in an effort to bring down the planes, or at least dissuade the Russians from retaliating. U.S. and Russian defenses destroy all but one of the planes, but that one continues on its way to drop its bombs on a Russian target. We learn that the Russians have put in place a Doomsday System. If an atomic bomb explodes anywhere in their territory, nuclear weapons will be automatically launched toward every major city in America.

An integral part of our military leadership is Dr. Strangelove, a wheelchair-bound ex-Nazi. He is the head of the United States' weapons development program and a trusted advisor to the president. As soon as he enters the story, we realize he is insane. He speaks in a distinct German accent, and his black-gloved robotic hand is not completely under his control. It seems to have a mind of its own and even tries to strangle him.

When the last plane gets through and drops its payload, Dr. Strangelove calculates that the radioactive fallout from the incoming Soviet weapons will exceed lethal levels for the next hundred years. But Strangelove has a plan. He advises the president to gather a large number of beautiful women and virile men in a ratio of ten to one, and send them into mines where they and their offspring will be protected from the radiation.

They can emerge when it is safe, in about a hundred years. All the men in the war room with the president and Strangelove expect to be among the male component of this orgy.

The concept of Mutually Assured Destruction in the movie was closer to truth than fiction. The film was released just two years after the Russians had installed missiles with atomic warheads in Cuba. Several military consultants to President Kennedy advised him to use atomic weapons in response. The generals even went so far as to put the U.S. military on high alert—without the knowledge of their commander-in-chief. Fortunately, Kennedy kept his head and negotiated a peaceful end to the crisis. If that is not scary enough, records indicate that Kennedy won office by only 110,000 questionable votes in Chicago. Had the election gone the other way, Richard Nixon, whose judgment has been questioned at times, would have been president, and we all might have been incinerated. Put that together with the many false alarms that have jarred our missile defense system and we realize that Dr. Strangelove, even though a voice of insanity, may have sounded our final warning.

In the early twenty-first century, the possibility of vast destruction is still with us. Worldwide, thirty thousand nuclear warheads still exist. More than ten thousand are in the former Soviet Union, where safeguards are questionable. If terrorists take over a weapons *system* with thousands of nuclear warheads, then Dr. Strangelove will be relevant once more.

Bond, James Bond—#51

The best of men, ace of spies in the game of international intrigue, sensuous man of mystery, Mr. Bond is the last vestige of

British pride in the U.K.'s postcolonial era. Once, the sun never set on the Empire, but nowadays even the Scots are talking about independence. Such is the way of the modern world. Those uncomfortable with the loss of the Empire can retreat into memory, fantasy, cocaine, or sherry, but we suggest Bond. He'll lift your spirits.

The profession of spying is nothing new. Spies are mentioned in the Bible (Josh. 2.). As a recruited saboteur, Delilah was able to seduce and defeat Samson (*Judg.* 16.). Kipling's 1901 novel *Kim* revolves around the Great Game, as international intrigue was called in those days.

Every nation recognizes the value of "inside information," or, better yet, someone on the inside who can influence planning. With outright payoffs, or more subtle approaches such as the companionship of an exotic lover, spies have long been effective agents of war. The game of spy versus spy has a long and colorful history, and it is likely to continue well into the future.

Ian Fleming's James Bond, Agent 007, created a new dimension in espionage by intertwining it with the highest technologies of our modern era. Technology, especially that of warfare, has always needed the protection of secrecy, from the Egyptians and their secret formula for bronze, to the encrypted software of today's world. And high technology has served spying well. Bond elevated this to an exciting new level.

Some of the high-tech devices used by Bond were well ahead of their time. He introduced us to such real tech-toys as the personal minisub, the jet ski, the Acrostar minijet, the rocket pack, and the surgical laser. Other "gadgets," from speedboats to the legendary Aston Martin DB-5, illustrate the range of playthings available to the wealthy and the military. Safe in our local theater, we enjoy expensive vehicles and high-precision stunts performed with them.

Women in espionage have typically been used either to acquire information—pillow talk—or to "neutralize" an opponent by blackmail, but Bond has changed that image and championed the role of women. Bond's era, the late 1950s, was a sexist world, still burdened by Victorian attitudes. The girls were mere eye candy. But since the earliest Bond movies, women have moved on to become effective heroines and important villains.

James is an exceedingly effective man, gifted in a variety of pursuits. He may be a womanizer, but he always treats women with respect and truly warrants the attention he receives from them. Bond is such a capable and sensitive lover that he is able to turn an adverse female spy to his own side. Over the years, Bond has been portrayed by the most handsome of men: Sean Connery, Roger Moore, and Pierce Brosnan. And, for two generations, the standard of male excellence has been how James looks in a tux, while the standard of a tuxedo was whether it made the man look and feel like James Bond.

Great Britain was an imperialistic country that imposed their domineering will on people around the world for nearly four centuries. In the aftermath of World War II, when England mislaid their empire, James Bond appeared as an echo of imperial power and expertise. As the Brits resigned themselves to the loss of India and other colonies, they found reassurance in the creation and rise of Mr. Bond. James Bond is more than just the embodiment of the new way of doing the spy business; he is the best of the old traditions amid the newest technologies and sensitivities.

We have enjoyed more than twenty Bond films. Plus, there are too many spin-offs to mention, but a few examples include *In Like Flint, The Thomas Crown Affair, Austin Powers: International Man of Mystery,* and *The Tailor of Panama.*

On television he gave birth to *Mission: Impossible; The A-Team; I Spy; The Man from U.N.C.L.E.; The Wild, Wild West; The Avengers; Get Smart; Charlie's Angels;* and *The Prisoner,* in which Patrick McGoohan played a spy referred to only by his number (#6).

James Bond is far more than a number. He is the cultural weathervane for the civilized world.

Atticus Finch—#57

Harper Lee's novel, *To Kill a Mockingbird,* introduces us to Atticus Finch, a widowed lawyer raising two children in southern Alabama during the Great Depression.

Atticus is going to remind us, in his own calm, intellectual way, of several important moral values we may have misplaced.

Early in the story, his six-year-old daughter, who is called Scout, tells her father that she is distressed by the way school is going for her. (Atticus knows that she will face insults stemming from his evenhandedness toward black citizens, and he astonishes us.) He does not tell her to fight for her point of view, but says the problem is that she does not fully understand people. In his opinion, we cannot fully understand another person until we consider things from their standpoint, until we climb inside their skin and walk around in their shoes for a while.

In another incident, his twelve-year-old son, Jem, destroys the flowerbed of a neighbor because she shouted bigoted epithets at him when he walked past her house. When Atticus learns of what Jem did, he tells Jem that he will have to accept penance for his act of destruction: he will read to the woman every afternoon for a month.

The main current of the novel is the ceaseless flow of racial hatred that runs through the South in the 1930s. But Atticus shows us that in a society immersed in bigotry, we can still act with tolerance and dignity. We are reminded that our conscience tells us what is right and what is wrong; once we understand what is right we must follow that course regardless of the cost.

The court calls on Atticus to defend a black man falsely accused of raping a white woman. The judge who picks Atticus knows that he will present the best defense possible.

Soon after he accepts the case, Atticus anticipates that his client may be lynched, the usual course of vigilante justice in the South. At great personal risk, he sits alone on the steps of the jail and, as he had suspected, a group of white men shows up intent on murdering his client. Atticus stands firm and dissuades the men, all of whom he knows. As the tension rises, we find ourselves reflecting on our own values as we see the strength of a man we now admire.

At the trial, Atticus clearly shows that the man, who has a disabled arm, could not possibly have committed the offense. But the jury, including at least one of the men who wanted to lynch the defendant, convicts him. Atticus plans to continue his service to the black man by appealing the conviction. However, the man tries to escape and is shot dead, thus bringing the episode to an end.

Atticus is but a small voice in the wilderness. But it is the cumulative effect of such small voices that eventually bring about social advances.

Atticus Finch tops the American Film Institute's list of the Top 50 Heroes, and well he should. He is a quiet man whose exemplary strength of character is a timeless inspiration for us all.

HAL 9000—#66

On the campus of Carnegie Mellon University, a concept emerged at the dawn of the twenty-first century: The Robot Hall of Fame. Among its first inductees was HAL 9000, the pivotal character in Stanley Kubrick's groundbreaking 1968 film, *2001: A Space Odyssey*.

HAL 9000, the first serious robot known to a large audience, was the first to achieve star status. He was twenty-five years ahead of his time: he has machine vision and speech simulators. He can learn. He can speak. He can even sing. And he is now the highest-rated robot on The American Film Institute's 2003 list of the Top 50 Villains in one hundred years of cinema. That's right: one of the top fifty *villains*. HAL, the *H*euristically Programmed *A*lgorithmic computer, murdered four astronauts on a critical mission to Jupiter.

From the dawn of time, mankind has been looking for ways to do things more easily. At first, the simple machines: hammer, knife, lever. Then the windmill, the industrial loom, and the steam engine. And, almost a century before any practical computer, we had the idea of mechanical men who could do our work for us, but, unfortunately, who would take our jobs from us and also do away with us. The idea that a race of androids would decide to murder all of humanity comes from Karel

Kapek's 1923 play *R.U.R., Rossum's Universal Robots*. The robots (Czech for *worker*) are mass-produced by the millions. They fill every function (how convenient), then take over the world.

In modern times, fictional robots include Robbie of the 1960s TV series *Lost in Space*; Mr. Data of *Star Trek*; and The Terminator, portrayed by Arnold Schwarzenegger.

HAL 9000 stars in *2001: A Space Odyssey*. He is the mission-computer on a space ship that is on an important mission from Earth to Jupiter. The craft carries two men who stay awake through the long outward journey, three astronauts in hibernation, and HAL, the sixth member of the crew. The ship is his body, and he is its brain and central nervous system. Of the three conscious astronauts, only HAL knows the ship's real mission is to investigate a—something—that's in orbit around Jupiter. The "something" is a companion object to an alien monolith discovered on the Moon. Is it hostile? We have to find out. To prevent worldwide panic, almost no one has been told of the alien device the crew is heading for. Not even them.

HAL becomes unhinged by the conflict between secrecy and truth, and he has 100 million miles to brood over it. He's going quietly insane. He asks the astronauts in his coldly polite voice whether they are having second thoughts about the mission, if they've heard rumors of some sort of object dug up on the Moon. They think HAL's questions are part of a routine psychological test. But this is not a test. HAL incorrectly predicts that a radio component is going to fail, and suddenly the astronauts start wondering about how they will deal with him in his imperfect state.

But HAL knows exactly what the humans are planning to do. They're going to shut him down, just as the mission approaches its critical phase. He can't allow that. He becomes the first computer to humanize itself. Sadly, the human traits that emerge are paranoia and schizophrenia. HAL now uses his mistake as an excuse to send the crew outside the hull. He uses the ship's controls to kill four of the astronauts, managing to trap the fifth outside in one of the service pods.

The last man, Dave Bowman, is stunned: the computer doesn't obey his commands. HAL refuses to open the air lock, and their conversation has become famous. When dealing with defective equipment, a scientist has four options: use a hammer, call repair, turn the power off, or take it apart. When he manages to get back in through a manual airlock, Bowman tries the last one. That always works. At least, the parts you're left with aren't any more broken than what you started with.

Isaac Asimov's robot stories, of the same vintage as Clarke's, hinged on three laws of robotics, but his First Law—a robot is not allowed to injure a human being—has been left out of HAL 9000, even though the scientists in this story almost certainly read Asimov's books.

2001 was based on Arthur C. Clarke's 1948 story "The Sentinel." Sir Arthur (and Stanley Kubrick, whose transcendental film gave the story its popularity) and HAL stimulated and inspired those who worked in computers, robotics, and artificial intelligence. Clarke didn't just anticipate today's technology: flat-panel displays, microwaves for cooking, and computers in navigation; he created a to-do list for the next fifty years.

Today, the Pittsburgh region, home of Carnegie Mellon, is one of the key centers for mobile robotics. NASA has been developing a Remote Agent computer to handle the exploration of deep space.

Wish them luck.

Did You Know

HAL 9000 is villain number 13 on the American Film Institute villains list.

The Robot Hall of Fame is under the School of Computer Science (www.cs.cmu.edu).

In "Moxon's Master," by Ambrose Bierce, 1894, a mechanical computer refuses to lose a chess game and attacks its human opponent.

"Robbie," by Dr. Isaac Asimov, was first published in 1940 as "Strange Playfellows" in Super Science Fiction, Fictioneers, Inc.

HAL 9000 was voiced by Douglas Rain.

13. Women's Liberation

The achievement of "equality" for women has been one of the main victories of the twentieth century, but there's plenty of room for improvement. To this day, a woman is "given away" in marriage, as though she were the property of her father.

Just look at national politics. Women have headed the governments of Israel, England, Germany, Liberia, Philippines, Nicaragua, even Pakistan, but in the United States how many women have run for president? For vice-president?

The denigration of women started thousands of years ago, and until the 1920s—when women won the right to vote—there was little or no practical improvement. It took a few centuries of romantic idealization and literary activism to achieve even that lowest of basics, but along the way, progress was being made, led by theater and literature.

In fiction, at least, women advanced. There is Portia, the clever heiress who solves the legal dilemma in Shakespeare's *Merchant of Venice*, and the strong-willed Hedda Gabler in Ibsen's 1890 play. We also know the wild adventure of *Thelma & Louise* (1991) and the law practice of *Ally McBeal (1997–2002)*.

In this chapter we examine some of those brave women

characters who led the battle back toward equal rights: Nora Helmer, Lady Chatterly, Mary Richards, and Buffy the Vampire Slayer.

Hester Prynne—#30

This victim of misguided social norms persevered and lived a productive life amid a sea of sanctimonious malevolence. And her legacy grows.

The Scarlet Letter, written in 1850, was Nathaniel Hawthorne's account of Puritan mercilessness, written with the shame of his own ancestors in mind. His great-great-grandfather, John Hathorne, had presided over the Salem Witch Trials, sentenced many innocent women to death, and was unrepentant when the suspected witchcraft was revealed to be a hoax perpetrated by a few girls. Hawthorne was so ashamed of this legacy he altered his family name by inserting the *W* into it.

The setting of the novel is Boston in the 1600s. Puritan life there was gloomy, joyless, and rigid. Puritanism was an American form of Calvinism, the basic tenet being the universal depravity of man through original sin. The theology was hard, cold, and devoid of any human feelings. Religion was the law and the law dealt harshly with any woman who showed the slightest sign of strength or independence. Punishment for private sinning was severe and public.

In the story, Hester Prynne is a young woman who thinks her husband has been lost at sea. Passion draws her to an unmarried pastor, Arthur Dimmesdale. He returns her affection and from this union an illegitimate child, Pearl, is born.

As a result of her adultery, Hester falls into disgrace and further alienates the Puritan community by refusing to reveal the name of the father. The local authorities, all men, put her in jail. When she is released she must wear a scarlet *A*, for adulteress, as a sign of her shame. She has few allies in this narrow-minded environment so she moves into a cottage on the edge of town. There she lives a quiet, dignified life with her daughter, earning her living by needlework.

Many years pass and when Dimmesdale realizes that he is fatally ill, he publicly confesses that he was Hester's lover and dies in her arms. Thereafter Pearl, now grown up, comes into a great deal of money from the estate of Hester's husband. Following this, mother and daughter return to Europe where Pearl marries a wealthy man.

The story could have ended there, but it does not. We are dealing with a strong, self-assured woman who sees a need for strength in her former community, and so she returns to Boston where she continues to wear the scarlet *A*. With quiet dignity she brings enlightenment to the community and soon women turn to her for solace and comfort. After her death she is buried next to Dimmesdale, and they share a common headstone bearing a scarlet *A*.

The story has helped society ease the stigma of adultery. By slowly distancing ourselves from the concept of sin, we have relegated adultery to the secular grounds for divorce, and we have come to accept the children of unmarried women as part of the social milieu.

Hester is not heroic in the usual literary meaning of the word. She is an ordinary woman with human compassion in a cold, intolerant society. And therein lies her power and influence: she exhibited all of the human frailty, affection, and perseverance we universally admire.

Nora Helmer—#25

Ibsen's 1879 play, *A Doll's House,* examines the destructive consequences that can occur when social norms interfere with marriage. The husband and wife in the story live a life of luxury and love each other passionately, but there is a dark side to their relationship. The husband considers his wife nothing more than a doll—incapable of independent thought or action.

Nora is the beautiful and loving wife of Torvald, manager of a bank, who adores her. Early in their marriage Torvald became ill and for his recovery they had to leave Norway and take up residence in Italy. They were not affluent at the time so Nora, unbeknownst to her husband, borrowed money by forging her father's name on the loan papers. She has paid off the loan, but the lender—Nils Krogstad—is a man of dubious character. He attempts to preserve his job at Torvald's bank by blackmailing Nora. She tries to help Krogstad by pleading his case with Torvald, but Torvald fires him anyway. As revenge, Krogstad makes the forgery known to Torvald. This results in the turning point of the play and their lives.

In the 1880s society was organized along strict patriarchal lines. The world defined a man's position in the community, and Torvald's moral code was entirely derived from social norms.

These are the personal values behind Torvald's actions after reading a letter from Krogstad revealing Nora's indiscretion. After reading the note, Torvald immediately becomes angry with Nora. If the letter becomes public, he will be ruined. He makes no attempt to consider her motives. Fortunately, a few minutes later he realizes that the information can be hidden from public scrutiny, and he is relieved. The danger has passed and he now forgives her. He belatedly interprets her actions as love for him, but recognizes her inexperience in the ways of the world.

Nora is taken aback. She realizes how deeply Torvald is dominated by the dictates of society; he has forgiven her only because the situation can be hidden from the community.

At the end of the play, Nora shocks us by walking out on her husband and children. Her exit is a metaphorical rejection of the social values that pervade her home and life, and hang so heavily on her. She says she has to find out who is right—society or she. She wants her life to have a value of its own: a reasonable expectation that women of the twenty-first century are enjoying, thanks to figures such as Nora Helmer.

Lady Chatterly—#15

Her name alone conjures sexual images, and her story has transformed sexual standards in literature and society.

In 1928, the British writer D. H. Lawrence completed *Lady Chatterly's Lover*, and had it printed in Italy. Lawrence's friends sold the one thousand copies to various individuals. Because it was published privately, under British law no copyright was issued. Almost immediately pirated editions appeared. In America alone we had at least four.

Straight away, the religious community was up in arms about the book. They complained to the authorities that the writing was obscene and evil. As a result it was banned in England and America. And it suffered the same fate everywhere else in the world including China, where merely possessing a copy could bring a life sentence in prison.

The story is erotic and passionate. Lawrence presents his readers with earthy language and descriptions of sexual intimacy between two vital, responsive individuals. By twenty-first-century standards, it might be considered sensual, but certainly it would not be looked on as pornographic, as it was considered in 1928.

Lady Constance Chatterly is the young, attractive wife of a wealthy man who emerges from World War I a paraplegic. Even though sex had never been of special interest, she finds herself attracted to Mellors, a straightforward, unrestrained fellow who is the gamekeeper on her husband's estate. She has a protracted sexual affair with the man and falls in love with him. She becomes pregnant by him and decides to leave her husband and marry Mellors. However, Mellors's estranged wife tries to move back in, and when she is refused she raises a scandal that doesn't implicate Connie, but Mellors is fired anyway. In addition, Sir Clifford refuses to give Constance a divorce. He accepts the fact that his heir will be the son of a commoner. And on this ambiguous note, the story ends with each of the three principles living apart from the others: Sir Clifford continues to live at his estate and Constance moves to London, where she awaits her lover who may, or perhaps may not, choose to join her.

Grove Press published the novel in 1959 and immediately Postmaster General Arthur E. Summerfield banned it from the mail. The dispute was litigated before U. S. District Court Judge Frederick van Pelt Bryan, who decided that the book was "an honest and sincere novel of literary merit," and decreed that it be allowed in the mail. Thereafter, several publishers sold a total of more than 6 million copies.

The first movie version (1955) also evoked horror among those squeamish about sex, and the state of New York banned it. However, the U.S. Supreme Court, in a decision that dealt an almost fatal blow to U.S. film censorship, said that New York had violated our constitutional rights: we should be allowed to view the film. Thereafter followed the sexual revolution of the 1960s and widespread open-mindedness, with X-rated movies such as *Last Tango in Paris,* stand-up comics Lenny Bruce and George Carlin, and radio personalities such as Howard Stern.

Lady Chatterly helped society move forward. She brought her sexuality into the public domain. She paved the way for *Sex and the City.*

Nancy Drew—#62

Nancy Drew appears in more than four hundred books as well as several movies and other spin-offs. She has strongly influenced several generations of women during their most formative years, instilling in them the spirit of a woman who competes with men on their own terms and wins.

She was the brainchild of Edward Stratemeyer, who was also responsible for The Hardy Boys, Tom Swift, and The Bobbsey Twins. He saw the untapped market potential and enlisted the assistance of Mildred Wirt Benson to appeal to this audience.

Stratemeyer gave Benson the basic plot outlines, and she converted those into full-length stories. Author credit was given to Carolyn Keene, a generic pseudonym established by the Stratemeyer Syndicate so they could use any number of actual writers.

Benson was tired of what she called the "namby-pamby"

characterization of women, so she gave Nancy Drew a substantial measure of spunk and individuality. The first three stories appeared in print in 1930, just one month before Stratemeyer died. They were an instant, dramatic, and long-term hit. His two daughters, Harriet and Edna, took over the enterprise after his death, with Harriet doing most of the writing.

The basic plot outline follows a winning formula. Nancy often faces two distinct mysteries that turn out to be connected. She receives a warning to abandon her pursuit. She befriends an innocent victim who might be ruined if the mystery isn't solved. There are ominous encounters with villains, a number of mishaps, and captivity of Nancy, the innocent victim, or both.

She has sidekicks, Georgia and Bess, and a boyfriend, Ned (but no hanky-panky ever ensues). When Nancy needs heavy lifting, her boyfriend, her father, or the local police chief step in. But Nancy provides the drive to delve into the mystery, the spunk to pursue the leads, and the wits to solve the problem.

Nancy is the sixteen-year-old daughter of the wealthy criminal defense lawyer, Carson Drew, a widower since Nancy was three. She is presented as a sophisticated young lady who dabbles in adventures. Though she is wealthy, she never shrinks from getting her hands dirty. She succeeds at everything she tries—not just well enough, but spectacularly. Her flower arrangements win the blue ribbon. She replaces an ill actress after a single rehearsal. She rides horses bareback in the circus, and she has forensic skills that Sherlock Holmes would have envied. She assists a visiting doctor with a confidence and dexterity that astonish him, even though she has had no medical or nursing education.

Starting in 1950, Nancy became less refined. Now eighteen years old and attending college, she continues to operate with

the poise and intellect of a thirty-year-old. Meanwhile, Stratemeyer's daughter Harriet revisited the entire series and over-
hauled many of the stories to make them more politically
correct: she removed the racism and anti-Semitism that de-
tracted from the originals and updated the props to keep them
current with new technology. Nancy's Depression-era roadster
morphed into a Mustang convertible, still in Nancy's signature
blue.

The Nancy Drew enterprise had also expanded its scope.
There were four Nancy Drew movies between 1938 and 1939,
and 14 TV episodes in 1977. While the original Nancy Drew
Mystery Stories series targeted girls ages eight to eleven, several new series were introduced: The Nancy Drew Notebooks
for younger readers, Nancy Drew on Campus for a slightly
more mature audience market, and the Nancy Drew Files for
still older readers interested in a bit more romance. (Tradition-
alists need not worry: Nancy remains virginal.) In addition,
starting in 1988, Nancy Drew participated in a series of sixteen
books comprising the Nancy Drew & Hardy Boys Super Mysteries (note her top billing). Her books have been translated
into at least thirteen languages. She currently has more than 34
million copies in print.

In addition to the various story lines, there has been a
Nancy Drew cookbook (*Clues to Good Cooking*), board games,
and computer games. In 2003, Gumshoe Girls began selling a
line of Nancy Drew loungewear and accessories. There have
been two television series.

The Nancy Drew Mystery Stories, in print since 1930,
ended in 2003, with the 175th title. In 2004, a new series,
Nancy Drew Girl Detective, was launched, with richer and
more descriptive stories. We still get our favorite sleuth, Nancy,
but different stories for a new audience. Though she's been

around for more than seventy years, Nancy Drew is still capti-
vating and inspiring generations of young women.

Maybe You Didn't Know

Nancy Drew is not the only fictional female sleuth; the Judy
Bolton series has her fans, though because Judy actually
ages and grows and gets married, the potential stories have
been more limited.

To learn more about Nancy Drew, we suggest
    The Girl Sleuth: A Feminist Guide by Bobbie Ann Mason.
    Girl Sleuth: Nancy Drew and the Women Who Created Her
by Melanie Rehak.

Mary Richards—#39

Mary Richards, the unlikely icon of the feminist revolution,
enchanted the world as the title character of *The Mary Tyler
Moore Show* from 1970 to 1977.

Mary led the way in the battle to bring women equality in
a so-called man's world. She was the first television star to
portray an unattached woman living an independent life
while doing a man's job where she was treated as an equal. In

1970, that was a shock. The media still pictured feminists as army-booted uglies, but Mary was as beautiful, gracious, and competent as Ms. Moore herself. A subtle feminist, Mary Richards was the role model for feminine success in an age of change.

Comedienne Carol Burnett had cracked the gender barrier as hostess and comic in her own right, but television's staple, the half-hour situation comedy, was a family format in which complete families were the rule and women were dependent creatures. Actress Marlo Thomas, daughter of famed comic Danny Thomas, had come close to breaking the barrier in her show *That Girl,* but her character had no great responsibility and was firmly attached to a regular boyfriend.

Created by the team of Allan Burns and James L. Brooks (also of *Taxi* and *The Simpsons*), *The Mary Tyler Moore Show* focused on Mary's job. Mary had boyfriends, neighbors, and romances, but the workplace was the main interest. She was a producer in a TV newsroom, WJM, Minneapolis. Men were not objects to be sought but friends or competitors. Her family relationships were the friends she established through her workplace.

The show's setting was no accident. While at present women can be found in almost every career, that was not the case in 1970. Journalism was one of the few careers open to women, as it has been from Nellie Bly to Barbara Walters. Nor is it accidental that the show was placed in Minneapolis, Minnesota, when most shows were set in New York or California. Home territory to liberal vice-presidents Humphrey and Mondale, Minneapolis is a cosmopolitan city where you can find forty kinds of bagels in the grocery and Vietnamese balloon-flowers at the farm market.

We remember Mary Richards as one of the first women

characters to have romantic and sexual affairs, however gently implied. She was also one of the first television characters to bridge the chasm between fiction and reality, a trend followed by Candace Bergen's similar workplace comedy *Murphy Brown* and Murphy's verbal battle with the real vice-president, Dan Quayle.

The characters of Mary Richards's world, unlike the static characters of earlier sitcoms, matured and developed. Her boss, Lou Grant (Ed Asner), was divorced; her friend Georgette (Georgia Engel) joined the show in its third year and married coworker Ted Baxter (Ted Knight). Her friend Rhoda (Valerie Harper) moved away (and had a show of her own). At the end of the show's seven seasons, the final episode presented most of the staff being fired by *their* network, and Mary is the last to leave—literally turning out the lights.

In each show's opening sequence, Mary paused on a street corner, turned, and threw her hat into the air, the traditional gesture of graduation, a celebration of freedom. At that corner, Nicollet and Seventh, now stands a statue of her in that pose. In the dedication ceremony on May 8, 2002, Ms. Moore reminded us that she is still a force for progress. That's right, Mary, you made it after all.

To learn more about Mary Richards, we suggest
   The Education of a Woman: The Life of Gloria Steinem by Carol G. Heilbrun.
   Bachelor Girl by Betty Israel.
   The Museum of Broadcast Communications, *www. museum.tv/archives*

Buffy the Vampire Slayer—#44

Few of the creators of the characters in *The 101 Most Influential People Who Never Lived* are alive. This is to be expected: influence usually takes time to develop, so most of the characters in this book are decades or centuries old. The subject of this essay is a relative newcomer to this scene, but that has not stopped her from becoming a cultural icon with the sort of influence usually reserved for gods. She was chosen for a world-saving mission.

Joss Whedon created Buffy the Vampire Slayer for the 1992 film of that name. Whedon fashioned a woman who refused to be victimized, and he placed her in a setting that reinforced her attitude. He blended a Dracula-fighter with Wonder Woman and a bit of Valley Girl.

From the beginning, Whedon said, "I wanted Buffy to be a cultural phenomenon . . . That was always the plan."

And what a phenomenon she has become. Several books have been written about Buffy and her crew. She embodies today's typical teenager, and she has been likened to the heroines of Greek mythology. Buffy has explored such Big Questions as "How do we deal with suffering and loss?" and "What should we wear to the prom?" (Candace Havens, *Joss Whedon: The Genius Behind Buffy*). Buffy Summers plumbs the depths of teenage angst, while remaining perky and flippant.

Professor: So you're the Slayer. We thought you were a myth.

Buffy: You were myth-taken.*

---

* Season 4, "A New Man"

As with many other creations of science fiction and fantasy, Buffy is not just a character, but an entire universe (a "Buffy-verse") populated with vampires, ghouls, demons, and mad scientists.

She has a support staff to help her find, identify, and vanquish the evil creatures. The core of this support crew are her mentor Giles ("I'm afraid we have a slight apocalypse."*), the computer-savvy Willow ("I've Googled 'til I just can't Google no more."†), Willow's childhood friend Xander ("I'm seventeen. Looking at *linoleum* makes me wanna have sex."‡), and rehabilitated demon Anya ("I provide much-needed sarcasm."§).

The idea of the Slayer started out of the observation "High school is hell." It didn't take much beyond a freewheeling imagination to move from that to "High school sits on a hellmouth, the portal for entry of all sorts of monsters into this world, where they wreak havoc and jeopardize the future of humanity."

> **Giles:** It's the end of the world.
> **Buffy, Willow, and Xander (together):** *Again?*‖

She, with her sidekicks, appeals to everyone who can still remember the hell of their teen years.

---

* Season 7, "Bring on the Night"
† Season 7, "First Date"
‡ Season 2, "Innocence"
§ Season 7, "Get It Done"
‖ Season 4, "Doomed"

———

Buffy suffers through high school—and then college—while successfully dealing with classmates, clueless teachers, principals, and other adults, and at the same time she keeps the world safe from demons. The series lasted seven seasons, a substantial accomplishment for any television character. And she went out with a bang: the series concluded with not just Buffy, but many girls, heroines in training, becoming victors instead of victims. In the end, she and her universe continue to empower and enable future generations of women.

Interlude: Who's Fictional?

The toughest part of this project is judging who is really fictional.

First, we got complaints about characters people thought were real. Next, other people complained that we were using characters that were obviously fictional, as if we'd set out to debunk a few legends. How dare we include fictional characters? Others just wanted to argue. Sure, some stories are fictional, but King Arthur? Spock?

This is not a scholarly work. You may have guessed from the low price, the absence of obscure characters, and the occasional bit of humor. Still, in scholarly terms, what we think of as deliberately fictional characters do not appear until about the year 1500. Before then, stories were written only about people who were known to have lived or believed likely to have lived. The tales were written to illuminate a known event, using what the characters were likely to have said or what they should have said. Fictional creatures were used to teach morals—Aesop's animal stories and the allegorical "everyman" plays. In these stories, and the Germanic folktales that prepare the child for the larger world, a great many of the characters are general roles—the prince, the old father, the witch, the beauty, the miser—rather than specific people. The modern notion of fiction, a created character just believable enough to be worth reading, dates from about the time of Cervantes. And the transition isn't a clear one. For example, many of Shakespeare's characters were based on real people. And people in our own century continue to produce historical novels about the French Revolution or Roman history. Movies and television programs based on fictional and quasi-fictional characters are also popular.

It's in modern times we develop enough of an interest in character and culture to justify pure fiction. Molière's plays and Dickens's novels depict social stereotypes, not purely fictional characters. But the novels of Eliot, the Brontës, Dumas, Melville, Hardy, and Hawthorne appear in such detail that we can believe we are reading the private lives of actual people. Modern works such as *One Hundred Years of Solitude* are fantastic dreams, full of possibilities, and devotedly fictional. And the Road Runner cartoons exist only to make us laugh.

In this collection, we have genuinely fictional characters like Ebenezer Scrooge, created by novelist Charles Dickens as part of his fight against greedy and corrupt businessmen. Scrooge was another allegorical character, but did Charles Dickens base Scrooge on someone he knew? Was Fred Scrooge a creditor, a landlord, a neighbor who said "Bah, humbug!" on every St. Swithens' Day? When you deal with writers, you find bits of real people here and there. In Woody Allen's film *Deconstructing Harry* (1997), Woody's character Harry Block alienates everyone around him by using their private lives as source material for his books.

If we weren't sure a character was fictional, we asked ourselves what was more important about their life, the facts of their life, or the stories woven around them. When we lose sight of the real person, the character becomes fictional. Finally, if we couldn't find something interesting to write about a character, we dropped it. That's our ultimate decision maker. Reality can be tough, even for fictionals.

14. Comics and Animation

Animation trumps almost every other story form. Peter Pan is a good example. Never mind that he opened on the London stage before our grandparents were born, that Mary Martin made him the star of New York theater, that book versions are sold and films with live actors have been made. Nothing tops Walt Disney's animated version. It's the same with Cinderella. The animated version is the clear winner.

Telling a story with images goes back to the Stone Age, so it's not surprising that we react to it so strongly. In modern times, the simplest form is the newspaper comic, which usually tells a joke in four panels. *Blondie, Beetle Bailey,* and many other strips run every day, and we love them. The comic book was originally just an odd collection of short strips on a newsprint sheet folded in half. These days a comic book has perhaps fifty to two hundred panels per story, a full range of colors, and can run for several dozen issues on a single plot line.

An animated film uses up to 100,000 images and can give every character lifelike motion in glowing color. Animation traces its roots to the Magic Lantern, invented by Kircher about 1645, but the modern process dates to 1909 and artist

Winsor McCay. The first full-length cartoon shown in the United States was *Snow White and the Seven Dwarfs*, 1937, and that launched Disney's long string of classic movies. But there are other characters who were more important.

Mickey Mouse—#18

Walt Disney introduced his most famous character on November 18, 1928, in the first synchronized sound cartoon, *Steamboat Willie.* Mickey became an overwhelming success, overtaking Felix the Cat, and since then he has become an international personality. He was the "cash mouse" who laid the financial foundation for Walt Disney's empire of animated motion pictures, television shows, comics, and theme parks.

Mickey is an American icon held in such high esteem that the federal government changed the copyright laws to protect him. Disney's copyright on Mickey Mouse was due to expire in 2003, but Congress—with him specifically in mind—extended the term of protection for ninety-five years with the Copyright Term Extension Act.

During the 1930s, Mickey Mouse starred in cartoon shorts and became the most charming symbol of the twentieth century—a sympathetic, well-meaning little guy, born out of the Depression, but who satirized people's foibles and taught them to laugh. He always tried to do his best and symbolized all of the good aspects of folks. He was not a social symbol or given over to moralizing. His favorite expressions were, "Oh boy!" "That's swell!" and "Gosh!" He was the symbol of innocence, happiness, and delight. He always had big dreams, and his dreams had universal audience appeal.

Initially, Walt himself supplied Mickey's voice. In 1946, Jimmy MacDonald took over for thirty years, and Wayne Allbright followed.

Walt and his head animator, Ub Iwerks, gave us a mouse that played such roles as aviator, fireman, electrician, plumber, detective, and cowboy. Along the way Disney generated an entire clan of animated characters, including Minnie Mouse, Goofy, Pluto, and Donald Duck.

Mickey Mouse won Disney an Oscar in 1932. In 1935 the League of Nations presented him with a special medal that recognized Mickey as a symbol of universal goodwill.

The peak of Mickey's success came with his starring role as the "Sorcerer's Apprentice" in the feature film *Fantasia* in 1940.

During World War II, Mickey Mouse served his country as the password of the Allied forces on D-Day, June 6, 1944. And he may get to serve his country again: If the number of write-in votes he gets for president gets any higher, he may be elected. We have done worse.

From 1955 to 1959, the *Mickey Mouse Club* was a popular children's television series. The show featured twelve school-age Mouseketeers who sang, danced, acted, and generally entertained us every weekday afternoon. It was the most successful children's show ever presented.

Mickey Mouse moved to Disneyland in 1955 to become chief host of the theme park, welcoming millions of visitors every year. On his first television show from Disneyland, Walt said, with humility, "I hope we never lose sight of the fact that this was all started by a Mouse." In 1971, Mickey helped open the Walt Disney World Resort, including the Magic Kingdom Park, in Florida; in 1983 Tokyo Disneyland opened, followed by Disneyland Paris in 1992.

Mickey is one of the best-known and beloved characters of all time. We thank Walt Disney for Mickey Mouse and all that Mickey represents. He has touched the hearts and minds of almost every child and adult in the Western world.

Betty Boop—#96

In the 1930s, brothers Max and Dave Fleischer created Betty Boop, the most memorable and entertaining female cartoon character ever invented. As no one had before, she brought jazz, drugs, and sexuality to the cartoons of her day. She was the archetypal flapper and the sexiest woman on the screen. Her coy assertiveness helped pave the way for the more liberal attitudes we enjoy today, not only in the magazines that feature the provocative beauty of women, but also in the sexy nature of MTV and nudity in movies, television, and the Broadway stage.

The Fleischer Studios provided cartoons to Paramount, and their Betty challenged the preeminent animated cartoon character of that time—Felix the Cat—as well as the Disney characters that were then emerging.

Betty was one of the first animated cartoon personalities presented as a human, and she was also one of the first to be recognizably female. First drawn by Grim Natwick, she had a slim waist, broad hips, shapely legs, and feminine gestures. She wore a short, sleeveless dress, and in many cartoons the dress came off, leaving her clad only in her sexy underwear. Definitely not children's fare. In one story, she wore only a grass skirt and a lei that swung from side to side and periodically exposed her breasts as she danced a hula. Her stories were meant for adults. Hot stuff.

Betty had no fixed persona although, always sexy and provocative, she was variously depicted as the daughter of a Jewish refugee, a black African, a Samoan, a circus performer, and dozens of other roles. Betty also ran as a daily and Sunday comic strip in the 1930s. Betty was a dumb but endearing character who said such things as, "I guess the people who moved out don't live here anymore."

Some of her cartoons opened with live-action black-and-white film of jazz greats such as Duke Ellington and Cab Calloway, both with their Cotton Club orchestras, and Louis Armstrong and his orchestra. After they performed, the film transitioned into an animated story, with the 'toons often imitating the stylized posture and movements of the live performers.

Several of the cartoons referred to drugs. Don Redman sang "Chant of the Weed" and Cab Calloway sang about "kicking the gong"—smoking opium.

In the story entitled "Boop-Oop-A-Doop," Betty is a circus performer. Her act is so hot that after a performance, the ringmaster follows her into her tent and tries to force himself upon her. Fortunately, Koko the Clown comes to her rescue. Then he whispers something in her ear and she replies, "No! He couldn't take my boop-oop-a-doop away!"

Betty often said or sang the ambiguous expression "boop-oop-a-doop." It was the hallmark of her virginal but sensuous approach to life.

Alas, in 1935, Congress passed the Hays Act to desexualize the media, and Betty Boop morphed into an array of unprovocative sexless characters. Her dress, now extended well below her knees, had a high collar and long sleeves. Betty's career might have ended with her last cartoon in 1939, but she persisted in a long string of broadcasts on children's television in the 1950s, extending her run to about thirty years. In 1988, she appeared in *Who Framed Roger Rabbit*.

Betty was a pioneer in animation as well as women's rights, and she introduced black jazz musicians to a large audience.

Those of you attracted by the Snow White approach to life, please join the line on the left and await the next appearance of Prince Charming. The rest of you, please join us on the right and "boop-oop-a-doop."

Buck Rogers—#84

Rocket ships and ray guns are such staples of science fiction that few remember when they first appeared. Fans of *Star Trek* and *Star Wars* might be astonished to learn that they emerged in the pulp fiction about Buck Rogers.

Philip Francis Nowlan created the character in 1928 in the story *Armageddon 2419 A.D.* Buck Rogers was an instant success, and his adventures triggered a large audience reaction to the entire science fiction genre—especially boys growing up during the Depression—readers who sought escape in cheap novels, comics, and a future in which anything would be possible.

Buck Rogers burst on the scene through a Rip Van Winkle–like mechanism. He fell into unconsciousness in the twentieth century when he was overcome by fumes in an abandoned mine. The gas also served to preserve him in suspended animation for five hundred years. When he emerged from his stupor, America had been taken over by Mongols. And, as was true in Woody Allen's film *Sleeper,* the character—a relic from the forgotten past—is recruited by the resistance and with him they are able to catalyze the defeat of the tyrants.

Following the liberation of his home, Buck participates in adventures involving alien attacks, space travel, and many other features that are now standard sci-fi fare.

Thanks to a receptive audience, Buck Rogers became the inspiration for an entire generation. And with the improving economy after the end of World War II, Americans found an outlet for their dreams in the space program during the 1960s and 1970s. After that, Buck Rogers's technology, considered extraordinary during the Depression, now set the standard for science fiction novels, comics, TV programs, and movies.

Buck Rogers and Flash Gordon are frequently lumped together. Their first-run lifespans overlapped during the Depression. Buck Rogers's adventures started as serial novels in pulp magazines and migrated to comics, whereas Flash Gordon—another science fiction space adventurer—got his start in comics and moved in the reverse direction to novels. They both kindled the imaginations of teenage boys starved for adventure. Girls were there, but only along for the ride. Buck Rogers was in the driver's seat.

A short Buck Rogers movie was shown at the Chicago World's Fair in 1933–1934. Republic Pictures produced a movie serial of twelve episodes starring Buster Crabbe (of Flash Gordon fame) in 1939. This was later edited and released in 1953 as the movie *Planet Outlaws* and in 1965 on television as *Destination Saturn*. A radio show ran from 1932 until 1947, while the comic strip started in 1929 and continued to 1967. A live-action television series appeared in the 1950–51 season.

But as the real space program satisfied our need for adventure, Buck Rogers moved into the background until 1979, when a third movie launched a new television series, with a nuclear holocaust replacing Asian warlords as the agent of destruction. Buck Rogers morphed into a space shuttle pilot who was frozen for five hundred years following a space accident. Interest in a renewed comic book and newspaper comic strip followed. In 1990, a series of illustrated novels appeared. Other spin-offs included several novels, a board game, and a video game produced first for arcades and later released for the first generation of home computers.

During the course of fifty years, Buck Rogers has fueled the imagination of a generation that dreamed of expanding our world. And they, in turn, inspired the next generation into real-life space adventures. More than any other fictional character, Buck Rogers can properly lay claim to be the godfather of the Space Age.

Superman—#64

June 1938 introduced Superman, in the dangerous days before the start of World War II. Sixty-five years later, *People* magazine honored him as one of the top icons of the twentieth century.

His creators, Jerry Siegel and Joe Shuster—two kids in Cleveland—came up with the character on a hot night in 1932. They combined all the strongmen they knew into one character, made him impervious to bullets and able to leap great heights. A man of action, in his first appearance he smashes through the doors of the governor's mansion to get a pardon for an innocent woman facing execution.

They had a hard time selling their work, and six years later, Siegel and Shuster were paid just $130 for signing away the rights to Superman. Don't feel sorry for them. Times were hard—unemployment was about 25 percent in the United States—and these two boys were lucky to become employees of National Periodicals.

In those days comics were among the lowest of pulp fiction, but Superman hit big and his success created a mass market. "Comic books" had started as cheap collections of picture jokes but had branched out into action, romance, crime, and horror. The comic book as we know it today—illustrated tales of a continuing character—owes its success to Superman. Within three years he had the bestselling comic book in the Unites States and ran as a daily strip in 230 newspapers. His popularity spread worldwide, and the Man of Steel starred in several titles plus a prequel—*Superboy*. Superman spawned a rush of second-string superheroes and spin-off series featuring his cousin Supergirl and his pals Jimmy Olsen and Lois Lane.

The basic myth of Superman was present in the very first pages: infant son of a Kryptonian scientist, sent to Earth by rocket ship just before their world was destroyed. He was adopted by Midwestern farmers and soon developed great abilities. Superman has every quality a young boy wishes for—strength, speed, invulnerability. Flying, x-ray vision, and heat-vision were added later. So too was his sole vulnerability—kryptonite, chunks of his home planet. Anything connected with home is trouble. There's green kryptonite—which can kill—and several other colors, each with its own effect.

The Superman story fits the standard hero format: a heavenly child is sent away from danger, is raised in poor surroundings, and proves to be a great asset to his new family. Note that Luke Skywalker was raised by his uncle, a farmer, just as Superman was raised by Martha and Jonathan Kent, also farmers. Jesus saves his believers by providing a path to Heaven; Superman saves the world from monsters, natural disasters, and criminals, repeatedly, several times a month for more than sixty years. Face it—we do need a lot of saving.

He doesn't quite fit the single exploit hero, though. He loses his father in his teens in most versions, but he doesn't find that key magic helper, such as Obi-Wan Kenobi or a fairy godmother. No wonder he has to work so hard.

Superman generally doesn't do very well socially. He's reserved with everyone he meets, burdened by his secret identity and busy schedule. As Clark Kent, his alter ego, he's never in touch with his real self. He's mild-mannered, clumsy, and shy. He's got the social skills of a squid, as if he's from another planet. Wait. He is.

He has no success with women (faster than a speeding bullet—yep), although in several newer versions he settles down with Lois Lane, the love of his mature years.

Superman is the embodiment of the yes-man, devoted to authority from the start. He's a nice fellow here to help out, a devoted citizen from the first issue. After several years on radio, Superman made the jump to television in 1951. Played by George Reeves, Superman defended "Truth, justice, and the American way." More recently, he's the star of several movies and television series, including *Lois & Clark* and the more recent *Smallville*. DC Comics generally has at least two Superman series going, but between new plot lines, spin-offs, and specials, it could be more than a dozen. He's still a major player in the entertainment industry. Still going strong.

Maybe You Didn't Know

Superman's Kryptonian name is Kal-El and his father was Jor-El.

Superman has been played by George Reeves and Christopher Reeve.

Superman cartoons done by the Max Fleischer Studio (1941) are generally rated as the best Superman animation and the best work to come out of that studio.

Super-abilities: You can see bones in your hand by red light, a poor sort of x-ray vision, and the heat from the eyes does project outward as a very weak sort of heat-vision. Dreams of flying are common, but most people can only fly straight down.

To learn more about Superman, we suggest

A Smithsonian Book of Comic-Book Comics, edited by Michael Barrier, M., and Martin Williams.

The World Encyclopedia of Comics, volume 2, edited by Maurice Horn.

The Great Comic Book Heroes by Jules Feiffer.

Comic Book Nation, The Transformation of Youth Culture in America by B. W. Wright.

The Death of Superman by Simonson, Louise, et al.

Bambi—#41

Usually it is not a good idea to make enemies of people with guns. But you can get away with it if you have Walt Disney on your side. The Italian word *bambino* is the origin of the name of the ungainly and winningly innocent deer that stars in the 1942 animated film *Bambi*. The character quickly became the rallying point of the antihunting circle. This one deer has polarized modern society into the nature lovers versus animal hunters. And it is the hunters who are on the retreat.

In Disney's film, Bambi is hailed as the "Prince of the Forest" when he is born. As a young deer, he makes friends with the other small animals of the forest, especially Thumper, a rabbit. However, Disney's dreamscape is shattered when hunters arrive and kill Bambi's mother. This awkward spindly fawn grows up very quickly, discovers love, and outlasts the hunters, who are destroyed by a runaway fire of their own making.

Disney claimed that this was his favorite of his films, and audiences overwhelmingly agree. With the success of the movie, the whole of nature has become personified by a single deer. Bambi speaks initially with the squeaky voice of a child, and both children and adults empathize with him and appreciate the simple pleasures of his woodland home.

The film was an instant hit, providing a clear escape from the horrors of World War II, which was raging at the time the film was first released. It is still a classic, still disarming hunters. Even died-in-the-flannel hunters know that Bambi is off-limits or they will be branded Bambi-killers.

The story first appeared in print in 1923. It was titled *Bambi: A Life in the Woods* by Felix Salten, the pen name of Siegmund Salzmann, a Hungarian raised in Vienna. It is worth noting that much of Europe had been heavily settled by then, to the exclusion of the larger predators that might have threatened Bambi. Without appreciable numbers of wolves and bears, the forest was no longer a place of drama and danger, but a resting place for birds, deer, rabbits, and weary city-dwellers. Europe was still struggling to recover from the horrific devastation of World War I, and this story might have been intended as a thinly veiled manifesto against killing of all sorts.

The story reached America in 1928, translated by Whittaker Chambers (see sidebar). In 1936, the Nazis banned the book, recognizing its antimilitaristic implications. Salten escaped to Switzerland, and died there after the war.

The novelist Thomas Mann introduced the story to Walt Disney, who translated the tale into the sentimental movie that has enchanted generations of children. It premiered in London on August 8, 1942, and in the United States five days later. The movie has only nine hundred words of dialogue, using visuals rather than voice to establish both the story and the underlying message. Disney retained Salten's depiction of the simple beauty of nature and the intrusive, disruptive cruelty of man. The American Rifleman Association and other prohunting organizations have attempted to protest the film's harsh representation of hunters, to little success.

Bambi continues to shield wild animals—both prey and predators—from culling by human hunters, thereby leaving them to their own and nature's harsh devices. This whitewashing of the real world of nature—"red in tooth and claw," to use Tennyson's expression—continues to blind many of us to the cruel realities of the world. Such is the power of Bambi.

The Disney organization has capitalized on the appeal of Bambi as it has on its other successes: They market small statues of Bambi and his girlfriend, Faline, which remind the audience of the appeal of the two characters and extend the influence beyond the movie. Bambi thereby entered many American households well before the invention of the DVD, and his influence extends well beyond opposition to hunting. It is not unreasonable to suggest that the entire vegetarian, antivivisection, and animal rights movements owe a considerable debt to the influence of Bambi.

Maybe You Didn't Know

The translator of Bambi was the same Whittaker Chambers who was the accuser in the Alger Hiss spy case brought to national attention by . . . Richard Nixon, later president.

15. Commerce

The advertising geniuses of Madison Avenue are the ultimate in persuasion. A few images of how grand life would be with their brand of fish sticks, and we're ready to buy. In the usual advertisement, it's a real person who gives the sales pitch, but a fictional spokesman has several advantages. Take the Michelin Man: He may not be handsome, but he's never going to change brands. He won't get arrested in a sex scandal, demand higher pay, collect residuals, or grow old. Captain Morgan, the buccaneer of rum, will never be brought to court on piracy charges, and Ernie, the Keebler Elf, will not gain weight, no matter how many cookies he eats.

There are hundreds of such untiring salesmen, and we certainly can't mention them all. We didn't include Mr. Clean, Mr. Whipple, or the California Raisins. We didn't include the various soap girls of the 1900s and such classics as Aunt Jemima, Tony the Tiger, Josephine the Plumber, and Ronald McDonald. We include two from the tobacco industry, however, because they really do deserve our attention.

This chapter looks at the three most influential commercial characters and examines their history and effect. Two icons in this chapter clearly altered the buying habits of many people over a long course of time. One changed the image and expectations of women in our society, the other killed thousands of people. There's no question that their impression on society has been huge.

The Marlboro Man—#1

Dawn. Purple haze punctuated by swirls of frost as red cattle move in the darkness. Heat from the great beasts. An orange glow nearby. A burly man holds fire in his hand, brings it to his face, and breathes it in as a ruddy glow stretches across the sky. Congratulations. You've just met the most famous killer of the last two hundred years: The cigarette. Welcome—to Marlboro country.

Advertising Age picked the Marlboro Man as the most powerful brand image of the twentieth century and one of the top advertising campaigns of that era. Previously marketed by Philip Morris tobacco as a ladies brand of cigarette called "Mild as May," Marlboro's new image boosted its sales fourfold from 1955 to 1957, and by 1972 it had become the top cigarette brand both in the nation and the world. In 2000, its market share was 35 percent of U.S. cigarette sales, outselling the six next most popular brands *combined*. Winston had only 5 percent of market share; Camel 5 percent; Salem 3 percent.

Between 20 and 30 percent of the U.S. population now smokes, down from about 40 percent of the population in the 1950s. According to the CDC, deaths attributed to smoking total about 440,000 per year in the United States, plus another 9 million serious illnesses (1995–1999). Marlboro has held at least a third of U.S. cigarette sales for decades, at times as high as 46 percent of the market. By the end of the twenty-first century, the Marlboro Man will have triggered thousands of American deaths. Why not millions? Be patient. Lung cancer takes years to develop—forty years, fifty, sixty. So the kids who started smoking in 1957 are just starting to wheeze into the cancer wards.

Tobacco is perhaps the only product you buy knowing that its intended use will cause cancer, emphysema, heart disease, and stroke. Nicotine, the natural stimulant responsible for tobacco's kick, is a powerfully addictive substance. Of all cigarette smokers trying to quit in any year, only 1 in 40 succeed. But we are a determined lot, and there are roughly 50 million smokers and 50 million former smokers in the United States.

Why do we start? Advertising doesn't merely inform us of price and performance, it tells us what products make us successful and attractive. In the late 1950s, advertising men Jack Landry and Leo Burnett tried several approaches to boost Marlboro sales. Burnett is generally accredited with the creation of the Marlboro Man as we know him today, the cowboy. This was exactly what adolescents wanted to be—tough, independent, and free of their parents. Burnett wanted the strongest male image for his campaign, and that's the cowboy. And thus the Marlboro Man came into existence, not to sell trips to Wyoming but to plant the idea that the right brand of tobacco would give you independence and strength.

In 1987 David Millar died; in July 1992 Wayne McLaren departed this life; and in October 1995 David McLean followed. Who were they? Men from the Marlboro ads. The original Marlboro man and two other actors used for the role.

They died from emphysema and lung cancer. Did you have to ask?

To learn more about the Marlboro Man, we suggest
The Image-Makers by William Meyers.
The Want Makers: The World of Advertising: How They Make You Buy by Eric Clark.
Advertising Age Magazine, "The Advertising Century."
McMurty, Larry. "Death of the Cowboy", *The New York Review of Books*, volume 46, 17.

Barbie—#43

The role model for little girls everywhere, the most popular doll in the world, Barbie was created as an alternative to the infant and toddler dolls of the early 1950s. By today's standards, Barbie is a ridiculous extreme, ultra thin and impossibly pretty. But half a century ago, most dolls were lumpy infants. Adult and teen dolls existed, but mostly as expensive figurines for adults or cheap paper cutouts for children. Nothing in the middle. Ruth Handler, disappointed in the dolls her daughter was playing with, approached her husband with an idea for a fashion doll with the proportions of an adult woman. The doll would be named for their daughter, Barbara, and made of plastic. The Handlers and Harold Matson owned a plastics company, Mattel Creations, but they had doubts that such a toy could be made affordably. Ruth persisted and found a German novelty doll named Lilli that was close to her idea. That proved it could be done.

In 1959, the toy that debuted was sleek, saucy, and sophisticated: teenage Fashion Model Barbie. Soon she'd be a commercial icon, one of the bestselling, if not the top doll, for more than forty years, about a *billion* made.

To attain and hold her popularity, Barbie has gone through several physical transformations, changing with the culture. At first she was almost as sultry as the German Lilli (who was not a child's doll but an adult party gift). The full figure, sunken cheekbones, and pursed lips of the Parisian haute couture Barbie of 1959 quickly evolved into a slim doll with a more girlish athletic body, a plainer face, and the wholesome grin of a Midwestern cheerleader.

This doll was not about satisfying the ambitions of motherhood. Barbie's career interests have gone through far wider transformations, from Malibu Barbie to Astronaut Barbie, to surgeon, swimmer, executive . . . just about everything. An overachiever, if ever there was one.

She has careers and clothes without limit.

Clothes, especially. Barbie first appeared in a striped one-piece swimsuit with ten or more fashionable outfits illustrated on the box. The clothing sold the doll, and then you just *had* to buy all the accessories, an endless vicious cycle known to every parent. A hundred new outfits a year, all a woman could want. And the car, the playhouse, the beach house, sunglasses. The girl has everything.

She embodies a new sort of physical ideal. Barbie's not a mother-goddess. She doesn't have the heavy hips of heavy responsibilities. The trailer-park Barbie with three menial jobs and a dozen kids is not one you're going to find in Toys "R" Us or any place else. She's still a girl. Barbie's world is about the limitless possibilities of youth. Parents aren't important: she has none. Children—well, none that we know of. The emphasis has always been on clothes, fun, cars, friends, and boyfriends.

It's not mere coincidence that Barbie appears in the era of beach-blanket movies and *Playboy* magazine. The nation was enjoying a burst of prosperity after thirty years of depression and war.

Barbie dolls sold for $3 in 1959, and a vintage Barbie will easily run you $500–$5000 nowadays. Few characters on our list are so reflective of our commercial culture and its obsession with material goods, youth, beauty, and thinness. Part of Barbie's importance is that she distills the aspirations of America down to an eleven-inch rod of plastic.

Barbie holds a place of honor in the Dwight D. Eisenhower Library in Abilene, Kansas, as one of America's achievements in his two-term presidency. There was a Barbie Hall of Fame in Palo Alto with more than twenty thousand dolls (and who knows how many outfits?).

But there's another side to Barbie. Almost as much as she is admired for her success, Barbie is despised for being too perfect, for setting unreachable goals, for thoughtless sexism, materialism, and selfish political and social amorality. She's banned in Saudi Arabia. She has been blamed for waves of bulimia and diet disorders. She's seen as a figure of sterile oppressive intolerant affluence. There's even said to be a Barbie Liberation Organization. Lot of good that'll do.

Barbie made the news in 2004. She and longtime companion Ken announced they would be going their separate ways.

Successful woman, on her own after a forty-year relationship. Maybe she's not so far from the real world after all.

Maybe You Didn't Know

- Trailer-Park Barbie is a parody title. So far.
- Barbie has at least two videos.
- Barbie is in the Smithsonian Institution's Legacies collection.
- Ken had a makeover in 2006.
- Barbie's versions include Malibu, Mexican, Malaysian, Moroccan, and Nigerian.

Joe Camel—#78

Joe Camel debuted in the late 1980s, a cartoon character, and the last of only three commercial icons on our list. He's unique in appearance and mission, for Joe Camel can be interpreted as nothing less than a set of male genitals sandwiched between a tuxedo and a pair of sunglasses. His assignment was equally obscene: He sold cigarettes to children.

Sex in advertising is nothing new. A Coca-Cola ad from 1906 features a waitress in a low-cut dress. Attractive women in bikinis pose atop motorcycles and work the auto shows in satin gowns. In the 1960s, subliminal advertising techniques were made famous in Vance Packard's consumer caution book *The Hidden Persuaders*. Camel cigarettes had long been accused of placing the image of a nude, erect man within the front quarters of the realistically drawn camel that appears on every cigarette pack. We don't see *that* image as anything other than a camel.

Joe Camel was deliberate, in several senses of the term. Perhaps the character started out as an accident, but certainly, no camel looks like that. Joe's rubbery jowls bulge at just about the right position, and the bulk of his nose is very much like a limp phallus. This emblem of male chic sits between two other stylish elements: a nifty pair of dark sunglasses and a jacket, usually a dinner jacket or tuxedo that would do James Bond credit. Holding a pool cue or a saxophone, Joe is the epitome of cool. He's in the nightclub, he's attracting a lady, he's playing jazz, he's IT. Gotta have that cigarette.

The so-called teen market has been estimated at a billion packs per year. It now appears that RJ Reynolds Tobacco saw its market share among teen smokers slipping and decided as early as the 1970s to target an even younger population. Preteen cigarette sales are minimal, but in time these kids have both the cash and the inclination to buy cigarettes. Brilliant, but not unique. Hess Gasoline still sells model trucks to kids, and children play with Matchbox Mustangs and assemble plastic models of PT Cruisers and other cars a decade before they can drive. But cigarettes? In 1994, Joe Camel was the advertising character most often recognized by children ten to seventeen years old. Even six-year-olds recognized the Camel with his cigarette. Their brand loyalty had been set in stone long before they made their first purchase.

The ad campaign was a brazen gamble that paid off, but it couldn't last. The public's resistance to the character was nearly immediate—not to the pornography, which went unchallenged, but to the use of cartoon characters in cigarette advertising.

With the discovery of memos establishing that tobacco companies were deliberately targeting children, lawsuits blossomed left and right. In 1997, the Federal Trade Commission got into the act, and soon, at least in the United States, the character was gone and the lawsuits began to settle. The impact, however, is permanent. As we all know, a really good advertisement, whether it's selling Anacin, Alka-Seltzer, Gilbey's Gin, or Lucky Strikes, stays with us for years.

This character, for nearly a decade, was one of the few male seminudes in advertising, an approach also used with much more modesty in Calvin Klein and other blue jeans commercials, a step to equal exploitation. Joe revitalized the "hook-'em-early" strategy used decades earlier by car and oil companies. Joe Camel has been called the Pied Piper of Emphysema. In 2013, the five-year-olds of 1997 will be old enough to legally buy cigarettes. Which brand do you think they're going to buy?

16. Propaganda

Each of the characters in this chapter was created to sell an idea to an unsuspecting public. Maybe we should call it political advertising. Big Brother is the villain of the terrifying story *Nineteen Eighty-Four* by George Orwell. Look around you, and you'll see evidence of his world. Big Brother would have loved the Patriot Act. If the political process in our country is moving toward an Orwellian nightmare, we can't say we weren't warned.

Rosie the Riveter, as American as apple pie, influenced American opinion and brought women into the workforce, for a while, anyway. And Smokey Bear certainly called our attention to protecting our forests, but the actions taken in his name proved to be more dangerous than the original problem.

Do any other characters belong in this chapter? Sure. We could include Dr. Strangelove and Godzilla, who both helped sell nuclear disarmament; William Tell, who became a national symbol for Switzerland; and our own Uncle Sam; and Uncle Tom, Nora Helmer, King Arthur, Macbeth, and many more. Perhaps you have your own candidate. Let us know.

Smokey Bear—#21

Smokey Bear is the mascot of the fire prevention strategy adopted by the Forest Service for close to a century. But the USDA Forest Service has pursued a broader, misguided, strategy—fire *suppression*—and the two strategies have been confused, creating serious problems.

The Smokey Bear campaign actually predated the adoption of the mascot. During World War II, we realized that wood was a crucial wartime resource, and the Forest Service adopted protection of the public forests—fire suppression—as a priority. Enter Smokey Bear in May 1950. He was a three-month-old cub, fleeing a fire. Ray Bell, a local forest service official, adopted him and nursed him back to health. By the time the cub was relocated to a zoo in Washington, D.C., the forest fire prevention campaign had been retooled around him with the tag line "Only you can prevent forest fires."

". . . Suppression tactics became so effective by the 1970s that the U.S. Forest Service boasted it could stop wildfires by 10 A.M. the day after ignition." (Jay Lininger, Klamath-Siskiyou newsletter, Spring 2001.)

It was only with the growth of ecological concerns in the last two decades or so that the problems with the fire suppression strategy have been discussed. "We need to change our ways of thinking about fires," notes Michael Castagnola, a firefighter with the San Francisco Fire Department.*

As John Kitzhaber, governor of Oregon, stated (*The Christian Science Monitor,* June 27, 2002), "For decades we've been

---

* www.tompaine.com/feature2.cfm/ID/6131, "Smokey Bear Got It Wrong."

suppressing wildfires that used to naturally thin many of our forests. The unfortunate result, however, has been to raise the potential for dangerously large and intense wildfires." This is because the material that doesn't burn in small fires accumulates and feeds much larger fires.

Controlled burns, adopted gradually as a maintenance mechanism over the years, do not solve all these problems. Forests are dynamic, living systems, not static objects. The life of the trees in the forest, in many cases, actually depends on fires. As Stephen J. Pyne wrote, "Fire shapes the forest."* Many varieties of plants have evolved that require exposure to fire as the trigger to set and spread their seeds into the newly nourished and prepared ground. In the absence of fire, these plants grow old and die without reproducing. Animals that feed off the fresh growth from such plants lose nourishment. Tinder accumulates rather than recycles, setting the stage for a devastating fire.

People, to escape the congestion of cities, have moved into expensive houses out in the suburbs, close to the forests. The success of Smokey Bear's fire *prevention* campaign, perceived as a successful fire *suppression* campaign, has lured people to build in harm's way. The eruption of major fires close to houses began to expose the defects with the fire suppression strategy.

A year after the Yellowstone fires of 1988 lit a firestorm of criticism in the U.S. Congress, a new discovery was made: fire is not an unmitigated evil. Visitors to Yellowstone noticed the new growth and some could not even identify where the fires had burned. Behind the scenes, both plant

* *Fire: A Brief History.* (See sidebar.)

and animal life had quickly begun to recolonize the burned landscape, resulting in an ecology that, if anything, was healthier than it had been before. According to the Fire Ecology home page, "The supposedly catastrophic results that the public came to believe and fear were greatly exaggerated by the media."

As George Wuerthner wrote (*Cascadia Fire Ecology Education Project,* 1994), "Large fires are not disasters, nor do they damage the land. Rather, they are an essential part of the ecological setting that no amount of suppression can ultimately prevent—nor should we want to. . . . Without fires, dead material accumulates, locking up essential nutrients necessary for plant growth. Fires release these nutrients, and enhance the production of nitrogen-fixing plants that often revegetate recently burned areas. Fires are thus analogous to river floods that each year provide a new layer of life-giving soil for plant growth. . . . Fires also cleanse forests. Many tree pathogens are killed just by the smoke. . . . Some species like the Ponderosa pine, Douglas fir, western larch, Jeffrey pine, and sequoia are specifically adapted to survive fires by having a thick bark, and tall limbless trunks which protect them from small, quick burns. . . . Smokey lied. Studies have shown that under natural fire conditions, few wildlife species or individuals are hurt."

Smokey Bear died in 1976. It is long past time to retire the fire suppression campaign founded on the presumption that fire is a controllable evil. It is, in fact, neither. Smokey Bear raised national awareness to the value and delicacy of natural lands, and he may have inspired much of the environmental concerns that try to preserve wilderness areas. The Forest Service may have meant well, but Smokey's negative influence on the nation's public forests has been enormous.

It's Official

Title 16 of *The United States Code* section 580p declares the name and character *Smokey Bear*—no *the* in the middle—to be the property of the United States. The Forest Service collects fees for use of the character and is required to use those fees to help fight forest fires.

Stephen J. Pyne, who teaches at Arizona State University West in Phoenix, is recognized as the world's leading authority on wildfire.

Rosie the Riveter—#28

Rosie the Riveter was the icon of one of the most successful propaganda campaigns ever conducted by our federal government. In 1940, the traditional belief among Americans was that women belonged at home and not in the workplace. However, as we inducted more and more working men into the armed forces during World War II, the government knew that women would have to fill the men's jobs, especially in war-related industries. The drive was so successful it drew more than 6 million women into jobs formerly held by men.

The challenge was to overcome the strong male-oriented bias against women's employment, so women were recruited only when it became a necessity. Therefore, a woman taking a defense job was portrayed as fulfilling her patriotic duty by working to benefit the country's war effort. At first, only single women were targeted—married women were likely to be mothers, and the presumption was that a mother's "job" was tending her home and children—but as the war continued, married women, too, were recruited; industry needed as many women as they could get.

The newly formed Office of War Information coordinated the propaganda, and the figure of Rosie the Riveter made the idea of working outside the home acceptable to women. They could "Do the Job He Left Behind." The campaign included billboards of women doing men's work and wearing overalls. In addition, the government encouraged magazines to publish stories about women who worked and were enjoying newfound freedom and financial independence.

During the course of the war, employment for women increased to nearly 20 million, from a prewar figure of 12 million. The portion of the work force filled by women increased from 25 percent in 1941 to 36 percent in 1944. The greatest number of women held factory jobs, but they also worked as bus drivers and mechanics as well as mail deliverers, air traffic controllers, and welders. Inequity in pay continued, however. The average woman's salary in the defense industry was $31.21 a week while men made $54.65.

At the end of the war, male-oriented values were reinstated, and by the summer of 1945 about 75 percent of previously employed women had lost their war-related jobs. By 1946 the number of women still employed had dropped back to prewar levels. Most left the workforce altogether while others returned to the stereotypical women's jobs: secretaries, maids, beauticians, sales clerks, nurses, and waitresses.

There were problems for women who wanted to move into the work force. For the most part, labor unions ignored the rights of working women and actively engaged in forcing them out of their jobs when the war was over. The war department allowed industry to discriminate against black women.

The women's work force began growing again in 1947 and equaled the wartime peak by 1950. But women lost the traditionally male, higher-paying jobs in industries such as iron and steel, automotive, and machinery production. They were pushed back into the lower-paying jobs in light manufacturing and the service industries that had customarily welcomed them. And discrimination in pay continued. In 1950, women earned only 53 percent of what men did.

In the difficult march to equal rights, Rosie's achievement, although intended to be temporary, was a major step in the right direction. She helped pave the way for the next generation of women, who made major moves into jobs that had previously been identified as belonging to men. And their stories inspired their daughters and granddaughters to consider traditionally male careers. Rosie's legacy has clearly been significant.

Did You Know?

The mythical Rosie may have been based on Rose Monroe, a woman who worked at an airplane plant in Michigan. She appeared in a government film campaign to sell war bonds. The movie's poster featured the now-famous picture of Rosie wearing her red bandunna, flexing her muscle. The title read, "We can do it!" From then on, all women who joined the wartime labor force were referred to as Rosie.

Big Brother—#2

Nineteen Eighty-Four quickly became a classic in the world of political/social fiction. Orwell warned us that, without realizing it, we were heading toward totalitarianism. Big Brother was the fearsome master of the welfare state, in which citizens had given up their liberty in expectation of security. Now they had a measure of safety—but the only thing that was certain was their loss of liberty.

Within Orwell's novel, Big Brother is the false front, the reassuring face of the oppressive welfare state, inviting the people to turn over all decisions, all responsibility for their lives to a new master: the bureaucracy.

There are two biblical touches in Orwell's allegory. Just as the elder Esau sells his birthright for a bowl of porridge (Gen., 25), the people in the modern welfare state give up control of their lives for protection and security. And Big Brother is overlain with the taint of Cain, who murdered his brother (Gen., 4). When God asked Cain where Abel was, Cain responded, "Am I my brother's keeper?" In the Bible, the implied answer is yes, you *are* your brother's keeper. In Orwell's novel, Big Brother is your keeper.

With a brother such as Cain, Abel had no need for an enemy. With keepers such as Big Brother, Orwell advises us, we have no need for family of any kind. Unquestioning obedience to the government, he cautions us, ultimately involves turning over responsibility for everything, including thought and love.

Among the most pervasive intrusions of Big Brother into the everyday lives of the citizens was two-way television, with sinister overtones. The broadcasts were strictly controlled by the government and could not be disabled. This was overt brainwashing. The scarier dimension was the other side of that two-way technology: Big Brother constantly monitored the citizens, making privacy almost impossible. "Big Brother Is Watching You" was the ordinary state of things; it was more a threat against individuality than an assurance of protection.

The state argued that it needed to protect its citizens from an enemy, Goldsmith. The enemy was invisible and might not even have existed. This doesn't bother the brainwashed citizens. If they suspected something, there was no record that would contradict today's announcement. History was constantly being rewritten. Big Brother employed vast offices to rewrite newspapers and official records, removing all inconsistencies.

In our own day, two wars—on drugs and on terror—have been used to justify massive intrusions into our private lives. These have been done allegedly in our own interests, the same rationalization that Big Brother exploited.

The father is the usual metaphor for the state, the fatherland, Patria, patriotism. By the middle of the twentieth century, paternalism had earned a bad reputation. So Orwell used a more personable figure, brother rather than father. It is more comfortable having an older brother looking out for you than having a domineering father making your decisions for you. Big Brother's totalitarianism is paternalism softened with a velvet glove.

We all exhaled a sigh of relief when the year 1984 came and went and we saw no obvious trace of Big Brother. And we went about our business as if nothing important had happened.

Nothing important *had* happened. Not on the surface. We had heeded Orwell's warnings and had apparently backed away from the mind-control state he had revealed to us.

Meanwhile, we must remain vigilant. All governments want control, all officials want freedom from embarrassing questions, no person likes to admit a mistake, and few bureaucracies ever will.

Total government supervision is never more than a few steps away. With no new Orwell to warn us, we could yet become a "kept" population of mindlessly obedient nationalists ruled by an ever more intrusive government unable to admit its error. We can only hope that the influence of Big Brother and *Nineteen Eighty-Four* is as strong in years to come as it has been in the past.

17. Television

Television is the most intimate medium. We welcome the characters of our favorite shows into our homes every week. TV shows can go on for years, and we get to know the characters as if they were members of our own families.

It doesn't matter that Perry Mason started in literature, or that *The Ghost and Mrs. Muir* was a movie, or that Neil Simon wrote *The Odd Couple* for the Broadway stage. Once they're on television, nothing else matters—that's what we remember.

Consider the variety of people we invite into our living rooms: Fred Sanford, Estelle Costanza, J. R. Ewing, Sergeant Bilko, Ralph Kramden, Archie Bunker, and Flipper (did we say "people"?).

Television actors frequently find themselves hailed on the street by fans calling them by their character's name. After all, we wouldn't hesitate to greet an old friend. And we trust them like old friends: we ask ourselves what Ben Casey would do for such an illness, or John Carter? What would Perry Mason or Jack McCoy tell us for legal advice? If only the professionals in our own lives were as fast, or as good. Now that's influence.

Perry Mason—#86

Lawyer Joke #1: How many lawyers does it take to stop a run-away bus? Never enough.

Lawyer Joke #2: How many lawyers does it take to roof a house? It depends on how thin you slice them.

We can blame Perry Mason for inspiring several entire generations of lawyers in their chosen profession, and the appearance of Erle Stanley Gardner's character on television amplified that inspiration. Perry Mason is the most famous fictional lawyer. Gardner created him without any character flaws and placed him in contrived situations, engineered to enable him to trap the villain in novel and interesting ways. The repeated embarrassment of District Attorney Hamilton Burger and LAPD lieutenant Arthur Tragg was just gravy.

Lawyer Joke #3: If I had but one life to give for my country, it would be a lawyer's.

Lawyer Joke #4: How do you stop a lawyer from drowning? Shoot him first.

Perry Mason first appeared in 1933, in *The Case of the Velvet Claws,* and continued in print until *The Case of the Postponed Murder* in 1973. In between, he was featured in eighty-five books and four anthologies of stories and novelettes. A radio series was broadcast from 1944 to 1955. The television series (271 episodes) ran from 1957 to 1966, and was revived for the 1973–74 season. There were also six full-length Perry Mason films.

Lawyer Joke #5: Four out of five doctors say that if they were stranded on a deserted island with no lawyers, they wouldn't need any pain killers.

The prospect of fulfilling the destiny of any savior or rescuing the innocent from their persecutors might have driven the career choice of many people. Change *persecutors* to *prosecutors* and the path is clear: become a criminal defense lawyer and you will save people, make money, and gain a popular reputation all at the same time. There's no downside. All the lawyer jokes came later. Well actually, lawyer jokes can be traced back to the Roman Empire.

Erle Stanley Gardner (1889–1970) was himself a practicing lawyer before turning to writing. Besides his Perry Mason stories, he published more than twenty-five novels about the detective team of Lam and Cool under the pseudonym A. A. Fair. He also founded the Court of Last Resort, forerunner of the Innocence Project—an organization to aid people falsely accused of a crime. Gardner died in 1970, but the Perry Mason legend continues.

Lawyer Joke #6: The trouble with the legal profession is that 98 percent of its members give the rest a bad name.

The basic scenario of a Perry Mason story is simple and consistent. A sympathetic innocent person becomes the victim of circumstantial evidence following a murder. Perry Mason, with the help of private investigator Paul Drake, arrives at the crucial evidence that not only clears their client, but also exposes the true killer. This person, who is usually on the witness stand when the evidence is revealed, ignores his Fifth Amendment right against self-incrimination and boasts that he did it, and is glad he did it. The episode concludes with the freed client celebrating with Mason, Drake, and Della Street, Mason's secretary. All the loose ends are tied up.

> Lawyer Joke #7: Anytime a lawyer is seen but not heard, it's a shame to wake him.

> Lawyer Joke #8: If a lawyer and an IRS agent were both drowning and you could only save one of them, would you go to lunch or read the paper?

As Perry Mason, Raymond Burr brought certain key qualities to the TV show. His imposing physique immediately impressed Gardner during the initial process of casting. Gardner is reported to have reacted strongly and favorably when Burr entered the room during the casting phase. Burr rode the success of the legal TV drama, establishing both the character of the most popular defense lawyer and the TV lawyer genre. His imprint can be felt in lawyer shows from (not a complete list) *The Defenders* to *Matlock* to *L.A. Law* to *Ally McBeal, The Practice,* and *Boston Legal.*

> Lawyer Joke #9: A busload of lawyers was hijacked. The hijackers announced that until their demands were met, they would release one lawyer every hour.

> Lawyer Joke #10: And God said, "Let there be Satan, so people don't blame everything on me. And let there be lawyers, so people don't blame everything on Satan."

The public attraction of the Perry Mason series echoed that of Sherlock Holmes: audiences enjoyed the game and delighted in the surprise endings and plot twists. They challenged themselves to guess the real criminal before Mason exposed him in the courtroom. And the strength of Mason's character etched an important positive image on the public perception of lawyers.

Lawyer Joke #11: Diogenes went to look for an honest lawyer. "How's it going?" he was asked. "Not too bad," he replied. "I still have my lantern."

Diogenes might have stopped looking if he had encountered Perry Mason.

You Have the Right

A poll of TV viewers conducted in 2001 by FindLaw Inc. (findlaw.com) revealed that Perry Mason is the favorite TV lawyer, the one people would most want defending them in court.

Archie Bunker—#32

Archie Bunker was the unabashed, ignorant loudmouth of Norman Lear's television sitcom *All in the Family*, a controversial comedy set in Queens, New York. The show centered on a reactionary blue-collar worker played by Carroll O'Connor.

The program started on CBS in January 1971, and by May of that year it was the top-rated series on television. It held that spot for five consecutive seasons. O'Connor won four Emmy Awards as Archie, and the show itself won four Emmys before it ended its run in 1983.

The show surprised, shocked, and offended almost everyone. Archie looked down on anyone different from him—anyone who wasn't a white Anglo-Saxon Protestant. The social changes occurring in America at the time confounded him. To Archie, gains by minorities came at the expense of him and other lower middle-class whites.

He denigrated all minorities: Italians, blacks, Poles, Hispanics, Jews. He was also against women's rights, anything beyond housework and child rearing. He backed up his intolerant opinions by saying that God agreed with him, that is, his own brand of god: white and American.

Archie brought our subconscious attitudes of intolerance and injustice to the surface, and he raised issues in a way that everyone could find distasteful. Conservatives thought the show made fun of them, and liberals contended that the program promoted bigotry.

Norman Lear, the creator of the show, didn't condone bigotry and hoped that the program contributed to improvement in the attitudes of Americans. However, in reality, Archie seems to have fired up the right wing and contributed to their political success in the twenty-first century.

Archie worked on a loading dock and also drove a cab, earning just enough to support his family: his wife Edith, whom he called "dingbat," their daughter Gloria, and her husband Michael Stivic, a closed-minded liberal Archie called "Meathead." Archie expressed what ultraconservative white people said behind closed doors on topics such as rape and poverty (the victims were to blame), homosexuality (perverts), militia groups (real Americans), welfare recipients (cheats who took hard-earned money out of his pocket), college students (all pinko Communists), and support for the Vietnam War (real patriotism).

When his socially tolerant, long-suffering wife, Edith, expressed an opinion, Archie invariably told her, "Stifle yourself." Edith was slow-witted, but not stupid. On the other hand, she was as ditzy as they come. While giving directions to a friend over the phone she asked, "Can you see Northern Boulevard from where you are? You can? Then you're lost."

Every minority character on the show was smarter than Archie, and he spent as much time with his foot in his mouth as one of his beloved cigars. We all saw that everyone Archie engaged and vilified got the upper hand. The audience knew it. Mike and Gloria knew it. Even Edith knew it. The only one who didn't know it was Archie, and that was the source of the show's irony.

Archie sat in his shabby, overstuffed green armchair and from that throne he held court and moralized. So central was this prop that it now resides in the permanent collection of the Smithsonian Institution in Washington, D.C.

We can think of no better way to characterize Archie than with his own words:

"Well, I'll tell you one thing about President Nixon. He kept Pat home. Which was where Roosevelt should have kept Eleanor. Instead he let her run around loose until one day she discovered the colored. We never knew they were there. She told them they were gettin' the short end of the stick and we been having trouble ever since."

"Tore, Feldman, O'Reilly, Nelson. That's an Italian, a Jew, an Irishman, and a regular American. That's what I call a balanced ticket."

"It ain't supposed to make sense; it's faith. Faith is something you believe that nobody in his right mind would believe."

Archie Bunker's ethnic insensitivity is still with us. It is alive and well, and it courses through the grassroots during each presidential election campaign.

Captain Kirk and Mr. Spock—#50

James T. Kirk, captain of the *Starship Enterprise,* is the most brilliant military tactician of the twenty-third century. He's a leader solving problems far from home, a hero of a new golden age that awaits us.

Kirk is the focal point of *Star Trek,* the first serious science-fiction series on prime-time television. It was our first exposure to science fiction as something other than battles with blobs, flying saucers, and giant spiders from Mars. *Star Trek*'s creator, Gene Roddenberry, envisioned the expansion of American culture into the year 2251 and beyond. The series portrayed Earth as a strong, peaceful, and prosperous civilization reaching out to the stars. The show's influence was such that a prototype U.S. space shuttle was named for Kirk's starship, *Enterprise.*

Star Trek's optimism was exactly the cure for the fears of its time, 1967, the height of the Cold War, with mutually assured destruction and Dr. Strangelove on our minds. Roddenberry's universe was built on a single insight: Can we survive the nuclear age? Yes, but only if we learn to take delight in the essential differences between cultures and between people. Mere tolerance is not enough. Out among the stars, if we act like savages, we will end up being treated like savages.

Star Trek gave a limitless frontier to a population that had just run out of frontier. The show and its successors follow Earth's future history into an era from about 2150 to 2400, in which American morals dominate a good part of the galaxy. It tapped into the frontier and Western mythologies of America and provided inspiration to the foundering space programs.

While the original series lasted only three seasons, 1967 to 1969, it launched four spin-off series and ten movies. For nearly forty years, some part of the "Trek" world has been in movies, cartoons, TV series, and syndicated reruns. Impressive.

Decades before America began to turn away from a purely WASP (White Anglo-Saxon Protestant) identity, the series provided a blueprint for a multicultural society. Kirk's partner in exploration is his second-in-command, Mr. Spock, a methodical officer with green blood and pointed ears. Spock was the first alien on television widely accepted as a serious, independent creature. By nature, as logical and unemotional as an encyclopedia (usually), Spock provided a rare contrast to our irrational beliefs. The Vulcan serves three functions: he's the outsider looking in, the technologist who speaks up, and the faithful friend. Spock's a marvelous character, but it's the captain who makes the decisions, and it's the captain whose style is the theme of the series.

Star Trek used or modified a few old myths in episodes like "Who Mourns for Adonis?" and "The Apple," but many of Kirk's exploits were simple morality tales in far-removed locales. Rod Serling, creator of television's *The Twilight Zone*, had pioneered that trick to get around the pervasive censorship of the 1950s. Jim Kirk accomplished the first Negro-Caucasian kiss shown on prime-time television, in an era when even biracial friendships were rare. While it was still considered offensive to show a black man and white man just working together, Kirk commanded a crew of different races, nationalities, genders, and species. He's a charismatic leader, and his crew are more than loyal to their captain and one another; they're steadfast friends.

Kirk operated under Star Fleet's "Prime Directive," a

doctrine of noninterference with the natural development of primitive cultures. In one episode, "A Private Little War," he restored the balance of power to a pair of warring primitive societies, while that year in the real world, the United States was busy providing sophisticated arms to tribal peoples in Cambodia and Vietnam (and much later, Afghanistan). Kirk defeated a race enslaved by entertainment (television), reformed a society modeled on the worst of human experience (Nazi Germany), and bested a supercomputer gone mad.

The show had many memorable characters, but Kirk and Spock stand out as influential. Kirk's strength is intuition amid technology, a theme that reoccurs in *Star Wars*. Outgunned, he bluffs his way out. Outnumbered, he invents a game so complex it distracts his captors. His adventures showed that there are still frontiers, new challenges, and new possibilities. He preserves his ship, his crew, his culture—American culture—well into the future.

Maybe You Didn't Know

- Spock's abilities include great strength and telepathy. He once had a small pet bear—with six-inch fangs.
- The episode "The City on the Edge of Forever" was written by Harlan Ellison.
- Kirk's middle name is Tiberius.
- Kirk was played by William Shatner, who also portrayed T. J. Hooker and Denny Crane.
- Never speak Klingon in an airport.
- Kirk first encountered Khan (Ricardo Montalban) in an episode entitled "Space Seed."

To learn more about *Star Trek,* Captain Kirk, and Mr. Spock, we suggest

The Making of Star Trek by Stephen E. Whitfield and Gene Roddenberry.

Deep Space and Sacred Time: Star Trek in the American Mythos by Jon Wagner and Jan Lundeen.

I am Spock by Leonard Nimoy.

J. R. Ewing—#63

The star of the TV soap *Dallas,* John Ross Ewing—J.R.—is the ruthless, unfaithful, backstabbing businessman who captivated American audiences for more than 350 episodes from 1978 to 1991. His character continues to this day as a prime example of the people we love to hate—the rich.

Soap operas were rare among evening shows, but *Dallas* was an immediate hit, the highest-rated show on television for three years and one of the ten top-rated shows for seven consecutive years (1979–1986). The show started as a five-part miniseries about an oil-tycoon family, with J.R. as the son of patriarch Jock Ewing (John Ross, senior), a tough rancher who raised his boy to be a man's man. J.R.'s not a character with many redeeming qualities, but he did the big things men dream of doing: making money, having affairs, drinking to excess; and he got away with it all. People who hated him tuned in every week to see what he'd do next and how he'd pull it off. Portrayed with oily charm by Larry Hagman, son of famous stage actress

Mary Martin, J.R. bullied his brother, cheated on his wife, and maneuvered his way to the top of his industry. He's the archetype of the crooked powerful businessman, and his charm was seductive.

After he was wounded in the 1980 end-of-season cliffhanger, the whole nation speculated on the identity of his unseen assailant. The question "Who shot J.R.?" became part of the national vocabulary. London bookies took bets on the answer. When the shooter was revealed in the following season, 76 percent of households in the United States watched, and news broadcasts reported it as though an important case had been solved.

Created by David Jacobs, the series featured the sexual and business exploits of the extended Ewing family, established on the Southfork Ranch in Braddock County, Texas. Hagman based his interpretation of the role on the infighting of a real Texas family, the sons of an oil magnate Hagman's father had represented. The series was initially filmed in an actual Texas mansion (since destroyed by fire) and then moved to a two-hundred-acre estate and its 8,500-square-foot building in Parker, Texas. The site continues to attract visitors.

Why is he an important character? Because his exploits and misdeeds were fascinating not only to Americans, but to viewers worldwide. The "Who Shot J.R.?" episode had a global audience of 300 million.

In 1991, five years after the end of the series, Larry Hagman happened to attend an OPEC conference in Vienna, and he was asked what the price of oil should be. He quoted a figure from one of the episodes, $36 a barrel, and the participants went wild with joy. The real oilmen respected him as one of their own. He got hate mail for propping up the price of imported oil.

And why did J.R. have such a following? Television programs live for decades in syndication and are also licensed overseas to broadcasters who can't afford to develop their own programs. It's a global market, and *Dallas* alone is said to have earned more than $1 billion.

What are the Americans like? How do they live? The opinion of the world is slanted by the image of J.R., the Rich American. This is the mark of great fiction—it informs people about a character and his culture, the way we think we know British society from watching *Upstairs, Downstairs* or *Benny Hill*.

And who would have thought, in 1978, that a Texas oil family could have any political influence?

To learn more about J.R., look for
www.ultimatedallas.com

Kermit the Frog—#67

Kermit is a frog in search of acceptance, and it is his perpetual journey that makes him special to all of us. He has had a weekly audience of more than 200 million people in more than one hundred countries, an annual appearance at the Macy's Thanksgiving Day Parade, and a starring role in at least four movies.

Puppeteer Jim Henson created the eventual star of stage and swamp out of an old overcoat in 1955. Soon the frog was doing commercials for Wilkins Coffee, and he appeared on a Washington, D.C. television show called *Sam and Friends*, which won an Emmy in 1959. Before long, Kermit was making the rounds of variety and talk shows. His big break came a decade later when he was included in the cast of *Sesame Street*.

According to the official biographies, Kermit was born in a swamp in Georgia. He had thousands of relatives and his biggest problem was being recognized as an individual. He headed out for the big city with a guitar, a bicycle, and an ambition to better himself. He soon encountered Miss Piggy, the love of his life, a lady-pig with an attitude: controlling, obsessive, temperamental, and vain ("Moi?"). Kermit accepted her attentions (not that she gave him much choice), and together they find happiness and accomplish their mission, whatever the episode requires, whether it's recovering a stolen diamond or just putting on a show.

He captured the imagination of a worldwide audience because he is calm, loyal, responsible, amiable, and cheerful. He's Bing Crosby, Mickey Rooney, and Fred Astaire rolled into one. A frog for all seasons. Among the Muppets, some of the most popular characters on television, Kermit has been the cohesive force holding this cast of characters together through its many Emmy Award–winning shows and seasons. He's a center of tranquility in a world of oddballs. Kermit's friends include a six-foot-tall yellow bird, a blue monster that devours cookies, a grouch who lives in a garbage can, and, of course, the indomitable Miss Piggy. This frog is a marvelous example of tolerance in a diverse society.

———

Kermit is also a child's introduction to the problems of identity. It's not easy being an individual, accepting your heritage, and finding a place for your own talents. Children are often uncomfortable with their individuality and follow fads in clothing and attitude, anything from Davy Crockett lunchboxes to Goth gear and gang colors. In each appearance, Kermit manages to neutralize every doubt or problem his frogness might subject him to. He deals with the problems of the moment: look out for alligators and avoid being stepped on, which is not easy if you're short and edible.

In the human world the child will encounter more serious problems of racial and sexual intolerance. Kermit's way ahead. He's got an interspecies relationship going.

The period of Kermit's creation was a time when a person who was gay or lesbian or black, antiwar, pro-Communist, or Jewish—anyone outside the WASP "norm"—risked physical attack. While Kermit isn't abused for his color within the show—it's always a question of situation rather than race—he's become an example of someone who *would* be victimized for his color or beliefs. Kermit's green is normal for the swamp, but in human society it's the color of sickness, mold, and Martian invaders. In human society, anything different is abnormal, something to be destroyed. Kermit is an example of perseverance in a dangerous world and helps children understand and survive the violent forces of the world.

"It's Not Easy Being Green" (written by Joe Raposo) has become Kermit's main legacy, such a familiar phrase that you'll find it as a subtitle for articles on monetary policy, lawns, artichokes, environmental policy, broccoli, Naderism, organic gardening, liberalism, and vegetarian cooking . . . almost anything different from society's average.

In 1990, creator Jim Henson died of pneumonia, but his creations live on. In 1994, Kermit became a permanent exhibit in the Smithsonian Institution's Legacies collection. Only one other of our characters (Barbie) has been so honored.

It has been reported that the Disney Company bought Kermit and the entire Muppet cast. But business deals don't always go through, and don't always last. If it's true, don't fret. They've gotten out of worse predicaments. Perhaps their next film will be *The Muppet Redemption: Escape from Anaheim.*

Did You Know

The original Kermit had rounded feet, and was not clearly a frog. His first TV appearance was in 1956.

Afterword

It is usual in books such as this to wrap up with some expression of a conclusion, of lessons learned, of take-home instruction of the Aesop's fable variety. There was a time, in fact, when we had the expectation of such an outcome, of making the exercise of our writing—and your reading—this book serve a higher purpose than mere entertainment.

No such luck. Try as we might, we could not identify any moral of this search. And we did want to find something that would make this collection something more than random.

Behind each of these characters hides a surprise or two, even our icons, our heroes and villains. All of these marvelous characters carry their own secrets and twists of fate that shock and amaze. Truly, we must be careful when digesting these tales, for the works of fiction are just as complex as anything in this world. What have we learned? That our favorite characters are richer than we imagined. That our fantasy life does more than sell books and movies, it drives technology, social change, war, and the everyday thoughts that fill our lives.

Appendix: Also-Rans and Near-Misses

In alphabetical order, here are twenty characters who almost made the cut.

Beowulf
Bugs Bunny
George Milton and Lenny Small
Golem, the
Gulliver
Harry Callahan (Dirty Harry)
Holden Caulfield
Homer Simpson
Jewish American Princess
Lancelot
Lolita
Medea
Mother Goose
The Phoenix
Pinocchio
Raskolnikov

Tom Joad
Uncle Remus
Walter Mitty
Winnie-the-Pooh

Our Thanks

The authors express their gratitude for the generous and valuable help they have received.

First and foremost, the untiring efforts of our agent, Claudia Menza, of the Menza-Barron Agency, and Carolyn Marino, Jennifer Civiletto, and Wendy Lee, our editors at HarperCollins.

We could not have completed the project without the generous advice and criticism of the Sunday Night Writers Group, Englewood, New Jersey: Eileen Watkins (who also contributed one of the essays), Susan Moshiashwili, Elisa Chalem, Ed Lataro, Elizabeth Larson, Marcia Sandmeyer Wilson, Ed Rand, and Seymour Rappoport. Also, we benefited greatly from the guidance of Barry Sheinkopf, The Writing Center, Englewood Cliffs, New Jersey, and his regulars: Eugenia Koukounas, Dan Balaban, Anna Radelescu, and Ana Doina. The Cresskill Writers Group under the direction of Henry Hecht was a consistent aid and a tolerant audience. The authors add their respects to Joan Braner, who introduced them to each other. Finally, all three authors offer a remembrance to the late Mary Brim Hess, for her suggestions, editing, and encouragement.

316 Our Thanks

———

Allan Lazar sends additional thanks to members of Henry Hecht's group: Sophie Ruszkiewicz, Tom Moorhead, Ed Thom, Frances Wilson, Jack O'Shea, Jim Genovese, Joe Giardina, Anne Gilmartin, Ken Effert, Blanche Hackett, and Rhea C. Levy. To the Writing Groups at the Englewood Southeast Senior Center for Independent Living: Gloria Jordan, Terry and Joseph Kneuer, Ann Zachs, Norma Burke, Sandor Halasz, Lilian Nissman, and Catherine Shedd. Also Mary Beavin. The Main Street Poets & Writers in Fort Lee, New Jersey, under the leadership of Patrick Hammer: Muriel Dickman, Alice Kanrich, Claire Lind, Jane Newman, Maryse Zeitouni, Ben Perlman, Rhoda Sklar, and Shirley Frank. In addition, Dr. Lazar benefited from the support and encouragement of Edna Lazar, ever-patient wife of the lead author, and their children who assisted in constructing the list of characters in the book: Jennifer Czahur, Julie Reskakis, Deena Berberich, David Lazar, Michael Lazar, Matthew Lazar, Judy Bendazu, Benjamin Lazar, and Pamela Halasz.

Dan Karlan would like to express triple appreciation to Martin Buchanan: for starting the three of us on this exercise by giving him Michael Hart's *The 100: A Ranking of the Most Influential Persons in History,* for suggesting some characters for our consideration, and for assisting us in the seemingly never-ending process of polishing the essays. Thanks also to Vince McCaffrey and the rest of the band at Avenue Victor Hugo Bookshop in Boston for coming up with particularly exciting suggestions for inclusion. Nenah Sylver was also helpful in suggesting characters. Special appreciation is expressed to his father, Jac, for his support, encouragement, and suggestions.

Jeremy Salter also thanks Anne K. Taylor, who made valuable comments on several essays, Laura Rindner, Steve Conte, Dr. David Pilgrim, Donna and Eduardo Campos, T. Velazquez, Mike Israel, and Jane Adelman.

He also thanks Kurt Hulit for his comments on film, the Hulit family, Steve Bronstein, Joanne Weck, Richard and Susan Feldman, J. Zingerman, John Wienke, and Jean Gastfriend.

Contributors who added to our list of characters include Janet Wilcox, Manie Barron, Catherine Stutzer, Burt Samuelson, David Zudkevitch, and Donna Campos. Many other people offered help or opinions. We thank them all.